JUDGING POSITIVISM

Judging Positivism is a critical exploration of the method and substance of legal positivism. Margaret Martin is primarily concerned with the manner in which theorists who adopt the dominant positivist paradigm ask a limited set of questions and offer an equally limited set of answers, artificially circumscribing the field of legal philosophy in the process. The book focuses primarily but not exclusively on the writings of prominent legal positivist, Joseph Raz. Martin argues that Raz's theory has changed over time and that these changes have led to deep inconsistencies and incoherencies in his account. One recurring theme in the book is that Razian positivism collapses from within. In the process of defending his own position, Raz is led to support the views of many of his main rivals, namely, Ronald Dworkin, the legal realists and the normative positivists. The internal collapse of Razian positivism proves to be instructive. Promising paths of enquiry come into view and questions that have been suppressed or marginalised by positivists re-emerge ready for curious minds to reflect on anew. The broader vision of jurisprudential enquiry defended in this book re-connects philosophy with the work of practitioners and the worries of law's subjects, bringing into focus the relevance of legal philosophy for lawyers and laymen alike.

Judging Positivism

Margaret Martin

HART
PUBLISHING
OXFORD AND PORTLAND, OREGON
2014

Published in the United Kingdom by Hart Publishing Ltd
16C Worcester Place, Oxford, OX1 2JW
Telephone: +44 (0)1865 517530
Fax: +44 (0)1865 510710
E-mail: mail@hartpub.co.uk
Website: http://www.hartpub.co.uk

Published in North America (US and Canada) by
Hart Publishing
c/o International Specialized Book Services
920 NE 58th Avenue, Suite 300
Portland, OR 97213-3786
USA
Tel: +1 503 287 3093 or toll-free: (1) 800 944 6190
Fax: +1 503 280 8832
E-mail: orders@isbs.com
Website: http://www.isbs.com

Hart Publishing is an imprint of Bloomsbury Publishing plc.

British Library Cataloguing in Publication Data
Data Available

ISBN: 978-1-84946-099-6

Typeset by Hope Services, Abingdon
Printed and bound in Great Britain by
Lightning Source UK Ltd

Judging Positivism

Margaret Martin

• HART •
PUBLISHING
OXFORD AND PORTLAND, OREGON
2014

Published in the United Kingdom by Hart Publishing Ltd
16C Worcester Place, Oxford, OX1 2JW
Telephone: +44 (0)1865 517530
Fax: +44 (0)1865 510710
E-mail: mail@hartpub.co.uk
Website: http://www.hartpub.co.uk

Published in North America (US and Canada) by
Hart Publishing
c/o International Specialized Book Services
920 NE 58th Avenue, Suite 300
Portland, OR 97213-3786
USA
Tel: +1 503 287 3093 or toll-free: (1) 800 944 6190
Fax: +1 503 280 8832
E-mail: orders@isbs.com
Website: http://www.isbs.com

Hart Publishing is an imprint of Bloomsbury Publishing plc.

British Library Cataloguing in Publication Data
Data Available

ISBN: 978-1-84946-099-6

Typeset by Hope Services, Abingdon
Printed and bound in Great Britain by
Lightning Source UK Ltd

For my parents

Preface

I have chosen to offer a sustained critique of one version of legal positivism and not (as the title may suggest) all versions of this theoretical position. My attention is focused on the account of law and authority offered by Joseph Raz. Raz is undoubtedly one of the most influential thinkers of our age. His ideas, original and complex, have gripped the imagination of legal philosophers of a generation. His key claims have even permeated debates about the nature of international law, constitutional law and beyond.

Philosophical discussions often proceed when those who are gifted enough to envisage a new way of thinking or conceiving of an issue or phenomenon put pen to paper. These are the castle-builders. They are the rare few. The rest of us spend our days contemplating the virtues and vices of the castles built by others. Both kinds of philosophic tasks are (ideally) undertaken with the same end in view: the hope of understanding the world around us, and in this instance, law. So edifices are built, and the stability of the foundation is inevitably called into question. The unceasing ebb and flow of this process over time speaks to the unbounded nature of philosophy and, perhaps, to a certain kind of restlessness of spirit. This sceptical posture likely has humble origins: the world as experienced seems to stubbornly refuse to live obediently within boundaries drawn by any one model.

One of the central aims of this book is to shine light on some fundamental difficulties with both the method and substance of Raz's account. While the focus is on his work, the conclusions drawn raise broader questions about the nature of the debate in jurisprudence. Are we able to conceptualize law without explicitly or implicitly relying on contestable value-laden assumptions? Does, for instance, an account of the nature of law inevitably rely on assumptions about the human condition? I will suggest that severing legal theory from political philosophy is a far more difficult task than is often assumed. Furthermore, it is often assumed that we are able to reflect on the nature of law without also reflecting upon the work of lawyers and judges. One of the conclusions that I draw is that there is a deep connection between Raz's positivist account of law and a positivistic (or formalist) account of adjudication. This is an old criticism of positivist thought that has been largely discredited. It was seemingly put to rest by those who characterized this argument as a simplistic error made by the misinformed. But once the legal philosopher aims to conceive of law as a whole, rather than to defend discrete theses in isolation, this old critique takes on new life.

The title is vulnerable to yet another criticism. One might argue that the label 'positivism' ultimately misrepresents the complex position staked out by Raz. The term itself has been used to mean a variety of things, the argument goes, and even if we can agree on a meaning, it is still unclear that this label is helpful. I am sympathetic to this view. One of my central arguments is that Raz has altered his position over time and that the alterations have created intractable problems for his account. In other words, Raz's positivist theses do not fit easily with his non-positivist ones. Let me explain in brief.

There are two central theses that are often associated with legal positivist thought: the separability thesis and the sources thesis. Those who champion the former maintain that there is no necessary connection between law and morality. While this claim has been a topic of considerable discussion, I will focus only on the second thesis. According to the sources thesis, which Raz famously defends, one need not rely on moral arguments in order to establish the content of a given law. The law of a given system consists of an aggregate of factually ascertainable norms. In other words, the law consists of an aggregate of *positive* laws. The label 'legal positivism' seems appropriate insofar as it captures this idea.

The label, however, does not adequately capture other central aspects of Raz's thinking. His account of authority is morally robust, as is his theory of adjudication (which is now sharply distinguished from his theory of law). The fact that the label is not a good fit in either instance should not lead us to prematurely abandon the label; rather, the lack of fit should prompt us to ask some serious questions about the way in which all of his theses fit together. As mentioned, I argue that the fit is poor: the castle must be renovated, or abandoned. Regardless of which of these options one chooses, it becomes clear that the assumption that legal theory can thrive as an independent, non-normative project must be discarded. It is not the case that philosophers who reject the dominant method are simply *interested* in different things (so that the choice between methods becomes but a matter of taste). Rather, I will argue that the non-normative 'conceptual' or 'descriptive' project rests on an extremely unstable foundation – the instability of which is best viewed from the inside of Raz's complex account. There are many promising theoretical paths worth pursuing, and many of these are well-travelled. Regardless of questions chosen and answers proffered, it is clear that the assumptions that currently dominate the debate cannot serve as unquestioned truths insofar as our collective aim is to understand the nature of law.

Acknowledgements

The central argument of this book was first articulated in my PhD thesis, defended in 2006 at the University of Cambridge. This was made possible by the support of the Social Science and Humanities Research Council, the Overseas Research Scholarship and the Cambridge Commonwealth Trust. I must also extend thanks to Wolfson College and the Faculty of Law at the University of Cambridge. I am very appreciative of the Faculty of Law at Western University, who have afforded me the time and the freedom to rethink and rework my ideas. And I remain forever grateful to Richard Hart and his remarkable team at Hart Publishing for supporting me and this project.

I had the pleasure of presenting the chapters at a number of exceptional institutions, including University of Oxford, London School of Economics, University of Edinburgh, Georgetown University, University of Notre Dame, McMaster University and McGill University. Specifically, I owe a debt of gratitude to the following individuals who asked excellent questions and challenged me to improve my argument: Benjamin Berger, Brian Bix, Tom Campbell, Jules Coleman, Dwight Newman, Richard Ekins, Timothy Endicott, John Finnis, Evan Fox-Decent, John Gardner, Michael Giudice, Andrew Halpin, Kristine Kalanges, Maris Köpcke Tinturé, Randy Kozel, Chandran Kukathas, Cormac Mac Amhlaigh, Mark Murphy, George Pavlakos, Jeffrey Pojanoski, Thomas Poole, Veronica Rodriguez-Blanco, Stefan Sciaraffa, Lawrence Solum, François Tanguay-Renaud, Neil Walker, Wil Waluchow, Charlie Webb, Grégoire Webber, Michael Wilkinson, Paul Yowell and Lorenzo Zucca. I must also thank the students who attended the talks and asked such insightful questions. A special thanks to Trevor Allan and William Lucy, my PhD committee members, whose many incisive comments were invaluable to the process of re-envisioning my argument.

My work, and my intellectual life more generally, benefited enormously from conversations with (and the support of) Alan Brudner, Julie Dickson, Antony Duff, David Dyzenhaus, Aileen Kavanagh, Sandra Marshall, Danny Priel, Kristen Rundel, Frederick Schauer, and the late Samuel Ajzenstat. I am forever grateful to my friend and colleague Valerie Oosterveld who has been my unofficial mentor since I arrived at Western. A special thanks must be extended to Sean Coyle for his ongoing support and for our many chats over the years. I will also remain deeply appreciative of the time I spent with Amanda Perreau-Saussine, who passed away in August of 2012. Thanks to her generosity (and that of her family) I was able to spend many productive summers in Cambridge, dividing my time between their home in Haslingfield and Amanda's office at Queens' College. I am also very grateful for the unwavering support of Gordon and Faith Johnson, who presided over Wolfson College during my stay. Their son, Orlando, is the artist who created the print which appears on the cover.

I would like to thank Andrew Botterell, Grant Huscroft and Bradley Miller who continually invite leading philosophers to speak at Western as part of our Public Law and Legal Philosophy Research Group. It has also been a pleasure to have the opportunity to work with Richard Bronaugh, who, as editor of the *Canadian Journal of Law and Jurisprudence*, has left his mark on our field. For those who edited the manuscript at various stages of completion (often with deadlines pending!), namely, Lawrence Burns, Ranjan Chaudhuri, Tigger Jourard and Anastasia Pasecinic, I am humbled by your remarkable efforts. And to Angela Prattas, who ensured that all of us at Western were greeted with kindness each and every day. It is difficult to embark on long-term projects without a lot of support. I am forever grateful to my family and friends.

Finally I must thank Nigel Simmonds, who was my PhD supervisor. It is hard to overstate the debt I owe him, or the amount of admiration that I have for him. Those supervisions at Corpus Christi College are some of my finest memories. I was so very lucky that he was able to cast his sharp philosophical eye over the manuscript in its first incarnation. This book, and my academic life more generally, are a direct result of his efforts. But, of course, my mistakes remain my own.

Contents

1

Setting the Stage: Practical Reason and Norms *Reconsidered*

IT IS HARD to conceive of living in a peaceful society that is not governed by law; it is equally difficult to comprehend the nature of law despite the essential role it seems to play in our lives. It has a presence that is at once familiar and elusive.[1] Laws are used to perform a set of rather well-known tasks, such as setting speed limits, regulating relations between landlords and tenants, and setting tax rates. They also address the darker side of human co-existence, through prohibitions against murder, rape and theft, laws set moral limits, albeit shifting ones, about the kind of behaviour that will be permitted in the society. The totality of laws serves as a reservoir for our collective history while simultaneously working as a force that shapes us individually and collectively. Of course, the views that find expression in legal form do not necessarily represent the views of all, but nonetheless the law offers a snapshot of lives lived.[2]

At times, the law has also operated as an instrument of injustice, working against the tide of good. History is littered with instances where the force of the law has been harnessed by rulers to bring about the unthinkable. At such times, law seems to be a tool of domination and subjugation. But, at other moments, the very idea of life under lawful rule is lauded as a cornerstone of civilization. It is viewed as a shield that protects individuals against arbitrary exercises of government power. How do we begin in our attempt to make sense of law's many moods?[3]

One seemingly obvious starting point is to attempt to say something about the way in which law works in the world. More precisely, it seems reasonable to begin with questions pertaining to law's role in bringing about and sustaining order in society. This starting point need not presuppose that the answer will be singular (or simple) in nature, but if we do not start with an enquiry into law's work in the world it seems rather hard for the inquiry to even get off

[1] HLA Hart, *The Concept of Law*, 2nd edn (Oxford, Oxford University Press, 1994) 14.

[2] See, eg N Lacey, 'The Jurisprudence Annual Lecture 2013 – Institutionalising Responsibility: Implications for Jurisprudence' 4 *Jurisprudence: An international Journal of Legal and Political Thought* 1, 4–11.

[3] L Fuller, *Anatomy of the Law* (Middlesex, Victoria, Penguin Books, 1968) 12.

the ground. Few would challenge the view that without law, achieving an orderly society would be difficult (if not impossible) insofar as the population has surpassed a certain numerical threshold. However, when philosophers give voice to the precise way in which law contributes to order, opinions quickly splinter. There are, nonetheless, dominant narratives that are readily identifiable in the literature. A number of philosophers, stretching back to Cicero, offer a story about law's coming into being which is supposed to illuminate the nature of law. Gerald Postema eloquently outlines this 'creation myth':

> Political authority and laws, Cicero tells us, were invented for the same reason: to establish and secure justice and equality of rights. When people were satisfied that this task could be accomplished by a single man, they accepted the rule of a king. However, they were forced to invent laws when they realized that they could not count on their kings being just. The special virtue of law, says Cicero, is that it is able to speak on matters of justice and rights to all citizens at all times with a single voice. In Pufendorf's version of this creation myth, royal faithlessness exposed not only the lack of royal accountability, but also, and more troubling, the people's inability to agree on standards by which to judge the king's justice. As their numbers increased, so too did the jarring dissonance of social life. People needed standards more dependable than the king's faulty sense of justice and more public than their particular and often dissonant judgments. The faithlessness of the king may have been the immediate problem, but the deeper need was to unify the judgment of the people, to enable them to speak the language of justice to each other in a single voice. Law taught them this language.[4]

Law, on this view, is conceived of as a set of public norms that serve to unite a populace that would otherwise descend into chaos. Law is able to unify judgment because it offers a set of rules that enjoy autonomy – that is to say, the citizenry can identify the content of any given legal norm without relying on moral arguments. This is important as moral issues are the source of disagreement and law's ability to unify judgment is therefore (according to this account) dependent on the ability of legal norms to offer practical guidance without recreating the very disagreements that legal norms are introduced to solve. This particular creation story reappears in various forms in the writings of a rather diverse list of philosophers, including 'Aquinas and Bentham, Hobbes, Pufendorf, Locke and Hume, Hart, Raz, MacCormick, and John Finnis'.[5]

Joseph Raz, one might object, does not belong on this list. If one reads *The Morality of Freedom*, for instance, we do not discover an account whereby concern with justice is weaved together with an understanding of law's order-

[4] GJ Postema, 'Law's Autonomy and Public Practical Reason' in R George (ed), *The Autonomy of Law: Essays on Legal Positivism* (Oxford, Clarendon Press, 1996) 79 (footnote omitted).
[5] *Ibid*, 80.

engendering role. Instead, Raz works to articulate the conditions under which legal norms enjoy moral authority. The considerations that factor into this enquiry include, but are not limited to, the ability of law to facilitate co-ordination and co-operation.[6] A close reading of this influential text could quickly lead any fair-minded legal philosopher to insist that Raz's account remains untouched by Postema's critique. In fact, Raz himself has responded in this fashion: he rejects the notion that he is committed to any particular account of law's function while simultaneously suggesting that legal philosophy, properly construed, does not place this question at its centre.[7]

At first glance, this response may appear to be satisfactory. In what follows, I will suggest that this conclusion is too hasty. We only have to return to his earlier works to see that, at least at one point in time, his theory of law is easily slotted into the list of thinkers whose lineage traces back to Cicero. Most notably, in *Practical Reason and Norms* Raz offers readers a clear vision of the way in which law creates and sustains order.[8] Raz does not offer any musings on justice, but the other key elements of the familiar narrative are nevertheless in place. Legal norms are understood as a set of public practical reasons that enjoy autonomy and, consequently, order is able to overtake chaos.

At the heart of this account lie Raz's core positivist commitments. As I elucidate further in this chapter, legal norms are understood as a set of factually ascertainable reasons for action that are identifiable based on their pedigree alone (the sources thesis). Moreover, legal norms do not simply offer citizens reasons for action, but reasons for action of an 'exclusionary' kind whereby all other competing reasons for action are displaced by legal norms (the pre-emption thesis). In *Practical Reason and Norms* we find another thesis, which may be less familiar to his readers. At the very centre of his account of the nature of law is an understanding of the role of judges: judges, Raz argues, are under a duty to apply the law.[9] That is, they are under a duty to *exclude* extra-legal considerations, including moral ones. Not only are individual legal norms thought of as exclusionary reasons for action, but the legal system in general is understood as exclusionary in nature. In light of these views, it is easy to see why the label 'exclusive legal positivism' is an apt one.[10] In this early work,

[6] J Raz, *The Morality of Freedom* (Oxford, Clarendon Press, 1986) 56.

[7] J Raz, 'Postema on Law's Autonomy and Public Practical Reason: A Critical Comment' (1998) 4 *Legal Theory* 1, 2,11. Also see ch 7.

[8] J Raz, *Practical Reason and Norms* (Oxford, Oxford University Press, 1999)

[9] *Ibid*, 137.

[10] Exclusive legal positivism is often contrasted with inclusive legal positivism. Inclusive legal positivists are united by their commitment to the separability thesis rather than the sources thesis. The claim is that law and morality are contingently connected. More precisely still, the criteria for validity of legal norms in a given system can include moral criteria, but it need not. It is 'conceptually possible' that legal systems exist where pedigree is the only determining factor for legal validity. I do not offer a direct challenge to this view. I do, however, share Coleman's recent thoughts on his own position: it occupies a logical space rather than a 'real world one'; indeed, its creation was

Raz insists that the judicial duty to apply the law is the very thing that accounts for the existence of order. If judges were not bound in this way we would return to a state of chaotic lawlessness. By applying the law, judges uphold and reinforce the practical force of the aggregate of legal norms. Discretionary activity, while an unavoidable part of the occupation of judging, is represented as a destablising force. Luckily the very existence of legal systems serves as a testament to the relatively marginal role judicial discretion plays in the courtroom (or so it is assumed).

This is a self-conscious attempt to articulate what law *is* – Raz's account is not meant to serve as a warning to judges to suppress any inclinations to use their discretionary powers unnecessarily. In what follows, I argue that the claim that judges have a duty to apply the law is the theoretical 'weight bearing plank' – it supports the significance of the other thesis. But, Raz has long abandoned the claim that judges are under a duty to apply the law; instead, he now argues that judges are moral reasoners while situating his positivist thesis within a morally robust conception of authority. As mentioned above, he even eschews the suggestion that legal philosophers should concern themselves with accounts of law's function. Can Raz discard his claim that judges have a duty to apply the law without displacing his other theses which are at home in this early account? Can he find a new home for his core positivist theses and still retain their significance?

I argue that if we pull this particular thread – if we explore whether Raz can abandon his functional account of law – then the Razian edifice unravels. He never successfully combines his positivist theses, which are at home in his function-based account, with his morally robust non-positivist elements (including his moral theory of adjudication and his account of legitimate authority). Raz's influential positions, while creative and complex, are also deeply unstable. Specifically, I argue that Raz has changed his theory over time and that these changes have created deep inconsistencies and tensions that render his position untenable. My argument will focus on four of Raz's central works – *Practical Reason and Norms*, *The Authority of Law*, *Ethics in the Public Domain* and *The Morality of Freedom* (in chronological order) – in order to map the changes, before exploring the implications of these alterations. Attention will also be paid to a more recent work, *Between Authority and Interpretation*.[11]

motivated by the Hart/Dworkin debate and not by reflections on the world. J Coleman (2009) 22 *Ratio Juris* 359. This book will focus on 'exclusive legal positivism' and the term 'positivist' will be used to refer to Joseph Raz's version of positivism (which is often referred to as exclusive legal positivism). I will not directly address the arguments of the inclusive legal positivists. For a defence of this position see: J Coleman, *The Practice of Principle* (Oxford, Oxford University Press, 2001) ; WJ Waluchow, *Inclusive Legal Positivism* (Oxford, Clarendon Press, 1994); M Kramer, *In Defense of Legal Positivism* (Oxford, Oxford University Press, 1999).

[11] J Raz, *Between Authority and Interpretation* (New York, Oxford University Press, 2009).

While this book will offer a critical assessment of Raz's central theoretical commitments in some detail, his works are also a foil for exploring the assumptions that inform the dominant approach to jurisprudential enquiry today – an enquiry that can be traced back to the works of HLA Hart.[12] In his famous work *The Concept of Law*, Hart set out to carve a space between traditional natural law theory and legal scepticism and, in so doing, held out the promise of progress.[13] The animating idea is that an accurate understanding of the nature of law is available only when law is viewed through the cool eye of the detached observer. According to this view, the job of the legal philosopher is to determine the features necessary for the existence of a legal system, without dipping her toe in the murky world of political theory, wherein philosophers of past and present, championing contestable conceptions of human nature, are locked in a perpetual battle. Instead of clarifying the nature of law, political philosophy only leads us back to a debate about foundational value commitments, a quagmire in which the tradition remains embedded. In the face of such a dire prospect, Hart offers the promise of escape. This is why *The Concept of Law* is often viewed as the starting point for legal theory.

Raz endorses a similar approach. His defence of this method in *The Authority of Law* is clear and bold. He adopts the 'assumption of universality according to which it is a criterion of adequacy of a legal theory that it is true of all the intuitively clear instances of municipal legal systems'.[14] He then draws a sharp line between the work of the philosopher and that of the sociologist. The philosopher lives in the world of abstraction, while the sociologist wades into the messy, ever changing, world of particulars:

> Since a legal theory must be true of all legal systems the identifying features by which it characterizes them must of necessity be very general and abstract. It must disregard those functions which some legal systems fulfill in some societies because of the special social, economic, or cultural conditions of those societies. It must fasten only on those features of legal systems which they must possess regardless of the special circumstances of the societies in which they are in force. This is the difference between legal philosophy and sociology of law. The latter is concerned with the contingent and with the particular, the former with the necessary and the universal. Sociology of law provides a wealth of detailed information and analysis of the functions of law in some particular societies. Legal philosophy has to be content with those few features which all legal systems necessarily possess.[15]

The line in the sand has been drawn; the providence of jurisprudence has been defined. However, this is the very line I wish to call into question.

[12] See Hart, *The Concept of Law*, above n 1.

[13] *Ibid*, 154.

[14] J Raz, *The Authority of Law: Essays on Law and Morality* (New York, Oxford University Press, 1979), 104.

[15] *Ibid*, 104–05.

The tenability of the Hartian project rests on the viability of the sharp distinction between non-normative conceptual analysis and normative philosophy. The distinction between a non-normative theory of law and a normative theory of adjudication is eventually erected to protect the first, more foundational one. If this project is going to work, value assumptions about the nature of law must be kept out. In particular, if a theory of adjudication is fundamentally moral in nature, then it must remain quarantined in a separate sphere.[16] I will call into question the stability of both sets of distinctions, thereby raising serious doubts about this particular methodological approach.

The burden of defending a non-normative account is a heavy one to bear. As we shall see, it is remarkably difficult to keep value judgments out of one's theory. Value judgments do not simply take the form of morally robust claims about what law ought to be, but contestable assumptions about law and the human condition more generally are also threatening. For the positivist project to work, it must be a matter of fact that law is best understood as a set of facts.[17] To defend the foundational assumptions would be to admit that positivism rests on contestable philosophical underpinnings, immediately reconnecting it with the philosophical debates of old. But such assumptions are difficult to excise. The very attempt to preserve this particular methodological commitment (and the substantive commitments born out of it) negatively impact jurisprudential enquiry. Legal philosophers are easily led to adopt a defensive posture wherein their role is to ensure that any perceived value-commitments are kept out. The object of study becomes the theories themselves, and the pre-existing theoretical commitments all too often act as constraints on what can be said about law. In such instances, what should be the output of one's reflections enquiry often becomes the input. To the extent that this shift of focus has occurred, legal philosophy has lost its way. While there is no single way forward, there are certainly many dead ends.

In the remainder of this chapter, I set the stage for the central argument of this book by offering a close textual reading of *Practical Reason and Norms*. What is striking about *Practical Reason and Norms* is that Raz does not offer a theory of law that is separate from his theory of adjudication. Rather, his positivist theory of law is itself grounded in a positivist (or formalist) theory of adjudication. Admittedly, it is a creative account that is elegant in its symmetry. It also has the added advantage of presenting the relationship between the various theses in a transparent manner: all the parts of this concept of law are mutually supportive and interconnected. Nevertheless, as mentioned above, the entire

[16] Not so, of course, for the inclusive legal positivists.

[17] Note this point is made specifically in reference to positivists who are commited to the sources thesis, although the general point – that if an argument is offered to justify the starting point, the project is compromised – holds for all versions of non-normative positivism.

theory is dependent upon the claim that judges have a duty to apply the law, and this constitutes a fatal flaw. I will argue that Raz's non-normative account in *Practical Reason and Norms* is vulnerable to a powerful counter-example: common law adjudication. This practice fits uneasily with his claim that judges have a duty to apply the law (insofar as 'law' is defined as a set of fact-based norms). It is a point he acknowledges and attempts to grapple with but never resolves in a satisfactory way.[18] Raz has two options: he can either become a normative positivist and advocate reform of the common law (like Hobbes and Bentham before him) or he can try to account for this practice within his non-normative framework. He selects the second of the two options, although one of the central arguments of this book is that only the first option is available. Normative positivism, I will suggest, is all that there is, insofar as he desires to maintain his positivist theses.

In chapter two I explore certain notable arguments in *The Authority of Law*. In this work, Raz introduces us to his sources thesis, which holds that discerning the content of law is a fact-finding mission and not an evaluative one.[19] Significantly, he defends this thesis by relying on the same functional account of law that appears in *Practical Reason and Norms*: law offers us a set of public practical reasons for action that serve to unify judgment in society. Raz is cognisant of the fact that if this account is going to be plausible, he must accommodate judicial practices where judges do not seem to be applying fact-based norms. In a later chapter in *The Authority of Law* he offers readers what he calls a rule-plus-exception model of common law adjudication that is supposed to achieve this end.[20] Upon close examination, this model proves to be little more than an artificial regimentation of the practice. Not only is his model vulnerable to counter-examples, but it also collapses from within. In the wake of that collapse, Raz inadvertently affirms some of Dworkin's basic ideas. The limitations of the fact/value dichotomy, which underpins his sources thesis, will also be investigated along the way.

Raz reconfigures his positivist account in *Ethics in the Public Domain*, and I evaluate the success of this move in chapter three.[21] He relies heavily on the distinction between a theory of law and a theory of adjudication, hoping to solve all of the aforementioned difficulties by means of this essential distinction. I

[18] This is not a novel claim. See AWB Simpson, 'The Common Law and Legal Theory' in AWB Simpson (ed), *Oxford Essays in Jurisprudence 2nd Series* (Oxford, Oxford University Press, 1973).

[19] Raz, *The Authority of Law*, above n 14, at 39–40. Raz writes: 'A jurisprudential theory is acceptable only if its tests for identifying the content of the law and determining its existence depend exclusively on facts of human behaviour capable of being described in value-neutral terms and applied without resort to moral argument'.

[20] *Ibid*, 185.

[21] J Raz, *Ethics in the Public Domain: Essays in the Morality of Law and Politics* (New York, Oxford University Press, 1994).

argue that the shift in his account of adjudication negatively impacts his theory of law, especially the relevance of the sources thesis. The manner in which his theory of adjudication affects his account of law becomes visible when his thoughts about the nature of legal rights are explored. Raz, I will argue, becomes an accidental realist, echoing Holmes instead of Hart. The sharp divide between his theory of adjudication and his theory of law cannot be maintained, which has serious implications for Raz's theory and for legal philosophy more generally. I also argue that his thesis that all law claims authority cannot solve all the aforementioned problems.

In chapter four I examine Raz's attempt to connect his positivist account of law with a morally robust account of authority. I demonstrate that his pre-emption thesis sits in tension with his normal justification thesis. The pre-emption thesis requires individuals to pre-commit to treating a law or a set of laws as reasons for action; conversely, the normal justification thesis demands that individuals assess the moral worth of the norm. Raz spies the problem, but he fails to adequately address it. Instead of offering readers a coherent account, he vacillates between two incompatible models of authority. The tension can be traced back to incompatible methodogies: unlike the pre-emption thesis, which was born out of his positivist methodology, his morally robust account of authority is the product of the focal method. I propose that only a natural law conception can rid Raz's account of these deep tensions.

In chapter five I revisit the idea of law as a set of public practical reasons. This is the account of law's function which Raz originally champions and never successfully discards, despite many attempts. I argue that the pre-emption thesis is to blame and that Raz is still committed to the account of law that he champions in *Practical Reason and Norms*. Whenever he defends his pre-emption thesis, this vision of law's function follows closely behind it. Raz's many attempts to account for law's complexity prove to be unavailable to him because of the demands of his sources thesis, and more specifically because of his pre-emption thesis. It is not surprising to discover that the very same issue that doomed his original theory (in *Practical Reason and Norms*) continues to haunt his account. Moreover, in an attempt to secure a place for his sources thesis in the courtroom, Raz transforms the sources thesis into an ideal of legal reasoning.[22] I will argue that one of the implications of this move is that a normative version of positivism is the most he can strive for insofar as he wishes to maintain his positivist commitments.[23] Ultimately, I conclude that

[22] Raz, 'Postema on Law's Autonomy' above n 7, at 15.

[23] In this context, 'normative positivism' refers to the view that judges ought to seek to factually ascertain and then apply pre-existing legal norms. At other junctures the term may be used more broadly to capture the view that law should work as a set of public practical reasons. In ch 7 I explore the connections between these two versions of normative positivism.The precise countours of any of the normative positivist positions matter are of little relevance in this book: I am more interested in drawing the readers attention to instability of Raz's non-normative account of law.

Raz fails to account for the work of judges and this is why we must move beyond positivism and beyond the Hartian method altogether.

In chapter six I travel down the path not taken by revisiting the question of how law contributes to the preservation of order in society. I offer the beginning of an answer to this question by starting with the concepts and ideas that both Raz and Hart originally introduced us to. For instance, if we reflect further on Hart's notion of the 'critical reflective attitude', then an ideal account of the nature of law takes root, one that is competitive with the substance and method of legal positivism. A legal philosopher need not aim at constructing a legal ideal from abstract principles and normative concepts; it can grow from very prosaic roots. By telling (at least) two stories about the manner in which law can contribute to creating and sustaining order, we can learn about the nature of law and about ourselves.

Finally, I turn my attention back to *Practical Reason and Norms* and I explore the underlying contrast between legal order and a state of confusion. Raz blames judicial discretion for creating uncertainty, but this is not quite right. Not only can discretion be a stabilizing force, but the causes of instability and uncertainty are many. When we begin to identify them, a more accurate account of law materializes. Guided in part by the insights of Lon Fuller, my analysis leads to the doorstep of natural law theory. While I do not walk through the door, the questions of natural law (broadly construed) cannot be avoided. This poses a problem for positivists of all stripes.

In chapter seven I explore in detail the exchange between Raz and Gerald Postema.[24] By drawing on the arguments I make in the book, I maintain that Postema is correct in his assessment of Raz's position. This particular analysis allows me to discharge my argumentative burden while demonstrating the precise nature of Raz's tactics: he deflects every complaint, but he does not reconfigure his theory for his readers. Not only are his deflections misleading, but one of the main points of this book is that it will be very difficult, if not impossible, for Raz to fit all his theses together in a coherent whole.

My overriding concern, however, is not soley with Raz's position, but with the terms of the debate of which Raz is one voice, albeit a powerful one. The problems identified in Raz's account bring into view the way in which the debate is being carried out within artificially narrow boundaries. When the cracks and fissures appear in Raz's account, we should turn our gaze to law as it is manifest in experience and think afresh about law's complexity. My hope is that the debate will include a broader spectrum of theories and ideas and that the focus will return to law as it is manifest in the world. The internal

[24] Raz rarely responds to his critiques, but he does offer a lenghtly response to an article written by Postema. See Postema, 'Law's Autonomy and Public Practical Reason', above n 4. While originally published in 1998, it has been republished as the appendix of his recent book, *Between Authority and Intepretation*, above n 11.

collapse of Raz's account illustrates the manner in which the philosophical questions of old – questions about the nature of the human condition – remain relevant. Just as relevant, as we shall see, are the work of the lawyer and the concerns of the layman.

I. *PRACTICAL REASON AND NORMS* AND EXCLUSIONARY REASONS

A return to Raz's original theory of law as articulated in *Practical Reason and Norms* is crucial for a comprehensive understanding of Raz's exclusive positivist position in its more recent form. An understanding of *Practical Reason and Norms* foreshadows the nature of the challenges that Raz will encounter when he replaces the claim that judges have a duty to apply the law with the claim that judges do (and should) reason morally. Given the interconnected nature of the concepts in his original articulation of the theory, such a move promises to have implications for his theory as a whole.

Let us begin where Raz begins: with a theory of practical reason, out of which his theory of law emerges. Raz seeks to establish that exclusionary reasons for action are a familiar part of our lives, even if they have yet to be identified as such. Note that in this early work Raz is aware that the burden is on him to establish that these kinds of reasons are commonplace. He is not simply making a point about what 'law claims' (as he does in his later works); rather he is interested in making sense of the practical workings of existing legal systems. The relationship between the exclusionary status of legal norms and the work of the judiciary is vital to this early account.

Exclusionary reasons are both first-order reasons that tell us what to do (or what not to do) and second-order reasons that serve to exclude all other competing reasons. To clarify these key ideas, he differentiates between two kinds of conflicts that can occur when we are deciding how to act. Resolutions of conflicts between first-order reasons are a matter of 'relative strength' or weight: we weigh up the pros and cons of acting in certain ways and the reasons for action that emerge as the weightiest are the ones that we act upon.[25] In such instances, we act according to the balance of reasons. For example, we might have a first-order reason to study and a first-order reason to go to a party: we decide which reason is more pressing (ie has more weight) and we act according to that reason.

Unlike conflicts between first-order reasons, conflicts between first and second-order reasons are different in *kind*. When first-order reasons come into conflict with second-order reasons, it is not a simple matter of *weighing* different reasons; rather, second-order reasons *exclude* all other relevant reasons. Raz explains:

[25] Raz, *Practical Reason and Norms*, above n 8, at 36.

> The presence of an exclusionary reason may imply that one ought not to act on the balance of reasons. The exclusionary reason may exclude a reason which would have been overridden anyway, but it may also exclude a reason which would have tipped the balance of reasons.[26]

Exclusionary reasons are game changers. They act like trump cards by excluding competing reasons for action. If I promised my mother that I would study, regardless of whether I would prefer to go to a party, my promise to my mother acts as a trump card that excludes other potential reasons for action. Raz is aware of the fact that the burden is on him to demonstrate that exclusionary reasons exist and that legal norms are best understood as exclusionary reasons. He must first overcome the fact that we do not commonly distinguish between first and second-order reasons when we speak about the process of decision-making. Raz uses examples to establish both that such reasons exist and that they are, in fact, an ordinary part of everyday life before turning his attention to the legal realm.

In one example, Raz introduces us to Ann. Ann is too tired to make a decision regarding the investment of her money. She does not weigh first-order reasons; rather, she excludes the very possibility of weighing first order reasons because she 'cannot trust her own judgment at this moment'.[27] This is an example of incapacity-based reliance on the exclusionary potential of reasons for action.[28] In another example, Colin promises his wife that when making decisions about his son's education he will only consider the interests of his son. Raz lists a host of potentially relevant considerations and states that Colin believes 'that because of his promise he should disregard such considerations altogether' unless they have an impact on his son's interest in having the best possible education.[29] In this regard, promises are best understood as exclusionary reasons. Raz's point is that 'Colin's promise, like Ann's fatigue, does not affect the balance of reasons' since it 'is not itself either a reason for sending his son to a public school or against doing so'.[30]

Finally Raz introduces us to Jeremy. Jeremy is a soldier who is 'ordered by his commanding officer to appropriate and use a van belonging to a certain tradesman'.[31] His friend points out that, on the balance of reasons, it is better to disobey the command. Jeremy concurs, but nevertheless recognizes that he must do as his commander says. Raz argues that the 'order is a reason for

[26] *Ibid*, 41.
[27] *Ibid*, 37.
[28] *Ibid*, 38. 'Ann's reasoning is typical of situations in which the agent cannot trust his own judgement because he is drunk or subject to strong temptation or to threats or because he realizes that he is influenced by his emotions, etc'.
[29] *Ibid*, 39.
[30] *Ibid*.
[31] *Ibid*, 38.

doing what you were ordered regardless of the balance of reasons'.[32] The order from the commanding officer is an exclusionary reason for action. Jeremy must do what his superior says, simply *because he says so*. It is the source and not the content of the command that matters. This last example, unlike the others, directly touches upon Raz's understanding of authority. Raz argues that 'Orders are orders and should be obeyed even if wrong, even if no harm will come from disobeying them'.[33] Indeed, this 'is what it means to be a subordinate'.[34] Raz argues that it 'may be that Jeremy is wrong in accepting the authority of his commander in this case', however, he adds: 'But is he not right on the nature of authority?'[35]

By obeying the command despite his reservations, Jeremy is recognizing his subordinate status and recognizing that the commander's directives are content-independent reasons for action. It follows from this that if Jeremy had disobeyed his commander, he would not have treated him as an authority. By suggesting that Jeremy has understood the nature of authority in general, Raz is signifying that the commander–subordinate relationship is indicative of authority as such. His military analogy brings into focus the difference between the conception of authority that he is operating within *Practical Reason and Norms* and the conception of authority that he uses in *The Morality of Freedom*. In the latter work, Raz grounds his conception of authority in general in a moral ideal of authority: legal norms are not authoritative simply *because* they are uttered by a superior (and then serve as content-independent exclusionary reasons for action); rather, such directives are only authoritative if and only if they have morally justified content.[36] Clearly this view cannot be squared with the military analogy: it accurately represents neither what does happen nor what should happen in the military. An understanding of Raz's military model of authority enables us to foresee the kinds of challenges Raz will face in reference to the coherence of his position when he alters the model in *The Morality of Freedom*.[37]

No doubt the idea of an exclusionary reason has great explanatory power in the military context. Subordinates are ordered to obey the commands (or face a severe sanction) and by and large they do. The key question becomes: is the same true of law? Can the idea of an exclusionary reason have the same explanatory power in the legal context? This idea of an exclusionary reason is an interesting one, but carrying it over to the legal sphere is a difficult task. In *Practical Reason and Norms*, Raz wants the idea to have near-complete explanatory power. The idea of an exclusionary reason is supposed to shed light on

[32] *Ibid.*
[33] *Ibid.*
[34] *Ibid.*
[35] *Ibid.*
[36] Raz, *The Morality of Freedom*, above n 6, at 74.
[37] See ch 4.

the nature of legal norms, on the nature of legal systems, on the nature of the judicial duty, and on the nature of authority more generally. Can it perform this demanding role?

The idea of an exclusionary reason is itself a demanding one. It takes us beyond the idea of law as social fact (which is a predominantly backward-looking claim) into the world of practical rationality (which is primarily forward-looking or action-guiding). On Raz's account, we first have to factually ascertain the content of the norm and then we must treat it as a reason for action, excluding all others. Yet, how do we know that, in any given case, an individual is actually treating a legal norm as an exclusionary reason rather than a weighty (first-order) reason for action? Raz's answer to this question leads him to consider the psychological state of the agent – a clear sign that the argumentative burden Raz must bear is weighty.

To begin with, Raz makes it clear that when agents rely on exclusionary reasons they can still *deliberate* about the merits of the authoritative directive in question; they simply cannot *act* on the defeated reasons. In other words, blind obedience is not at the core of his understanding of exclusionary reasons. Identifying cases where legal reasons are in fact treated as exclusionary reasons for action becomes even more difficult once we bear this qualification in mind. Consider, for instance, cases in which our personal judgment concerning the best path of action coincides with the requirements of the law in question. Are we acting for personal reasons only, or is the presence of the legal norm simply another first-order reason to be added to the list of reasons in favour of a certain action?

Raz spies this difficulty and maintains that we cannot act both for an independent first-order reason and for an exclusionary reason because if we did, we would be guilty of 'double counting'.[38] If the idea of exclusionary reasons is going to capture our reasoning process, our reasons for action must be simple and our intentions must be pure. If the idea of an exclusionary reason is going to illuminate the nature of law, then the norms must frequently serve as exclusionary reasons; otherwise, the idea of a weighty reason for action becomes the more plausible candidate.[39] Nevertheless, a degree of suspicion is warranted here. It seems that Raz has had to invent a crime of practical reason (double counting) in order to preserve his claim that people frequently rely on exclusionary reasons. In reality, people often have complex motivations and this fact

[38] *Ibid*, 58.

[39] This is not the way that Raz currently frames his argument. See chs 3 and 4 for a discussion of the idea that all law claims authority. Note that Raz does mention his thesis that law claims authority in *Practical Reason and Norms*, but he only connects it to the idea that law claims to be supreme (ie regulate any kind of behavior). There is no mention of the ideal of morally justified authority. See Raz, *Practical Reason and Norms*, above n 8, at 151.

is not accurately captured by Raz's account.[40] Without an additional argument, Raz has simply defined away the competition.

Raz does offer readers an additional argument. He articulates a test by which we can distinguish weighty reasons from exclusionary reasons. The test appeals to a familiar feeling of unease: if a feeling of unease is experienced, either by the decision maker or by one who is judging whether or not the decision made was in fact the correct one, then this is evidence that the agent has acted on an exclusionary reason. That is, we feel uneasy when we think someone should have acted on the balance of reasons instead of the exclusionary reason, or vice versa.[41]

To see how this test works, he asks us to consider Jeremy's plight once again. Recall that he has been given an order by his superior – an order that he thinks is wrong. Jeremy then proceeds to instruct his subordinate, Dick, to carry out the order. Dick also thinks the order is wrong and he chooses to disobey Jeremy. Raz argues that Jeremy is 'torn between conflicting feelings'.[42] Jeremy is convinced that Dick did both the right thing and the wrong thing: 'He wants to praise and blame him at the same time'.[43] Raz argues that this is a common situation, it also occurs frequently when children disobey their parents' instructions.[44] Now the main point that Raz needs to convince us of is that people who are experiencing a first-order conflict do not experience the same sense of being torn:

> The importance of these cases is that they can hardly be interpreted as ordinary first-order conflicts. When a person having full knowledge of all the relevant factors acts on the weaker reasons, either because he does not appreciate the full weight of the stronger reasons or for some other motive, we may find various mitigating circumstances but we do not feel torn in the same way. The peculiarity of the situations we are concerned with is that we are aware that the action can be assessed in two ways which lead to contradictory results.[45]

He concludes that 'when we judge that such mixed reactions are appropriate we indicate our belief in the validity of exclusionary reasons'.[46] We recognize both that an exclusionary reason exists and that it makes a claim on us. We would not feel uneasy when disregarding such reasons if we did not think that we should obey them. So Raz assumes that we believe that we should obey authoritative directives even if the content of those directives offends our moral sense of right and wrong.

[40] See ch 6 for an exploration of this point.
[41] Raz, *Practical Reason and Norms*, above n 8, at 41.
[42] *Ibid*, 43.
[43] *Ibid.*
[44] *Ibid.*
[45] *Ibid.*
[46] *Ibid*, 45.

Contra Raz, such mixed feelings can surely be felt in response to first-order conflicts of weight as well. When two paths of action are equally desirable, we may feel uneasy when we are forced to choose between them. As Sartre notes, a deep tension may arise if we are forced to choose between accepting a new position overseas and caring for one's sick mother.[47] It is more than likely that we regret the forsaken option and, further, we can see how either choice could warrant praise and blame at the same time. So the feeling of unease can occur even if an exclusionary reason is not in play. The test is not as helpful as it is meant to be. After all, the very point of the test is to shore up his claim that exclusionary reasons exist and that we can identify them.

There is yet another serious problem with Raz's proposed test: it only works in instances where there are conflicting reasons at play. That is, the test works in cases where an authority tells you to do something you do not want to do. So either the authoritative directive is morally bad and you are good, or your moral compass has gone astray and the law is good.[48] But again, if we are dealing with situations where the law coincides with what you want to do independently of it, it is far more difficult to determine if the legal norm is being treated as an exclusionary reason for action rather than as a weighty reason. The feeling of unease will not be present in such instances.

Again, the burden is on Raz to establish that legal norms are best understood as exclusionary reasons for action. In *Practical Reason and Norms*, Raz attempts to discharge this burden, albeit with limited success. Raz no longer aims at this end as he has re-conceptualized his position in a way that takes the emphasis away from empirical claims about the world and about the manner that we actually reason with rules. Instead Raz shifts to the features that law must have if it is *potentially* going to serve as an authoritative (or exclusionary) reason for action. Law, Raz insists, claims authority over us. It claims to give us pre-emptory (or exclusionary) reasons for action, but whether it actually serves as an exclusionary reason is of little moment from a jurisprudential perspective.[49] The focus is on determining whether a law or set of laws enjoy the moral authority claimed, rather than on the relationship between law and order. Implicit in this shift in Raz's account is new understanding of what kind of things we must think about in order to grasp law's nature: we can understand the nature of law without attending to the way in which law works in the world; we can understand the nature of law without thinking about the relationship between legal norms and those who are meant to be governed by them. When we explore Raz's conception of law in *Practical Reason and Norms* we find that his entire theory about law's nature is a functional account about the precise way in which law guides the conduct of the citizenry. As mentioned, at the centre of

47 Jean-Paul Sartre, *Existentialism and Humanism* (London, Eyre Methuen, 1948) 35.
48 See ch 6 for an elaboration of this point.
49 Raz, 'Postema on Law's Autonomy' above n 7, at 11–12.

his account is the thesis that judges have a duty to apply the law. Moreover, he is not simply worried about the promulgation of norms by legal officials, but with the relationship that those norms have with law's subjects.

There is no doubt that Raz has altered his position in a significant manner. The question that remains is whether these alterations are successful: is Raz's current position a viable one? In upcoming chapters, I will raise serious questions about the tenability of Raz's current accounts about the nature of law and authority. The remainder of this chapter will set the stage for the arguments to come. Raz, as we have seen, spends a lot of time establishing his core claim that exclusionary reasons exist and are commonplace. His next task is to demonstrate that legal reasons are best understood as exclusionary reasons. Instead of adopting the external perspective, offering observations about the nature of law from afar, Raz takes us directly into the world of the judge and the citizen in order to attempt to establish the salience of his contention that law is best understood as a set of exclusionary reasons for action. It is an ambitious and difficult goal, but the very fact that Raz no longer aims at this end may indeed be a sign that it is not a tenable project in this form.

II. EXCLUSIONARY REASONS AND THE LEGAL SPHERE: ISSUES OF METHOD AND SUBSTANCE

Raz's next move is crucial for the success of *Practical Reason and Norms*. He must connect his understanding of exclusionary reasons for action with his understanding of law. Raz argues that mandatory norms (such as legal norms) are exclusionary reasons for action.[50] Raz will, of course, have to substantiate this claim, but there is another feature of mandatory norms that must be dealt with first: mandatory norms are not simply reasons; they are usually rules or principles.[51] Raz argues that we must distinguish rules (a term he uses interchangeably with principles) from other reasons. Weight does not distinguish the two, since rules differ in their weight, as do reasons. Raz concludes that one 'is thus forced to look to content-independent features of rules to distinguish rules from reasons which are not rules'.[52] Here we have come across a key connection with the sources thesis. Rules must be identifiable in a *content-independent* way. This is a factual test for the existence of a mandatory rule because it is the pedigree of the rule, not its content, which determines whether or not it is a mandatory norm. Since mandatory norms are exclusionary reasons for action, we find that the notion of 'exclusionary reasons' is wedded to the notion of 'content-independence'.

[50] Raz, *Practical Reason and Norms*, above n 8, at 62.
[51] *Ibid*, 49–50.
[52] *Ibid*, 51.

Raz then turns his attention to legal institutions, which he divides into three categories: norm-creating, norm-applying, and norm-enforcing (otherwise known as the legislator, the courts, and the police force).[53] Raz argues that it is 'Norm-applying institutions and not norm-creating institutions' that hold the key to an accurate understanding of an institutionalized system.[54] In other words, the judiciary is the central institution that enables us to understand the nature of legal systems and the nature of law. Raz gives two main reasons for placing law-applying organs at the centre of his theory: (1) he identifies law-applying organs as a necessary (and hence *universal*) feature of legal systems; and (2) he identifies law-applying organs as key to the law's ability to perform the central function which he allocates to it, namely, the regulation of social relations.[55] While much confusion has surrounded what precisely it means to identify a 'necessary' feature of law, one can look to the way Raz argues for the centrality of law-applying organs for clues.

For one, Raz argues that force or coercion is not a necessary feature of the concept of law. He provides two reasons: first, a society of angels would need rules, but not force; and second, it is conceivable that legal systems with law-applying organs but no law-enforcing organs could exist.[56] He does accept that such a coercion-less system, while logically possible, might be humanly impossible.[57] Clearly, Raz is not considering the limitations of human society when discriminating between necessary and contingent features of law. The key point is that for Raz, the presence of law-applying organs is a necessary and universal feature that is shared by all existing legal systems. In other words, the *presence* of law-applying organs does not vary from country to country or time to time: such organs, according to Raz, necessarily exist if the system in question is to qualify as a legal system.

We have thus far established a key methodological assumption operating in *Practical Reason and Norms*: that one should look to identify features shared by all legal systems that are necessary to the very functioning of law. If such features were removed, then legal systems would cease to be legal systems. The judgment about what features qualify as necessary in this way is inseparable from Raz's view of law's function:

> The claim that the presence of a primary organ is a defining feature of institutionalized systems is based not only on our common knowledge of typical cases of legal and similar systems but also on the crucial role such institutions, when present, play in regulating social relations.[58]

[53] *Ibid*, 132.
[54] *Ibid*.
[55] *Ibid*.
[56] *Ibid*, 158–59.
[57] *Ibid*, 158.
[58] *Ibid*, 137.

Raz elaborates on this role, saying that law-applying organs serve to officially settle disputes, adding that 'the difference between normative systems which provide systematic and institutionalized methods of settling disputes and those which do not is of momentous importance to their utility and function in regulating social behaviour'.[59] The important function that law-applying organs have in society is one key reason why Raz isolates and prioritizes this particular institutional aspect of legal systems. Thus, we can see that in Raz's original articulation of his theory of law in *Practical Reason and Norms*, he is very concerned with the precise way in which legal norms (and the work of officials) engender order in society. He views this issue as intimately related to, and indeed responsible for, his theory about what law *is*. It is especially noteworthy that Raz now denies that his theory is connected to a theory about law's function in any philosophically salient way.[60] The reasons that may lead him to make this claim will be explored in upcoming chapters, but it is useful at this juncture to put the pieces of his conceptual puzzle together.

The next step of the argument, and the most crucial, involves looking at the details of Raz's theory of law. This will clarify both why Raz views law-applying organs as vital for an understanding of law as well as the implications of this choice. It will also become clear how precisely Raz ties in his theory of exclusionary reasons with his theory of law. The tidiness of his theory and the interconnectedness of its various elements will also come to the fore. All this will be achieved by focusing on the key distinction between legal systems and systems of absolute discretion.

III. BETWEEN CHAOS AND ORDER: JUDGES AS WIELDERS OF OUR COLLECTIVE FATE

The idea of exclusionary reasons is the cornerstone of Raz's theory of law and the judiciary (which he refers to as the law-applying organ) is the central legal institution. When combined, a markedly formalistic vision of law emerges from the pages of *Practical Reason and Norms*. Judges, Raz argues, have a duty to apply the law: legal systems 'contain, indeed, consist of, norms which the courts are bound to apply regardless of their view of their merit'.[61] This duty to apply the law is the thesis that unlocks Raz's account of law and brings his theory to life. Judges are not simply important players in a political game of power and principle. Instead, they are charged with the responsibility of maintaining a stable body of norms that the citizens can turn to for guidance. The very same norms that guide our behaviour serve as the standard by which

[59] *Ibid.*
[60] Raz, 'Postema on Law's Autonomy' above n 7. See also ch 7.
[61] Raz, *Practical Reason and Norms*, above n 8, at 139.

judges evaluate our behaviour. Judges must treat citizens *as if* they too are required to treat legal norms as exclusionary reasons for action. In this regard, the judicial duty to apply the law does not simply secure the exclusionary nature of legal norms. This duty also gives shape to the legal system more generally. Legal systems are themselves exclusionary in nature. This is Raz's account in a nutshell. By exploring the distinction between legal systems and systems of absolute discretion, we clarify the way in which his positivist theory of law connects to his vision of adjudication. Moreover, this distinction offers a kind of creation myth that is meant to highlight the features that all legal systems must possess. As we shall see, the features highlighted – an autonomous set of legal norms that can serve as reasons for action of the populace enabling order to triumph over chaos – places Raz within the tradition tracing back to Cicero, of which Postema speaks.

Systems of absolute discretion are hypothetical constructions that are meant to serve a specific didactic purpose in Raz's account.[62] By contrasting legal systems with what they are not, we are supposed to gain a better understanding of what they are. In purely discretionary systems, judges have no duty to apply the law and hence judicial decisions do not perform a guiding function. Judges are not required to follow precedents, nor are they required to apply any particular norms, whether they be legislated or customary. Rather, they are subject to a single instruction: 'they are always to make the decision which they think best on the basis of all the valid reasons'.[63] Raz argues that legal systems, by contrast, 'contain, indeed, consist of, norms which the courts are bound to apply regardless of their view of their merit'.[64] In other words, the law consists of norms that 'primary organs are bound to apply and are not at liberty to disregard whenever they find their application undesirable, all things considered'.[65]

To reiterate, for judges who are permitted to exercise absolute discretion, decision-making is a matter of weighing all the relevant reasons in each and every case. This does not mean, of course, that judges are entitled to decide in an arbitrary way. They must do what they think is best on a case-by-case basis and they may appeal to ultimate values such as justice and fairness in order to justify their decisions. However, such a system of law involves a great sacrifice, according to Raz: consistency over time is lost.[66] When judges create new laws instead of upholding pre-existing norms, citizens will be uncertain about what kind of behaviour is permissible and prohibited. In other words, the guidance function of law will be compromised. If judges

[62] *Ibid*, 137.
[63] *Ibid*, 138.
[64] *Ibid.*
[65] *Ibid.*
[66] *Ibid*, 139.

apply the law instead of exercising discretion, they reinforce the exclusionary status of legal norms. Not only do they maintain a stable body of norms, but the formalistic approach ensures that citizens can have the requisite motivation to allocate legal norms' exclusionary force. Judges, Raz argues, 'must judge individuals *as if* they should take the legal requirements as exclusionary reasons' (my italics).[67]

Indeed, only when judges apply the pre-existing set of norms can we (as citizens) identify our legal rights.[68] According to Raz, the judicial duty to apply the law is responsible for the creation and maintenance of stable rights; citizens look to these rights for guidance in order to determine how to act and they expect these rights to be reinforced by the courts. This point becomes clear when Raz argues that, contrary to systems of absolute discretion, legal systems do provide guidance because of the law-applying duty of officials:

> Legal and similar systems, on the other hand, do provide guidance to individuals. They contain norms determining the rights and duties of individuals. These are the very same norms that the primary institutions are bound to apply and that is the reason that they also provide guidance to individuals as to their rights and duties in litigation before the primary organs.[69]

When judges apply the law they reinforce the set of stable norms that serve to guide the conduct of citizens and function as the storehouse of their rights and duties. Citizens have a reason to treat legal norms as exclusionary reasons for action because they can expect judges to reinforce the exclusionary force of legal norms. The operative assumption is that the work of the courts has a direct influence on the motivation of the citizenry to treat legal norms as exclusionary reasons.[70] Conversely, in systems of absolute discretion, the lack of the said duty means that consistency is lacking. Given such frequent changes to the law, the system fails to produce a stable set of norms. Consequently, citizens cannot look to these norms to identify their rights and duties. Only when law is treated by judges as an autonomous set of norms can it serve as a storehouse of rights and duties; only when the system functions as a storehouse of rights and duties does it actually qualify as a legal system.

The over-arching message is clear: when judges act dutifully, society is richly rewarded with a stable set of norms that the citizenry can treat as reasons for action (of an exclusionary kind). When law's autonomy is breached regularly by appeals to ultimate values, the price paid by all is steep. An appeal to values on the part of judges threatens the predictability of decision-making, leaving citizens uncertain about what kind of behaviour is permissible and

[67] *Ibid*, 144.
[68] *Ibid*, 138
[69] *Ibid*.
[70] Raz now denies this connection. See chs 3 and 7 for an exploration of this point.

what kind of behaviour is prohibited. The exercise of judicial discretion moves society towards uncertainty and chaos. In *Practical Reason and Norms* it is the judicial duty to apply the law that holds the key to creating and sustaining an orderly society.

Not only is the law-applying function of judges responsible for guidance and evaluation, it is also responsible for identifying the discrete set of norms that belong to a given system (a task which is of interest to officials, citizens and legal philosophers alike). 'Indeed the test by which we determine whether a norm belongs to the system is, roughly speaking, that it is a norm which the primary organs ought to apply when judging and evaluating behaviour'.[71] This point adds another dimension to the tidiness of Raz's theory: the law-applying duty of judges is the basis for identifying the norms of the system and ensures that legal norms perform the double role of guidance and evaluation.[72] Excessive law-creation undermines the ability to identify the norms of the system, thereby reaffirming Raz's commitment to a relatively formalistic theory that meets the requirements of the strong autonomy thesis. Raz denies that he is committed to this thesis, and while his current views do not align with his former position (as considered here), I will argue that he has a very difficult time shedding this particular commitment.[73]

To be clear, the duty to apply the law is not to be understood in an overly simplistic way, as if judges mechanically identify a rule and apply it to situations in *every single case*. This view is clearly implausible and is a mere caricature of adjudication. Raz insists that judges are not 'computing machines always applying pre-existing rules regardless of their own views of which rules or which decision is the right one'.[74] Judges do not always apply the law. Sometimes they make mistakes and inadvertently create new law.[75] Of course, this particular qualification does not take the pressure off the law-applying duty of the judge. Discretionary activity enters at other junctures as well. It is possible, perhaps inevitable, for disputes to arise that are not regulated by law. When the law is silent, judges can appeal to ultimate values to fill the void. Furthermore, because of 'the vagueness, open texture and incompleteness of all legal systems, there are many disputes for which the system does not provide a correct answer'.[76] Here Raz echoes Hart's familiar point that laws, like language, have 'open texture'.[77] This is an inevitable feature of law and an inevitable source of discretionary activity.

[71] Raz, *Practical Reason and Norms*, above n 8, at 139.
[72] *Ibid*, 142.
[73] See ch 3.
[74] Raz, *Practical Reason and Norms*, above n 8, at 139.
[75] *Ibid*, 145.
[76] *Ibid*, 139.
[77] Hart, *The Concept of Law*, above n 1, at 128.

Raz tries to incorporate these qualifications into his general position. He argues that judges 'are to follow a certain body of norms regardless of their views of their merits and are allowed to act on their own views only to the extent that this is allowed by those norms'.[78] Herein lies perhaps the most powerful objection that a Razian could put forth to challenge the largely formalist interpretation of Raz's theory of law that I am currently setting out. The extent of discretion that a judge has depends on the extent to which the law (and the conventions that govern the interpretation of laws) allows judges to exercise their personal moral judgment. Some jurisdictions allow for more freedom in the courtroom, others less. Whether judges are instructed to create new law or apply existing law is thus a contingent matter that depends on the content of the master rule(s) in question. Defenders of Raz who launch this challenge might argue that *Practical Reason and Norms* should be read in the context of his later works. For instance, in *Ethics in the Public Domain*, Raz stresses that the law can give official directives – it can direct officials to go beyond the law in certain circumstances.[79] This newer argument sees the rule of recognition (the 'master' rule that contains the criteria of validity for all the legal norms) as a content-independent rule rather than an exclusionary one.[80] Despite any appeal this objection might have, it is not particularly powerful when set against the arguments forwarded in *Practical Reason and Norms*.

Raz's formalist conception of the judicial role is defended in an explicit manner in *Practical Reason and Norms*, leaving very little room for interpretation on the part of judges. Even if judges do not always apply the law for the reasons listed above, Raz insists that applying pre-existing norms is their job. To underscore this point, Raz asks us to compare the work of a judge with that of a minister of transport. The minister must consider economic factors, but his policy must be based on the assessment of *all* the relevant variables. He is *not* required to base his decision on what Raz refers to as a 'partial judgment' from the economic point of view.[81] Conversely, Raz argues that the judge 'both regards his judgment as based on a partial assessment of the valid reasons and as justifying action'.[82] Legal systems, Raz argues, 'possess their own internal system of evaluation'.[83] Such evaluation takes place from 'the legal point of view' – all extra-legal considerations are to be excluded.[84] The

[78] Raz, *Practical Reason and Norms*, above n 8, at 139.

[79] Raz, *Ethics in the Public Domain*, above n 21, at 333.

[80] The idea of a rule of recognition is introduced to us by Hart. This master rule enables us to determine whether a given norm is a valid legal norm. See Hart, *The Concept of Law*, above n 1, at 94.

[81] Raz, *Practical Reason and Norms*, above n 8, at 144.

[82] *Ibid.*

[83] *Ibid*, 139.

[84] *Ibid.*

legal system is itself an 'exclusionary system'.[85] Law offers a limited domain of reason – reasons that judges are under a duty to apply. It is this duty that, according to Raz in *Practical Reason and Norms*, has near-complete explanatory power. By understanding what judges do, we can then understand how law works and the precise job of legal norms. They are, as Raz famously maintains, exclusionary reasons for action.

The reason why Raz considers law-application to be the only necessary feature of legal systems is that systems of absolute discretion: (a) are not legal systems by definition and (b) do not exist. However, if Raz admits that the amount of discretion judges enjoy is a contingent matter, then he will have to acknowledge that discretionary systems are not merely a hypothetical concoction and that the distinction between discretionary systems and legal systems breaks down. Raz would then have to rewrite his entire theory of law, erasing the centrality of law-application and its implications: consistency would not be a virtue (or it would be achieved via means other than law application); guidance would not rest on the reinforcement of a stable body of norms; legal norms would no longer be a source of rights and duties; and citizens would have to be motivated to treat law as a body of exclusionary reasons despite knowing that they might not be able to rely on judges to treat laws as if they were exclusionary reasons. It is clear that once the law-applying duty of the judge is removed, Raz's entire theory unravels.

This, as we will see, is precisely what happens. The problem is that the discretionary activities of the judiciary are not limited to the hypothetical realm. They are a common feature of practice and Raz's failure to accommodate this point dooms his original theory. Raz ultimately fails to offer an explanation of common law adjudication that is consistent with his positivist story.

IV. COMMON LAW SYSTEMS: A COUNTER-EXAMPLE

Those familiar with Raz's theory often view his corpus of works from the perspective of his later works and hence agree with Raz that he can separate his theory of law from a theory of adjudication. But, in *Practical Reason and Norms*, it becomes particularly difficult to arrive at conclusions other than those drawn above. These conclusions are not without consequences for Raz's theory. If we accept Raz's theory as it stands, we find that it is an extremely tidy theory of law – in fact, it is too tidy and fails to appreciate the everyday practice of law in common law systems. Do pre-existing legal norms *really* play the double role of guiding conduct and serving as standards of evaluation for judges? If judges fail to apply the law, will it *actually* corrode into the chaos that is a system of

[85] *Ibid*, 145. Raz explicitly states that the legal point of view is 'an exclusionary point of view'.

absolute discretion? The answer to both these questions appears to be 'no'. The existence of common law systems, where no such law-applying duty appears to exist in the precise way that Raz has conceptualized it, provides a counter-example to his theory.[86] He realizes this and attempts to answer the challenge presented by such systems.

Raz acknowledges that in 'many legal systems, for example in ours, there are courts with power not only to settle at their discretion unsettled cases but also to overrule established precedent'.[87] He notes that they 'are entitled, in fact, to repeal laws and replace them with rules which they judge to be better than old ones'.[88] Raz is aware that the presence of these systems 'might be claimed to provide a counter-example to my claim that the law consists only of rules which the courts are bound to follow'.[89] He responds to this challenge by appealing to what he calls 'ultimate laws of discretion'. However, in the process of doing so, he points to one of his key commitments: the bindingness of rules. Raz writes:

> A rule which the courts have complete liberty to disregard or change is not binding on them and is not part of the legal system. But the courts in Common Law jurisdictions do not have this power with respect to the binding Common Law rules. They cannot change them whenever they consider that on the balance of reasons it would be better to do so. They may change them only for certain kinds of reasons. They may change them, for example, for being unjust, for iniquitous discrimination, for being out of step with the court's conception of the body of laws to which they belong.[90]

Here Raz restates his position on the bindingness of rules: rules are binding when the court is not at liberty to disregard them. How, then, are the primary rules of common law jurisdictions binding? Raz's answer is that they are not. Rather, his claim is that the 'Common Law rules' are binding on judges (ie the rules that determine whether and in what circumstances they can alter existing law).

We might wonder whether Raz escapes the challenge that common law systems present to his theory. Raz wants to turn to the bindingness of common law rules, the rules that direct the behaviour of judges, in order to shore up his theory. Up until this point in *Practical Reason and Norms*, Raz's discussion

[86] If the duty to apply the law is interpreted in a broad sense (ie to stand for the claim that judges must make reference to previous rulings and statutes) then no issue exists. I have argued that the duty to apply the law stands for a more narrow and robust claim whereby judges are duty-bound to apply factually ascertainable legal norms, regardless of the view of their merits. The fact Raz flags common law systems as problematic is further evidence that the narrow reading is correct. More will be said about common law adjudication in ch 2.

[87] Raz, *Practical Reason and Norms*, above n 8, at 140.

[88] *Ibid.*

[89] *Ibid.*

[90] *Ibid.*

of the bindingness of rules revolves around primary rules, not the rules of discretion that apply to judges (labelled by Raz as binding common law rules). Yet, recall Raz's argument that a legal system consists of 'norms which the courts are bound to apply regardless of their view of their merit'.[91] Since the duty to apply the law is a defining characteristic of law, how can Raz allow that this duty does not hold in certain systems without undermining his theory? In common law systems judges do not have a duty to apply pre-existing laws: the merit of the primary norms is precisely what judges are ordered to consider. Indeed, they are given discretion to change the primary rules if they happen to be 'unjust', 'iniquitous', or 'out of step with the court's conception of the body of laws to which they belong'.[92]

There are several causes for concern about this attempt to patch up the theory. First, one should note that judges who operate under such instructions seem to be given a great deal of leeway with the primary rules of the system. In other words, judges would be hard-pressed to disobey the rules of discretion of such a system. In fact, these instructions have more in common with the instructions given to judges in systems of absolute discretion than those in legal systems. Second, and perhaps more importantly, concrete decisions do not sit in a unidirectional relationship with the rules of discretion: the rules guiding judges can be given more specific content in light of particular decisions. In other words, changes in the law can impact on the rules and conventions that govern the behaviour of judges. Elsewhere Raz acknowledges this point when he argues that law-making procedures include conventions of interpretation.[93] He explains that 'a change in the conventions of interpretation of a legal system changes its law'.[94] The illustration Raz gives us is telling: if the legal definition of 'person' is extended to include 'foetuses', such a change has occurred.[95] Given that a change in the conventions of interpretation can be brought about by a judicial decision concerning the primary rules of a system (ie a decision that renders abortion illegal), this means that judges can change the rules that guide them. Hence, Raz's statement that judges in common law jurisdictions cannot alter the rules governing their behaviour is false.

As I have shown, the existence of common law systems threatens the viability of Raz's theory. Such systems violate the criteria of Raz's definition of legality, which is supposed to capture the universal and necessary features of *all* legal systems. At a minimum, the existence of counter-examples undermines the key elements of Raz's theory in *Practical Reason and Norms*. Consider the guidance function: if existing systems do not instruct judges to apply the

91 *Ibid*, 139.
92 *Ibid*, 140.
93 Raz, *Ethics in the Public Domain*, above n 21, at 236.
94 *Ibid*.
95 *Ibid*.

law, then clearly this duty is not necessary for the maintenance of order. In response to other notable attempts to accommodate common law systems, Raz attempts to devise a theory of common law that is consistent with his positivist theory while offering a theory of adjudication that coheres with the way in which common law judges perform their role. In later chapters, I will prove that neither strategy succeeds.

In chapter two, I illustrate why Raz's attempt to accommodate common law reasoning into his theory is unsuccessful. Instead of presenting us with a nuanced theory of common law adjudication, Raz presents us with an artificial regimentation that coheres with his pre-existing positivist commitments. This first attempt to accommodate the common law into his theory is made in *The Authority of Law*.[96] In his more recent book, *Ethics in the Public Domain*, he introduces a theory of adjudication in addition to his theory of law – a move that also proves to be problematic.[97] On the surface, this strategy seems successful, but a closer look at the interconnections between the elements of his theory reveals the source of tension: as chapter three will make clear, one cannot abandon the view that judges apply the law and hope to keep the other core pieces of the puzzle in place.

Once Raz's view of judges as law appliers is replaced by a view of judges as moral reasoners, he has quite a bit of work left to do if he is going to provide us with a coherent theory of law. Legal sources, which are of the utmost importance in *Practical Reason and Norms*, become less important. Recall that in *Practical Reason and Norms,* legal sources have a backward-looking and a forward-looking aspect: not only must citizens and judges ascertain the content of these norms, but judges also have a duty to apply them.[98] Once Raz states that judges are moral reasoners who do and should look to extra-legal moral reasons when making decisions, the sources thesis becomes problematic. That is to say, it only identifies pre-existing law (the backward-looking aspect) and it does not identify the set of norms that judges must apply (the forward-looking aspect). Raz also has to account for the motivation of citizens: if they cannot expect judges to reinforce the exclusionary status of legal norms, why should they grant these norms exclusionary force? If citizens do not do that in practice, then should we still conceive of law as a set of exclusionary reasons? These questions and a number of additional ones will be asked along the way. In his next book, *The Authority of Law*, Raz tries to avoid all of these difficulties. He offers us a model of adjudicative reasoning that is supposed to accommodate common law reasoning into his positivist framework.[99] It is to this argument that we will now turn.

[96] Raz, *The Authority of Law*, above n 14, at 185.
[97] Raz, *Ethics in the Public Domain*, above n 21, at 326.
[98] Raz, *Practical Reason and Norms*, above n 8, at 137.
[99] Raz, *The Authority of Law*, above n 14, at 180.

2

Between Fact and Value

THE SHARP DISTINCTION between fact and value that sits at the foundation of modern-day positivist thought can be traced back to earlier positivist thought. Bentham, for instance, distinguishes between expository and censorial jurisprudence. The expositor's job is to determine what the law *is*; only then can the censor seek to articulate what it *ought* to be. More precisely, according to Bentham, the expositor's job is to 'shew what the *Legislator* and the underworkman the *Judge* has done *already*'.[1] To perform this function, the expositor must rely on her apprehension, memory and judgment. She is interested in comprehending the past acts of legal officials. This first task sets the parochial factual stage for universal (or at least universalizable) moral judgments. The expositor, Bentham argues, is a citizen of a particular country who must seek to understand the content of the laws of that country. The censor, by contrast, is a 'citizen of the world'.[2] Her utilitarian judgments are supposed to transcend the particulars to capture what ought to be. She must 'suggest what the *Legislator ought* to do *in future*'.[3] To perform this important role, she must rely on a different mental faculty altogether. The 'sentiments of pleasure and displeasure' serve as the raw material for the utilitarian calculation that Bentham advocates.[4] However, for Bentham, the moral conclusions do not overtake the positive legal mandates. The positive law is supposed to do all of the practical work in our day-to-day lives: Bentham instructs us to obey punctually and censure freely.[5] Both tasks must be performed for Bentham's project to be realized and each, as we can see, requires a distinct set of intellectual capacities.

The distinct nature of the two interpretive undertakings set out by Bentham requires us to determine in advance what kind of reasoning we wish to engage

[1] J Bentham, *A Fragment on Government* in R Guess and Q Skinner (series eds), *Cambridge Texts in the History of Political Thought* (Cambridge, Cambridge University Press, 1998) 8. Unlike Raz, Bentham is primarily interested in what the law ought to be going forward. Furthermore, it is not clear that Bentham shares Raz's view that figuring out what law is is a fact-finding exercise. See P Schofield, 'Jeremy Bentham and HLA Hart's "Utilitarian Tradition in Jurisprudence"' (2010) 1 *Jurisprudence* 2.

[2] *Ibid*, 8.

[3] *Ibid*.

[4] *Ibid*.

[5] *Ibid*, 10.

in. Are we seeking to determine what law *is* or what it *ought* to be? The need to separate these two tasks does not pose a particularly onerous challenge for Bentham, insofar as we are solely concerned with the context in which he situates his arguments in *A Fragment on Government*.[6] However, once we shift our focus from the citizen to the judge, things become markedly more complicated. This distinction presents us with a very limited array of options. Are judges primarily expositors who are under a duty to apply the law? Do judges operate first as expositors and then as censors, relying on moral arguments? Or are judges primarily censors? I will argue that all three of these options fail to adequately conceptualise the work of the judge. In Raz's case it is the distinction between fact and value is to blame for this, as it is simply too sharp to reflect the phenomenology of judicial decision-making.

Raz, in the course of his career, struggles to capture the features of adjudicatory practice within his positivist framework, which is underpinned by the sharp distinction between legal facts and moral values. In *Practical Reason and Norms*, Raz locates the judicial role on the expositorial side of the dichotomy. Judges must identify the content of legal norms, which they are then under a duty to apply. The judge looks to moral standards only when gaps emerge, when mistakes are made, or when the law is unsettled. As I elucidate in this book, Raz eventually abandons this view and proceeds to locate his account of adjudication firmly on the censorial side of the dichotomy (insofar as we understand the term 'censorial' to stand for judgment about what *ought* to be done). Judges, Raz now insists, are moral reasoners who should appeal to moral principles when rendering their decisions. Why does Raz make such a dramatic shift?

One plausible answer is as follows: if Raz's account in *Practical Reason and Norms* is going to be tenable, he must account for the existence of common law adjudication. Recall that I have argued that Raz's initial attempt to account for this practice was insufficient.[7] Unless he can bring this potential outlier into the positivist fold, it will stand as counter-example to his account of law, which at this stage is still wedded to a theory of adjudication. In *The Authority of Law*, which is the focus of this chapter, Raz attempts to discharge the argumentative burden by articulating a model of common law adjudication that aims to account for the discretionary powers of the judiciary without sacrificing the idea that law is best understood as a discrete set of factually ascertainable norms that can serve as reasons for action. While creative and promising, Raz's rule-plus-exception model proves to be ill-suited to the job it must perform.

[6] There are deep problems with Bentham's theory, however. See A Perreau-Saussine, 'Bentham and the Bootstrappers of Jurisprudence: The Moral Commitments of a Rationalist Legal Positivist' (2004) 63 *CLJ* 346.

[7] See ch 1.

Following NE Simmonds, I will demonstrate that Raz's rule-plus-exception model fails to capture a key feature of common law adjudication: judges do not simply add exceptions to existing rules; sometimes they cast the law in a new light. That is to say, a new case may lead judges to a re-articulation of the intellectual underpinnings of an area of law. This possibility operates as a counter-example to the rule-plus-exception model, revealing it to be an artificial regimentation of the practice. I will then demonstrate that Raz's model is untenable for an additional, equally devastating reason: it collapses from within. Specifically, Raz's model collapses into a version of Dworkin's interpretive account of adjudication.

By exploring the relationship between Raz and Dworkin, an additional point about the debate comes into view: the constant vacillation between thinking about law as fact or as moral value (understood through the eyes of Hercules, Dworkin's ideal judge) hides from sight a third alternative: that the practice itself is infused with values that can, at times, inform the judicial decision-making process. This very possibility is brought to life in Simmonds's example, discussed below. While this possibility is explored at length by thinkers who seek to understand the philosophical foundations of the common law, such discussions are viewed as different in nature to the debate in general jurisprudence. By slicing through the fact/value dichotomy (as it is utilized by Raz and others), we can begin to see the way in which debates about the nature of contract law, for instance, are related to the questions and concerns that animate the debate between positivists and their interlocutors.

I will begin this chapter with an examination of the two-pronged argument that Raz offers us in defence of his sources thesis. As we shall see, the sharp dichotomy between legal facts and moral values mimics Bentham's distinction between expositor and censor: Raz, like Bentham before him, connects each job with a distinct intellectual task. However, the sharp lines are not easily reproduced in the complex world of legal practice, a point that Raz concedes but cannot accommodate into his core thesis.

I. THE SOURCES THESIS DEFINED AND DEFENDED

The sources thesis captures the claim that 'law' is best understood as a set of fact-based norms identifiable by their pedigree alone. Like some before him, Raz rejects the idea that content matters: the validity of a law is determined by its source alone and the merit of the norm is irrelevant. Raz provides us with two arguments that seek to justify the sources thesis. The first argument appeals to a familiar set of distinctions, while the second argument attempts to explain why these distinctions are important. To do so it focuses on elucidating the function of the law. The two arguments are mutually reinforcing and interdependent. The account of law's function will only be viable if the distinctions that underpin the sources thesis illuminate the nature of law and vice versa.

The sources thesis equates law with pre-existing rules that can be factually ascertained. For Raz, this thesis systematises a number of distinctions that are commonly used in reference to the law: namely, the distinction between a judge's technical skill and her moral character, between applying existing law and creating new law, and finally between settled and unsettled law.[8] Greater emphasis is placed on the first term in each pair. Judges use their technical skill to identify settled law and apply it and law-creation is limited to only those situations where the law is unsettled. When judges create new law, they employ moral arguments. In such instances, a judge's moral character comes into play rather than her technical expertise. Recall that Raz defends an account in *Practical Reason and Norms* whereby the judges apply settled law in most cases – discretion is a marginal, but inevitable, activity.[9] In Hartian terms, the core is much larger than the penumbra.[10] As we shall see Raz has yet to abandon this account by the time he pens the essays in *The Authority of Law*.

Notice that Raz's argument on this point echoes Bentham's inasmuch as the judge is determining either what law is (*qua* expositor) or what it ought to be (*qua* censor). Since these two distinct roles utilise different intellectual skill-sets, the judge must determine in advance whether the law is settled or unsettled and proceed accordingly. Again, it is not clear that the adjudicative landscape divides into such crisply delineated categories. Do judges have these two distinct jobs? Can we know this as a matter of fact, rather than interpretation? The phenomenology of adjudicatory practice suggests a more complex picture. Raz recognises the limitations of the dichotomy between law application and law creation, admitting that 'the courts, in most cases brought before them, probably neither merely apply an existing law nor do they merely initiate a new law'; rather, they 'may be doing a little of both'.[11] Once this qualification is made, it appears as though Raz has accounted for the observed practice. In this regard, legal positivism is an attractive theory because it *seems* to offer readers the clarity they crave without sacrificing the complexity that any viable account of law must exhibit. Nevertheless, the picture is misleading. Raz is attempting to soften his stark distinctions by qualifying his position and

[8] J Raz, *The Authority of Law: Essays on Law and Morality* (New York, Oxford University Press, 1979) 49.

[9] See ch 1.

[10] HLA Hart, *The Concept of Law,* 2nd edn (Oxford, Oxford University Press, 1994) 123. Hart famously distinguishes between the core of settled meaning and the penumbra of doubt: 'Nothing can eliminate this duality of a core of certainty and a penumbra of doubt when we are engaged in bringing particular situations under general rules'.

[11] Raz, *The Authority of Law*, above n 8, at 94.

by directing our attention to an empirical observation, but it is an observation that is *not* represented in his definitional architecture.

One might respond by insisting that it is useful to have clear distinctions even if most situations require the application of both concepts. In other words, notwithstanding some complexity, being able to draw clear distinctions allows us to comprehend and navigate a complex world. Despite any initial plausibility, there are problems with this response in the context in which it is forwarded. One notable difficulty with this approach is that distinctions may become infinitely receding. If we consider a given judgment, we should be able to identify those elements that involve the application of pre-existing law and those that are creative. This strategy will only succeed if one can identify a relatively clear boundary between the core and the penumbra, but Raz denies that such a boundary exists (even though his theory needs this very line to exist).[12] Unless the positivist establishes that such a boundary *does* exist (and the burden is theirs), we can never separate out and ascribe parts of any given judgment to law application and other parts to law creation: every part of any given judgment will exhibit both characteristics. Moreover, marking the point at which factual law-application ends and value-laden law creation begins must itself be a matter of fact and not interpretation if the set of distinctions is going to be useful.[13]

Raz employs a second strategy in order to deal with the gap that exists between his theory and the practice of law. He argues that his theory is supported by common usage. On those rare occasions when his theory goes beyond common usage, it should be seen as performing a 'tidying' function. According to Raz, the set of distinctions that underpin the sources thesis need not mirror practice at all times: 'If, in fact, the sources thesis coincides with the way these distinctions are generally applied, it has explanatory power and is supported to that extent'. When the practice does not line up with Raz's distinctions, the sources thesis 'can then be regarded as being a systemising or a tidying-up thesis where it goes beyond the ordinary use of these distinctions'.[14]

What justifies Raz's act of conceptual 'tidying' and how do we know whether the distinctions he draws clarify more than they obscure? One plausible response would be to claim that the distinction between law application

[12] *Ibid*, 73. See W Lucy, 'Adjudication' in JL Coleman and S Shapiro (eds), *The Oxford Handbook of Jurisprudence and Philosophy of Law* (Oxford, Oxford University Press, 2002) 220.

[13] Stephen Perry's assessment is correct: 'These distinctions to which Raz adverts, however, are not so much systematized by the sources thesis as they are implied by it, in the sense that they do not constitute incontrovertible social facts, hard empirical data which a theory of law must acknowledge and explain or else be accounted unacceptable; they are, rather, claims about the theoretical character of the legal process which presuppose the acceptance, explicit or implicit, of a certain philosophical interpretation of that process' in 'Judicial Obligation, Precedent and the Common Law' (1987) 7 *OJLS* 228.

[14] Raz, *The Authority of Law*, above n 8, at 50.

and law-creation must hold *most* of the time. This does not mean that judges must apply law more than they create it (although I argue below that Raz is committed to this view), but it does mean that in most instances judges must be clearly applying the law or clearly creating new law. Judges cannot often be 'doing a little of both', despite what Raz suggests above. In short, Raz cannot simply point to familiar features of the practice in order to dull the sharp edges of his distinctions. The observations must be accounted for in his theory; otherwise, he offers readers little more than the appearance of a nuanced account.

The second argument forwarded in support of the sources thesis (and the more central of the two) is supposed to illustrate the importance of the initial set of distinctions, while justifying any 'conceptual tidying' that might be required. The main reason why fact-based sources deserve centre-stage in our concept of law is, according to Raz, because of the important role such norms play in our society. Raz maintains that it

> is an essential part of the function of law in society to mark the point at which a private view of members of the society . . . ceases to be their private view and becomes (i.e. lays a claim to be) a view binding on all members notwithstanding their disagreement with it.[15]

Law can perform this unifying function by offering fact-based norms that give the citizenry 'publicly ascertainable ways of guiding behaviour and regulating aspects of social life'.[16] If law is going to play this role, legal norms must be factually ascertainable and followable, at least by most of us most of the time. Raz's understanding of what law *is* is thus grounded in a theory of what law *does* and how it does it. Legal norms must provide a fairly stable set of reasons for action if law is going to perform this function.

Raz, at this juncture, is silent on the precise role that judges must play in order to ensure that a stable storehouse of norms persists over time. Elsewhere in *The Authority of Law*, a familiar story is retold. We are reminded that legal systems are not discretionary systems, as only legal systems 'contain laws determining the rights and duties of individuals' and these are 'laws which the courts are bound to apply in settling dispute'.[17] The ability of law to guide the conduct of the population is very much dependent on and not independent of the judicial duty to apply the law.[18] Granted, he does qualify his position, noting there are disputes to which the existing norms do not provide a correct answer (even

[15] *Ibid*, 51.
[16] *Ibid.*
[17] *Ibid.*
[18] Raz also repeats his claim that the legal point of view is a limited one and that the test by which we determine whether a law belongs to a given system is whether judges are under a duty to apply it. See Raz, *The Authority of Law*, above n 8, at 112–13.

though they may rule out certain answers as wrong). Consequently, discretionary value-laden judgments can be limited, but cannot be eliminated. The idea of a settled core and a penumbra of uncertainty resurfaces once again.

Clearly, Raz still has work to do to shore up this account and he is well aware of this fact. Most importantly, he has yet to account for the discretionary activities of judges. In *The Authority of Law*, he forwards a more ambitious argument that, if successful, would bring common law adjudication into the definitional confines of legal positivism. Specifically, Raz champions a rule-plus-exception model of adjudication that explains how a set of fact-based rules can persist through time despite the fact that judges appear to have the freedom to change the rules. Not only does this view of adjudication assume the existence of a core and a penumbra, it also assumes that the core of fact-based norms is much larger than the penumbra of uncertainty that, when encountered, would prompt judges to create law anew. Significantly, the rule-plus-exception model of adjudication is not an account of what judges should do, but merely an attempt to conceptualise what judges actually do. Raz sets out to explain away the appearance of a degree of freedom in common law adjudication which would render the practice incompatible with his positivist theory of law.

A critical evaluation of the rule-plus-exception model is not simply of interest for the jurisprudential debate. This model gives theoretical voice to a familiar understanding of precedent in common law systems, where the ratio of the previous case becomes a kind of rule that is binding on future courts. The failure of his model demonstrates, in no uncertain terms, the inadequacy of a theory of precedent that views past decisions as fact-based rules that future judges are bound to apply. We need not, of course, argue that precedent has no constraining force; rather, we simply need a different story about its role in legal decision-making.

II. RAZ'S RULE-PLUS-EXCEPTION MODEL

The fluidity of common law decision-making – which is often characterized as allowing for incremental change – does not fit easily with the positivist's rule-based model. Raz acknowledges that the English system 'combines following precedent with considerable flexibility because it allows the courts, even those bound by precedent, to distinguish a previous decision rather than follow it'.[19] At first glance, the familiar act of distinguishing cases does not appear to be captured by categories of law creation or law application, thereby casting doubt on the salience of the very distinction on which Raz so heavily relies.

[19] *Ibid.*

Undeterred by appearances, Raz re-crafts the distinction in an attempt to capture this more nuanced gradation of change. The original distinction between law creation and law application is supplemented, furnishing us with four possibilities: 1) law application; 2) law modification; 3) over-ruling (or law creation); and 4) gap-filling. The second category of law modification stands out as especially important as it captures the gradual change that is characteristic of common law reasoning. Raz insists that the act of distinguishing cases, or law modification, is a very restricted form of law-making which involves adding an exception to an existing rule. The following two conditions constrain this process:

(1) The modified rule must be the rule laid down in the precedent that is restricted by the addition of a further condition for its application.
(2) The modified rule must be such as to justify the order made in the precedent.[20]

Consider the first condition: what does it amount to in practice? Judges who distinguish the present case from a past case can 'only narrow down the rules' – they 'cannot extend them'. Extension is possible only when there is a gap in the law, but gaps only appear when a judge is faced with an unregulated dispute.[21] Raz adamantly maintains that the 'new rule must be based on the old one with the new restricting condition', explaining that 'A, B, C, then X is transformed into A, B, C, E, then X'.[22] When distinguishing occurs, the previous conditions of the original rule are preserved and these conditions 'become the foundation of the new rule'.[23] The act of distinguishing, understood in this way, is a limited form of law-making. Notice that on this account, the source-based rule is constant as it remains virtually unchanged by the new decision.

The second condition adds an additional restriction to the decision-making process. The modified rule must have been a possible candidate for the original decision.[24] This second condition, like the first, helps to preserve the rule-based model of law. If the new decision could have justified the old one by subsuming it, then the old rule is preserved in a meaningful sense. Indeed, with a little imagination, the new rule is merely the application of what might have been the original rule, tailored to slightly different circumstances. Raz's vision of law as a stable set of rules that are capable of serving as exclusionary reasons remains very much intact in this model of adjudication.[25] A key ques-

[20] *Ibid*, 186.
[21] *Ibid.*
[22] *Ibid*, 207.
[23] *Ibid*, 186.
[24] *Ibid.*
[25] *Ibid.*

tion remains: does the rule-plus-exception model accurately capture the process of judicial decision-making in everyday practice?

To begin, we might ask whether Raz is concerned with the facts of the case or the facts as they appear in the public record. Raz argues that the judge is concerned with the public record.[26] This makes theoretical sense given that he is concerned with the public aspect of rules. However, Raz is incorrect to think that judges are only concerned with the public record of facts. The facts of the case as noted in the record may not capture the facts as they were originally presented at trial. However, while the original facts can become relevant, such occasions are rare and Raz may therefore feel untroubled by such counter-examples.

There is another assumption that underpins Raz's theory, although it is one that remains undefended. Raz assumes that the common law is best understood as a set of rules. Yet, most aspects of common law adjudication resist being understood as a set of rules. Rules tend to have a single, canonical formulation that is articulated in language.[27] While common law decisions are written down, the actual holding (or ratio) of the case need not be found anywhere in the decision (a point that law students quickly realise). As AWB Simpson argues, it is a familiar fact that if 'six pundits of the profession' were asked to write down a governing doctrine of common law adjudication, it is highly likely that they would all write down different formulations of the doctrine in question.[28] To think of precedents as a set of rules also takes attention away from the basic point that judicial decisions are case-specific. The judge rules on the fact–scenario presented and is not laying down (forward-looking) Hartian rules that are supposed to apply to the future actions of a class of people.[29]

This constellation of characteristics is precisely what worried the traditional positivists. Bentham, frustrated by the failure of the common law to fit into a rule-centred account of law, declared that 'As a system of general rules, the common law is a thing merely imaginary'.[30] Hobbes was also scathing in his assessment of the practice. Postema explains:

> Though the doctrine of artificial reason of the law Common Lawyers have sought to substitute their own opinions for the law of the land (*Dialogue* 9655). This is not only contrary to the fundamental law of England, since the king alone has legislative power, Hobbes argues (*Dialogue* 55), but it also defeats the basic purposes of

[26] *Ibid*, 187.

[27] AWB Simpson, 'The Common Law and Legal Theory' in AWB Simpson (ed), *Oxford Essays in Jurisprudence 2nd Series* (Oxford, Oxford University Press, 1973) 88.

[28] *Ibid*, 89.

[29] HLA Hart, *The Concept of Law* (Oxford, Clarendon Press, 1961) 21.

[30] J Bentham, *A Comment on the Commentaries*, CW Everett (ed) (Oxford, Clarendon Press, 1928) 125.

> law. For the judgments recorded in precedents are constantly in conflict; the law supposedly established by them is always unsettled; and the reasoning of many judges inevitably is discordant.[31]

If the reasoning of judges is discordant, it becomes very difficult for law to guide conduct in the way that Hobbes and Raz suppose that it does. Hobbes needs one voice (that of the sovereign) to cut through the subjectivity of preference that creates a state of war. Similarly, Raz needs rules to solve (not to recreate) the problem of how to act in a world filled with disagreement. After all, one of law's key functions, according to Raz, is to 'provide publicly ascertainable standards by which members of the society are held to be bound so that they cannot excuse non-conformity by challenging the justification of the standard'.[32]

The lack of fit between the practice of common law adjudication and the abstract theories of adjudication is more problematic for Raz than for either Bentham or Hobbes. Both Bentham and Hobbes are political philosophers who can (and do) advocate for reform, so they are not tied to current practice. Raz does not have this option. Insofar as he hopes to offer a non-normative account of law, he must account for this practice; otherwise, it will serve as a counter-example to his theory. The posture of traditional positivists towards the common law foreshadows the difficulties Raz will (and does) encounter. Raz continually struggles to describe what Hobbes and Bentham knew they could only hope to amend, namely, the value-laden practice of common law adjudication. A close look at Raz's rule-plus-exception model reveals the precise nature of the problem. Raz's adjudicatory model is itself vulnerable to counter-examples, which, in turn, renders it untenable as a non-normative model of what judges do. Moreover, as I examine in the next section, judges do not simply add exceptions to pre-existing rules; the facts of a new case may prompt judges to cast existing law in a new light.

III. CASTING LAW IN A NEW LIGHT

There is another, more common feature of common law reasoning that is not represented in the rule-plus-exception model. Common law judges do not simply add exceptions to pre-existing rules as this model suggests; they can also cast rules in a new light. This ever-present possibility presents a formidable challenge to the rule-plus-exception model, revealing it as an artificial regimentation of the practice. NE Simmonds forwards the most potent and

[31] GJ Postema, *Bentham and the Common Law Tradition* (Oxford, Clarendon Press, 1986) 49 (footnote omitted).

[32] Raz, *The Authority of Law*, above n 8, at 52.

nuanced argument on this point. A careful study of his critique is enlightening as it illuminates the inadequacies of Raz's adjudicatory model, demonstrating that it too is vulnerable to a counter-example. Simmonds's critique also points us towards a more accurate conceptualization of the adjudicatory process while setting up a second, equally devastating critique. The problem with the rule-plus-exception model of adjudication is not simply that it fails to capture certain important features of common law adjudication, but it also fails on its own terms. Raz's theory, I will argue, collapses from within, revealing that positivism's intellectual foe, Ronald Dworkin, has the proverbial upper hand.

In order to demonstrate the inadequacy of the rule-plus-exception model, Simmonds compares two cases: *Felthouse v Bindley* (an actual case) and *Belthouse v Findley* (a hypothetical case). The details of the actual case are as follows:

> In *Felthouse v. Bindley* an uncle wrote to his nephew offering to buy a horse for a certain price, and saying that if he did not hear from his nephew he would assume that the sale was agreed. The nephew was arranging an auction of his horses and, on receiving his uncle's letter, he instructed the auctioneer to withdraw the horse from the auction. The auctioneer failed to do so, and sold the horse to a third party. The uncle then sued the auctioneer for conversion of his (the uncle's) property. He argued that a contract of sale had been concluded and the title to the horse had, accordingly, passed to him before the auctioneer sold it.[33]

The outcome of the case turned on the Statute of Frauds, but Simmonds proposes that we consider the above case in the manner that contract lawyers conventionally construed it, namely, 'by interpreting it as holding that a contract cannot be concluded by mere silence'.[34] The nephew's silence meant that the contract never came into being, and consequently, the uncle's claim of ownership failed. In order for this holding to fit Raz's first condition, it must be stated in the form of a rule. Simmonds offers the following formulation of a rule that arises out of *Felthouse*: 'A contract is a bilateral relationship, binding on both parties, which will come into existence only when an offer has been accepted, and the acceptance communicated to the offeror'.[35]

Simmonds highlights the manner in which this recasting of rules transpires by reworking the facts of *Felthouse v Bindley* in his hypothetical case: *Belthouse v Findley*. While hypothetical, it is a realistic scenario that allows Simmonds to make a powerful theoretical point about the weakness of the traditional view that precedent establishes a rule that binds all of us in advance. Simmonds's example demonstrates that sometimes a case can lead us to re-conceptualise an area of law. The details of this second case are as follows:

[33] NE Simmonds, 'Bluntness and Bricolage' in H Gross and R Harrison (eds), *Jurisprudence: Cambridge Essays* (Oxford, Clarendon Press, 1992) 9 (footnote omitted).
[34] *Ibid.*
[35] *Ibid.*

> In *Belthouse v. Findley*, Belthouse wrote offering to buy Findley's horse for a sum of £1,000 and saying that, if he heard nothing from Findley, he would take it that the sale was agreed. Findley did nothing, and some time later he sought to deliver the horse to Belthouse and to claim the £1,000. Belthouse refused to pay on the grounds that Findley never communicated his acceptance.[36]

Simmonds suggests that the courts would probably distinguish the present case from the earlier one in the following manner: in *Felthouse v Bindley* 'the offeror sought to impose liability on another by stipulating that silence would be treated as consent'. Conversely, in the second case 'the offeror seeks to *escape* liability by pointing to the absence of a communicated acceptance'. This is not something that the offeror can do because, in general, 'the offeror has a right to be free of liability until acceptance is communicated'. In the facts of *Belthouse*, however, he has 'waived that right, and is liable for breach'.[37] If we applied the ratio of the previous case as it stands (namely, that both parties must give explicit consent) then we would have to conclude that no contract existed: the offeror would be free of liability.

The second case does not simply add an exception to the rule laid out by *Felthouse*; rather, it casts the law in a new light. Simmonds correctly draws our attention to the point that the 'two rulings move in completely different intellectual frameworks'.[38] The holding in *Felthouse v Bindley* 'assumes a world where contracts bind either both parties or neither party, and spring in and out of existence only as the bilateral bond is created or discharged'.[39] Explicit acceptance is required for the contract to come into existence. However, upon 'reflection on the facts of the latter case, we may conclude that it is sometimes right to hold that one party should be able to enforce the contract while the other should not'.[40] The foundational understanding of what is required for a contract to be formed has to be rethought in light of the facts of *Belthouse*. The ruling in this hypothetical case 'requires us to break with the language of contracts either having come into existence or not having done so' and thus we must abandon altogether 'the idea that the electric circuitry of offer and acceptance determines the existence or non-existence of the contract'.[41] It is not until the latter case is considered that the shortcoming of the previous model of contract law is thrown into relief.

Does Raz's rule-plus-exception model allow for this possibility? Consider the first condition: does it permit such fundamental change to the law? Recall that the first condition maintains that 'The modified rule must be the rule laid

[36] *Ibid*, 10.
[37] *Ibid*.
[38] *Ibid*.
[39] *Ibid*.
[40] *Ibid*.
[41] *Ibid*.

down in the precedent restricted by the addition of a further condition for its application'. If the first condition does not allow for such a recasting of rules, then it simply fails to account for the nature of common law reasoning. Conversely, if it does permit this kind of recasting, then the first condition becomes vacuous because it does not impose any constraints on the relationship between the precedent case and the new case.[42]

The only condition that remains (at this point) is Raz's second one, which states, 'The modified rule must be such as to justify the order made in the precedent'. The problem Simmonds detects is that if 'this second constraint is the only real one, the picture of case-law as a body of source-based rules has already been abandoned'.[43] According to Simmonds:

> As a matter of logic, the case might be subsumed equally well under an infinite number of different rules. There are few such rules that we would regard as acceptable *justifications* for the decision, but this restriction imports a moral element inconsistent with a view of case-law as a body of source-based rules: which rules count as acceptable justifications depends on whether they seize on likenesses and differences that we consider to provide adequate grounds for differential treatment. If the only restriction on propositions of case-law is that they should provide an acceptable justification of the individual decision, the content of case-law will depend not on source-based rules but on moral judgment.[44]

If we only focus on Raz's two conditions, then we get an infinite set of logical possibilities about which rules may be applied. But when we consider Raz's two conditions under real world constraints, there are far fewer possibilities. The viable contenders are determined by what similarities and differences between the two cases are deemed legally relevant. This determination itself rests on value judgments that are not part of the positive law. It is these value judgments that do the work in 'constraining' judges, as opposed to the two conditions enumerated by Raz. Therefore, Raz's search for de-contextualized rules that bind in advance proves to be a failure. Contextualized value judgments informed by the broader structure of an area of law emerge as the key to understanding the process of distinguishing. Notice here that Raz fundamentally misconstrues the practice even in those seemingly less controversial instances where judges are merely adding exceptions to pre-existing rules.

It is worth underscoring a subtle but critical difference between where Raz ends up and where Simmonds does. Simmonds highlights how the constraints on common law reasoning come from the broader normative landscape. What is and is not legally relevant is not determined by positive law alone. In this instance the constraints emerge from the nature of contract law and the

[42] *Ibid.*
[43] *Ibid*, 10–11.
[44] *Ibid*, 11.

values that are implicit in the practice. The path forward is not simply 'chosen' by the judge from an infinite set of logical possibilities. Again, Raz argues that the *judge must choose* the best option among all the logical possibilities. In reality, this simply does not happen. All of the logical possibilities can never (and thus will never) enter into their minds. As an account of what judges do, Raz's theory misses the mark.[45]

The language of choice, which Raz employs, is not accidental; it accompanies the assumption that pre-existing rules bind in advance. When the rules do not bind, we must choose between alternatives. This same assumption is found in Hart's *Concept of Law*: once we leave the comfort of the core of settled meaning where the answer is clear, we enter into the penumbra of uncertainty whereby 'all that succeeds is success'.[46] The collapse of Raz's model indicates that this problem is pervasive.[47] The point is not that there are no easy cases (there are), but rather that the positivists' story about what makes easy cases easy is too simplistic. Value judgments enter into the adjudicatory process and this must be accounted for. When we turn our attention once more to Raz's rule-plus-exception model, we find that Raz must also account for value judgments. However, the moment he does so, his model collapses from within into a version of Dworkinian interpretation.

IV. IDENTIFYING RULES: A HERCULEAN TASK

Consider, once again, the claim that the rule-plus-exception model generates an infinite number of logical possibilities rather than a single rule. This is a claim Simmonds makes, but it is also one that Raz himself recognises. According to Raz, whenever a judge attempts to apply the two criteria in Raz's rule-plus-exception model, she will realise that there are 'an indefinite number of different modifications of every rule conforming to the two conditions spelt out above'.[48] In response to the problem of how one chooses between the various rules that meet the two conditions listed in the rule-plus-exception model of

[45] Note that Raz may believe that a judge only needs two options. The point here is that Raz's own account commits him to a view wherein the judge is understood as choosing one option from an infinite set.

[46] Hart, *The Concept of Law*, above n 10 at 153, 'One form of "formalist" error may perhaps just be that of thinking that every step taken by a court is covered by some general rule conferring in advance the authority to take it, so that its creative powers are *always* a form of delegated legislative power. The truth may be that, when courts settle previously unenvisaged questions concerning the most fundamental constitutional rules, they *get* their authority to decide them accepted after the questions have arisen and the decision has been given'.

[47] Gerald Postema draws a similar conclusion. See G Postema, 'Positivism and the Separation of the Realists from their Skepticism' in P Cane (ed), *The Hart Fuller Debate in the Twenty-First Century* (Oxford, Hart Publishing, 2010) 262.

[48] Raz, *The Authority of Law*, above n 8, at 187.

adjudication, Raz insists that 'The court's obligation . . . is to adopt only that modification which will best improve the rule'.[49] The decision must both 'fit' Raz's two conditions and be 'justified' in reference to its competitors insofar as the option chosen must improve the rule. Given this characterization of judicial interpretation, Raz, it seems, becomes Dworkin in a fundamental way. Yet, whether this comparison holds or not hinges, of course, on exactly what Raz means by 'improve'.

What does 'improve' mean in this context? The determination of what improves the rule will be made by the judge and will likely be influenced, at least partly, by what a given judge believes the law is and what her job entails. Some judges may approach decision-making in a formalistic manner, prioritising positive law over other considerations; other judges may look to moral principles; others still may focus on what is best for society moving forward. In Dworkin's words, judges may be conventionalist, pragmatic, or principled.[50] Each interpretive theory can be comprehended as capturing a different understanding of 'improvement' of the law that is tied to a larger philosophical understanding of the nature of the law.[51] The manner in which, and the extent to which, moral views enter into the interpretive process will depend on which approach the judge adopts. The general point is that the determination as to which option will improve the rule is value-laden. The legal norm that emerges from the rule-plus-exception model of adjudication is therefore not a fact as such, but rather a value judgment about how best to go forward.

As I have elucidated in this chapter, Raz ultimately champions a version of Dworkinian interpretation. In order to determine what the law is in a given instance, we must interpret it in its best (ie 'most improved') light. Now, the 'best light' need not be a robust moral vision akin to the one that Dworkin ultimately espouses. One can agree with Dworkin that the process of adjudication is an argumentative one in which competing visions of existing law compete for primacy, without agreeing with him that judges should emulate Hercules in the pursuit of a single right answer that is available to us insofar as we view law through the lens of integrity. His more controversial claims build on, but are nonetheless separable from, his initial insight. In other words, Raz's argument ultimately lends support to *one* of Dworkin's key claims without confirming the truth of his more ambitious vision of 'law as integrity'. The point that judges must make value-laden choices about what decision will best improve the rule remains agnostic about (and thus detachable from) a defence of any specific vision of 'improvement'.

[49] *Ibid.*

[50] R Dworkin, *Law's Empire* (Cambridge, MA, Harvard University Press, 1986) 114–224.

[51] *Ibid*, 90. In Dworkin's words: 'So any judge's opinion is itself a piece of legal philosophy, even when the philosophy is hidden, and the visible argument is dominated by citation and lists of facts'.

Notice that we are now in a position to deflect a familiar line of argumentation. When Raz argues that judges must choose the option that best 'improves' the rule, we may wish to interpret the word 'improve' in a morally neutral way. The central difficulty with this line of argument is that the sources thesis (and his pre-emption thesis) needs facticity, not simply value-neutrality. Even if this argument were available to Raz, it should be resisted. While value-laden interpretations that are not moral in content are possible, it is implausible to think that judges are relying on this kind of reasoning with great frequency (or that they should try to reason in this way). For example, in the context of *Felthouse v Bindley*, what would a 'value-neutral' judgment look like? Why would a judge pursue it? Whether a given judge makes a judgment that is evaluative but not morally evaluative cannot be determined in advance and in abstraction from the relevant context. Moreover, such a determination will also turn on one's view of morality, making the job of identifying 'non-moral, evaluative' judgments all the more difficult. In Raz's case, any appeal to the idea of value-neutral interpretations is inspired by the need to maintain positivist commitments; the claim does not arise out of direct reflection on law under real world constraints. In the end, we are reminded that theoretical escape routes are rarely, if ever, illuminating. They only highlight the weakness of the theory and signal the need for fresh thoughts on law, even if that means one must abandon foundational commitments.

Consider another familiar line of defence: one might wish to defend Raz at this point by reminding us that Raz is not entirely hostile toward judges looking to morality. In *The Authority of Law*, Raz happily acknowledges that the law often instructs judges to rely on moral norms, even when there is no 'gap' in sight. Such instructions take the form of what Raz elsewhere calls 'directed powers'.[52] By rooting the instructions to apply moral norms in the positive law itself, Raz appears to have deflected a central criticism of legal positivism. The extent to which a given regime enables judges to behave in this manner is a contingent matter that need not deter theorists from defending positivism. Despite any appeal this line of argument may have, it fails to address the worries identified above.

The more we explore Raz's rule-plus-exception model of adjudication, the more Raz's positivist theory of adjudication begins to unravel. In order for Raz's account to be plausible, source-based law must be capable of being factually ascertained. However, if moral argumentation must be relied upon in order to decide between all of the alternatives that are consistent with the two conditions, we find that what the law *is* at any given moment cannot even be

[52] J Raz, *Ethics in the Public Domain: Essays in the Morality of Law and Politics* (New York, Oxford University Press, 1994) 243.

identified without relying on moral evaluations.[53] The fact that we must make evaluative judgments in order to determine the content of the law is fatal to the rule-plus-exception model. A list of possible contenders does not give us the law on an issue. Accordingly, the lesson that we learn from Raz's discussion is opposite to the one he wished to convey: the legal rules that result from the decision-making process rest on value judgments that are not themselves constrained by the two conditions of his rule-plus-exception model. What law *is* is very much a product of a judgment about what it *ought* to be.

In sum, Raz's rule-plus-exception model of adjudication is an artificial regimentation of the practice that collapses from within. The model was meant to account for the practice of common law adjudication in a way that allows Raz to preserve his positivist commitments.[54] Given the intractable difficulties with Raz's positivist theory of adjudication, it is not surprising to discover that he has since radically changed his position. His current stance – that judges are moral reasoners – takes Raz from the expository to the censorial side of Bentham's dichotomy. While this theory is more promising than the rule-plus-exception model, it too may prove to be inadequate. By moving between the two sides of the sharp dichotomy between legal facts and moral values, Raz glosses over many of the particulars of legal practice.

V. BETWEEN FACT AND VALUE

Dworkin understands what Raz inadvertently confirms above: Hart's idea of a settled core and a penumbra of uncertainty is a profoundly unhelpful way to think about adjudication. Hart offers readers a metaphor, and Raz gives content to it by trying to explain the practice of adjudication from within, rather than by simply offering a vague 'description' from the external perspective. Dworkin, of course, does not offer us only this bare claim about the argumentative nature of adjudication; rather, he asks his readers to think of law through the lens of 'integrity'. This is a full-blooded normative account of what judges *should* do in the courtroom. Each judge must seek a single right answer that is available when existing law is placed in its best moral light. Integrity is meant to combine the considerations of consistency, justice and fairness in a distinctly legal ideal.[55] It is this ideal that is supposed to allow us to understand the content of our legal obligations while also justifying the use of coercive force.

[53] This is the conclusion that flows from Raz's theory, whether judges operate in this fashion is a separate question.

[54] Dworkin makes a similar point. See R Dworkin, 'ThirtyYears On (Book review of *The Practice of Principle*)' (2001–02) 115 *Harvard Law Review* 1670.

[55] Dworkin, *Law's Empire*, above n 50, at 176.

Dworkin maintains that judges who value integrity adopt 'a protestant attitude that makes each citizen responsible for imagining what his society's public commitments to principles are, and what these commitments require in new circumstances'.[56] The unity of the law is the intellectual output from the judges' morally informed imagination. The worry, expressed by a number of legal theorists, is that Dworkin's approach takes the focus off the legal practice (and the values implicit in it) and places undue emphasis on the formation of a comprehensive moral theory that seeks to make sense of the legal system in its entirety.[57] The combination of Dworkin's theses into a moral vision (one which envelops or threatens to envelop the positive law) prompts some philosophers to quickly retreat to the more earthly world of legal rules, and the familiar confines of legal positivism. The debate itself vacillates between the world of positivism and that of idealism, traversing the intellectual void between these two extremes. Simmonds's discussion of contract law, as detailed above, points us to a third option: the possibility that some of the values relevant to adjudication are internal to the practice.

In order to demonstrate that the rule-plus-exception model is inadequate, Simmonds does not have to prove that the understanding of contract law as represented in *Belthouse* is correct; he merely has to demonstrate that casting law in a new light is a feature of common law adjudication that Raz's model fails to conceptualise. Nonetheless, we can see why Simmonds's assessment is persuasive. Recall the facts of the hypothetical case: Belthouse had written to Findley offering to buy his horse, informing Findley that he need not respond to indicate his acceptance; he only needed to show up on a given day with his horse if he wished to sell it. When Findley arrived with horse in tow, Belthouse had changed his mind. He no longer wanted the horse. In court, he argued that there was no existing contract as no explicit acceptance had been given by Findley.

The point is not simply that a decision in favour of the offeror (Belthouse) would be unfair (although it would be). In broader terms, the point is that the enterprise of contract law would not benefit from such a decision. Insofar as contract law is meant to stabilise relations between people through time, this general purpose would be undermined by a legal victory for Belthouse.[58] Unscrupulous offerors with knowledge of the law would be able to take advantage of less-informed individuals who would make agreements in good faith, only to discover that they had been intentionally misled. Therefore, it is accurate to say that an understanding of the purpose(s) implicit in the practice itself would likely guide the judge in such a case. For his part, Simmonds articulates his point in terms of rights: Belthouse waived his right to have explicit consent.

[56] *Ibid*, 413.

[57] NE Simmonds, 'Protestant Jurisprudence and Modern Doctrinal Scholarship' (2001) 60 *CLJ* 271, 292.

[58] See SM Waddams, *The Law of Contracts*, 6th edn (Toronto, Canada Law Book Inc, 2010) 11.

One might object that the claim that a right exists is not a fact about legal practice. Some deny that legal rights exist at all, while others debate the content of rights. However, Simmonds's point is not best understood as the statement of a fact, but as a persuasive argument about the content of our rights in contract law. His discussion directs us towards an ongoing philosophical debate about the intellectual foundations of the common law.[59] Different philosophical conceptions of the nature of private law attempt to explain the nature of the practice of adjudication in the private law context while simultaneously explaining how future cases ought to be decided.[60] Not only are many such theories deeply philosophical, but they are also practical. The hope is that judges will be convinced about the conception of rights on offer and that, when given the opportunity, they will give legal reality to the philosophical conception proffered. The divide between the two aims of seeking truth on the one hand and responding to practice on the other is only sharp if we adopt the assumptions of the debate in general jurisprudence. Because the foundational assumptions of the two debates are so different, the connection between the debate about the philosophical foundations of the common law and the debate waged in the general jurisprudence literature is rarely discussed. We are now able to see the connection (or the disconnection) between the two conversations. Raz, by moving across the blunt dichotomy between fact and value, 'jumps' over this third possibility. It is this third option that offers the more promising path to a philosophical understanding of law. It is not the only way forward, but it is a route worth exploring.

A far less fruitful path is the one down which Raz decides to travel. Instead of rethinking his positivist vision once his rule-plus-exception model fails to shore up his positivist account, he recasts his core theses, thereby furnishing us with the theories that are commonly associated with his name: namely, a morally robust theory of adjudication and the thesis that law necessarily claims authority. As I show in subsequent chapters, when Raz introduces readers to his morally robust theory of adjudication he shifts his account of judging to the 'value' side of the fact/value dichotomy. The sharp divide between fact and value is not discarded; his theory is merely recast within it. The distinction between fact and value is no longer primarily a distinction that is thought to map onto the practice of adjudication (as Raz argues in *The Authority of Law*). Instead, the distinction is understood to be of great theoretical value:

[59] A Ripstein, *Force and Freedom: Kant's Legal and Political Philosophy* (Cambridge, MA, Harvard University Press, 2010). R Posner, *Economic Analysis of Law*, 7th edn (New York, Aspen Law & Business, 2007). J Coleman, *Risks and Wrongs* (New York, Cambridge University Press, 1992). A Brudner, *The Unity of the Common Law: Studies in Hegelian Jurisprudence* (Berkeley, University of California Press, 1995).

[60] As an example of this approach, see JW Neyers, 'Causing Loss by Unlawful Means: Should the High Court of Australia follow *OBG Ltd v Allan*?' in J Edelman and S Degeling (eds) *Torts in Commerical Law* (Sydney, Thomson Reuters, 2012).

legal philosophy occupies the world of facts whereas normative theories of adjudication are value-laden by definition. The distinction between 'fact' and 'value' may serve as a dam that protects Raz's set of positivist theses from being overridden by the value-laden nature of adjudication. If the dam is breached, then legal philosophy becomes normative philosophy by association. Even though the distinction between a theory of law and a theory of adjudication is often treated as a matter of fact, the burden of ensuring that the distinction holds belongs to the positivists (and it is a heavy one). In the next chapter, I will challenge the viability of this distinction by looking closely at Raz's own arguments. Upon inspection, it becomes clear that Raz's theory about the nature of adjudication has implications for his understanding of the nature of law and vice versa. Indeed, not even his argument that all law claims authority can save his theory from the deluge.

3

The Perils of Positivism: Why Raz becomes a Realist

IT IS GENERALLY accepted that there is a distinction between a theory of law and a theory of adjudication. This distinction is treated as one of the foundational assumptions that frames, and limits, the current debate. Theories are quickly classified as 'normative' or 'conceptual' and the debates play out on these two distinct battlefields. Insofar as this distinction is treated as foundational, there is little impetus to explore the ways in which assumptions about the nature of adjudication may impact on the shape of one's general theory and vice versa. However, if the line between a theory of law and a theory of adjudication is not as sharp as is often supposed, and I will argue that it is not, then serious questions can and must be asked about the status quo in legal philosophy. The need to ask such questions is pressing given that the distinction is often used to exclude would-be interlocutors and not simply as a conciliatory gesture, as it may once have been.[1] The problem for the modern day positivist is that she needs the distinction to be watertight insofar as she hopes to keep normative assumptions sidelined. As we shall see, the argumentative burden is a heavy one and it is hers to bear.

The most common interpretation of Raz's work is that he has an independent theory of law in addition to a separate theory of adjudication. His theory of law is best captured by his sources thesis, which represents law as a set of factually ascertainable norms. In contrast, his theory of adjudication is morally robust: judges are moral agents who often appeal to moral principles when rendering decisions. It is often assumed that Raz's morally bare theory of law and his morally robust theory of adjudication form a coherent and complex whole. While the whole is undoubtedly complex, in what follows I will challenge the assumption that it is coherent. Raz cannot replace his original theory of adjudication with a morally robust one without displacing the other key elements of his theory, or so I shall argue. An understanding of the interrelatedness of the elements of Raz's theory in *Practical Reason and Norms*

[1] A Halpin, 'The Province of Jurisprudence Contested: A Critical Notice of *The Province of Jurisprudence Democratized* (2008) by Allan Hutchinson' (2010) 23 *Canadian Journal of Law and Jurisprudence* 515.

foreshadows the difficulties that Raz will encounter when he alters various elements of his account and seeks to defend them independently of each other.

As I elucidated in chapter one, Raz's conception of the nature of law in *Practical Reason and Norms* is grounded in a formalist theory of adjudication. Judges, Raz argues in this early work, have a duty to apply the law.[2] When Raz replaces this positivistic theory of adjudication with a morally robust one, significant implications for his account of law are raised. By focusing on the role that legal sources play in his revised theory, and particularly on his understanding of legal rights, it becomes clear that the sharp divide between his theory of law and a theory of adjudication cannot be maintained. Specifically, I will argue that when Raz draws out the implications of his morally robust account of adjudication for his view of rights, we find that his understanding echoes that of the realist Oliver Wendell Holmes rather than his positivist forebearer, HLA Hart. Instead of offering a single account of law, Raz vacillates between legal realism and legal positivism. When the conceptual dust settles, Raz is left with two mutually exclusive choices: he can become a card-carrying realist or a normative positivist.

Instead of travelling down one of these two paths, Raz seeks to blaze a new trail. For instance, in *The Morality of Freedom* he abandons his functional account of how the law preserves order, replacing it with an enquiry into whether and under what conditions law is morally legitimate. His positivist theory of law is meant to fold easily into his account of law's normative force: the thesis that all law claims authority is supposed to unite both views and solve all of the aforementioned problems. When Raz is armed with this thesis, all the worries which I have identified above seem to fade from view. Once again, I will suggest that appearances do deceive. Not only is the idea that all law claims authority a remarkably opaque one, but upon closer inspection we discover that Raz is unable to distance his new account from his old story about law and order (and all the attendant problems that I presented in chapter one). In short, this thesis does not offer Raz a way out. The pre-emption thesis, I will suggest, is to blame.

One reason why such changes in Raz's theory are not often recognized and explored has to do, at least partly, with the fact that Raz himself does not flag such changes. With rare exceptions, he has not offered a global reflection on his work. (Chapter 7 below highlights this issue in greater detail.) Another contributing factor pertains to the seeming independence of Raz's central theses. Notice, for instance, that the sources thesis does not directly address the question of the existence or non-existence of a judicial duty to apply the law. It is concerned only with the factual identification of legal norms. The reason the sources thesis is flexible in this way is that the question of identification

[2] J Raz, *Practical Reason and Norms* (Oxford, Oxford University Press, 1999) 137.

which it addresses is a backward-looking issue; by contrast, questions pertaining to the duty of the judge are forward-looking. Given this feature of the sources thesis, Raz is able to divorce it from the context out of which it arose: the sources thesis appears not to be wedded to Raz's theory in *Practical Reason and Norms* even if it was born out of reflection on it.

The seeming conceptual independence of the sources thesis allows Raz to preserve what I will argue is the mere illusion of theoretical stability and consistency through time. But if we shift our attention away from defending discrete theses in isolation and look instead at the practical role that Raz assigns to legal norms, the worry about the coherence of his position is illuminated. Once he introduces a morally robust theory of adjudication, legal sources have a diminished role in the courtroom and I will argue (following Postema) that this translates into a diminished role in the practical lives of the populace at large.

The same difficulties follow the pre-emption thesis. When it is examined in isolation, it seems to commit Raz to a rather minimal claim; however, upon inspection we find that Raz is never able to fully sever the link between the pre-emption thesis and the story of law and order found in *Practical Reason and Norms*, even though he expressly seeks to dissolve this connection. This is not surprising since the pre-emption thesis is merely the re-articulation of the idea at the centre of this early work; namely, the claim that law provides exclusionary reasons for action. In other words, the idea that legal norms could even potentially operate as pre-emptive reasons for action is diminished once it is argued that judges are moral reasoners who are not under a duty to apply the law. If legal norms are going to even potentially operate as Raz supposes, they must be factually ascertainable with relative ease (an assumption I explore in chapter five) and citizens must have the required motivation to accord legal norms pre-emptive status. Raz quietly admits that the work of judges does impact on the motivation of the populace at large.

I. LAW'S AUTONOMY CONSIDERED AND RECONSIDERED

Law may be regarded as a set of autonomous reasons for action. This is not a position that Raz has (to my knowledge) explicitly defended; nor is it a position to which he currently ascribes. It is, however, a position that can be attributed to him with relative ease. Recall that in *Practical Reason and Norms*, the legal perspective is a partial perspective whereby legal systems are understood to 'possess their own internal system of evaluation'.[3] Such evaluation takes place from 'the legal point of view'.[4] Raz illustrates the precise nature of

[3] *Ibid.*
[4] *Ibid.*

the legal point of view by contrasting the perspective of the judge with that of the minister of transport. The minister is not required to render 'a partial judgment from the economic point of view . . . his action is based on his total assessment of the situation'. Conversely, Raz insists that the same is not true of the judge.[5] The judge, he argues, 'both regards his judgment as based on a partial assessment of the valid reasons and as justifying action'.[6] Indeed, legal systems 'consist of norms which the courts are bound to apply regardless of their view of their merit'.[7] The key point is that moral reasons (which are extra-legal reasons) are not a part of the partial legal perspective and hence are meant to be excluded from the judicial decision-making process. Not only is each legal norm thought to be an exclusionary reason for action, but Raz insists that the system as a whole is an *exclusionary system*.[8] Law, one is left to conclude, enjoys a marked level of autonomy. Only when judges err, or when gaps appear, do they reach beyond the confines of positive law and create law afresh. It is due to the limited role that the discretionary activity is thought to have in existing legal systems that makes the 'strong autonomy thesis' an apt label for this early position. Legal norms are thought of as a discrete set of norms that can be identified and applied without recourse to moral norms.

This 'partial' legal perspective is of both intellectual and practical importance. The judicial duty to apply the law is responsible for furnishing us with a set of norms that qualify as law (thereby delimiting the contours of our concept) in addition to being the very thing that explains the existence of order in society. More precisely still, it is the central role that fact-based norms are thought to play in the real world that justifies their essential role in Raz's concept of law. Factually ascertainable legal norms are capable of guiding us thanks, largely, to the efforts of the judiciary in adopting the 'partial perspective' and to faithfully applying pre-existing positive laws when resolving disputes. The vital role played by Raz's positivistic theory of adjudication in shaping his early conception of law cannot be overstated. Even the 'test' for identifying the norms that count as 'legal' depends on this judicial duty: the law is comprised of the aggregate of norms that judges are under a duty to apply.[9] All paths direct us back to the idea that judges have a duty to apply the law. Again, in *Practical Reason and Norms*, one does not find a theory of law that is distinct from a theory of adjudication, quite the opposite: Raz's positivist theory of law is founded upon a positivist theory of adjudication. It is not the mere fact that Raz has changed his view that should give us pause; rather, the way in which his theses interconnect and

[5] *Ibid*, 144.
[6] *Ibid*, 143–44.
[7] *Ibid*, 139.
[8] *Ibid*, 145.
[9] *Ibid*, 139.

reciprocally reinforce one another in this early work foreshadows the difficulties to come when he alters his position.

Once Raz abandons the claim that judges are under a duty to simply apply the law and replaces this claim with its opposite – that judges have a duty to reason morally – everything changes. In *Ethics and the Public Domain*, Raz reconsiders a number of the same issues that were raised in *Practical Reason and Norms* almost 20 years earlier, but he arrives at radically different conclusions. In particular, he focuses on the issue of whether or not legal reasoning is a separate domain of reasoning: does it have its own logic? Is it something that only judges do? Is it distinct from any species of moral reasoning? Raz responds that legal reasoning is *not* a unique kind of reasoning. It does not have its own logic; nor is it exclusive to judges. Citizens can engage in legal reasoning as well, and when they do so, they are not simply imitating judges.[10] Significantly, he also argues that legal reasoning is best thought of as a sub-species of moral reasoning.

Raz observes that 'quite commonly courts have the discretion to modify legal rules, or to make exceptions to their applications, and where they have such discretion they ought to resort to moral reasoning to decide whether to use it and how'.[11] Despite the position that I ascribed to him at the beginning of this section, Raz rejects outright the idea that legal reasoning is autonomous, insisting, instead, that 'Legal reasoning is an instance of moral reasoning'.[12] Legal reasoning does not have a logic that is all its own. Moreover, Raz boldly declares that 'Legal doctrines are justified only if they are morally justified, and they should be followed only if it is morally right to follow them'.[13] Law is autonomous only in the weak sense according to Raz: legal norms are autonomous reasons for acting for those who are subject to the law, but not for judges who apply the law. Because the law is thought of as a set of factually identifiable norms, citizens are still able to identify the law and (at least potentially) treat any given legal norm as a pre-emptive reason for action. Inside of the courtroom judges are expected to appeal to moral argumentation.

[10] Raz, *Ethics in the Public Domain* (New York, Oxford University Press, 1994) 327.

[11] *Ibid*, 335.

[12] *Ibid*, 340. Raz famously argues that judges are human too, thus 'morality always applies' (J Raz, *Between Authority and Interpretation* (Oxford, Oxford University Press, 2009) ch 7). While this is an interesting way to frame the issue, it does not directly address the worries I am discussing in this chapter. One can argue that a judge is making a moral decision whether one applies a pre-existing legal norm or whether one opts to create new law. The question is whether Raz's positivist thesis means that he cannot be agnostic about whether judges apply the law rather than create it. The argument that 'judges are human too' also obscures the nature of the debate between inclusive and exclusive positivists. The former view is the possibility that moral criteria for legal validity can exist; the latter deny this. Raz is re-casting the nature of the disagreement, but the original point of contention remains.

[13] *Ibid*, 340.

The dramatic nature of this shift in his account of judicial reasoning is underscored when one recalls that in *Practical Reason and Norms* judges do not have the option under most circumstances to create new law by appealing to moral principles.[14] Discretionary systems in which judges appeal to moral norms with great frequency are not even an empirical possibility. In this earlier work, so-called 'systems of absolute discretion' are merely hypothetical entities that Raz invented in order to cast light on the features of legality that he views as central.[15] The comparison was introduced in an attempt to highlight the manner in which law contributes to the existence of an orderly society. Unless judges simply apply the law, we will find ourselves living in a chaotic, unpredictable world. As I elucidated in chapter one, this is a story of law and order which is told in the hopes of establishing that the law-applying function of judges is a universal and necessary feature that *all* legal systems share.[16]

It might be tempting to read *Practical Reason and Norms* through the lens of *Ethics in the Public Domain* as it would allow Raz's defenders to argue that Raz has now adjusted his theory by adding nuances without making wholesale changes. On this reading, his revised theory of adjudication merely shifts his account of what judges do towards the discretionary end of the spectrum without collapsing into a so-called system of absolute discretion. It is, after all, fruitless to try to identify the exact tipping point whereby a legal system becomes a system of absolute discretion. This is an empirical matter, not a philosophical one. While the latter point is sound, there has nonetheless been a marked modification of Raz's position that has significant implications that cannot be so easily set aside. The first indication that the shift in his thinking is a dramatic one comes from the mere fact that he chooses to introduce a morally robust theory of adjudication that is radically different from his theory of law. Raz has moved his account of adjudication from the 'fact' side of the dichotomy to the 'value' side – a difference in kind and not merely in degree. Raz is not simply making small improvements on his early effort; he is making wholesale changes.

Evidence of a fundamental reboot is easily found when we return to the test that Raz offers for identifying the norms of the system: norms are properly labelled 'legal' if judges are under a duty to apply them. If we apply this test to the morally robust theory of adjudication offered to us in *Ethics and the Public Domain*, Raz would instantly become a non-positivist: if judges are duty-bound

[14] Raz, *Practical Reason and Norms,* above n 2, at 143.

[15] *Ibid,* 137.

[16] The fact that Raz argues that citizens are not under an obligation to obey the law does not hurt my argument. My claim is that his early work seeks to explain the very existence of de facto legal systems; his later work is concerned primarily with questions of justification. That is, in *Practical Reason and Norms* Raz is seeking to understand law's role in engendering order and not whether citizens are under a moral obligation to obey. See ch 1.

to appeal to moral principles in deciding how to go forward (as Raz now claims), then the law would have to include both moral and legal norms. This, of course, is not the conclusion he draws, but it means that he must abandon this test (and he does). But his other theses are more entrenched and cannot be discarded with such ease. So the critical question is: to what extent are Raz's core positivist commitments impacted by the shift in his thinking about the nature of judging in a court of law? For instance, how important are fact-based sources in the courtroom? What becomes of the sources thesis, in other words?

In the same work, Raz offers us yet another sharp distinction in an attempt to secure a place for source-based reasoning in the judicial sphere. He divides legal reasoning into 'reasoning about the law' and 'reasoning according to the law'. Reasoning *about* the law involves determining the content of the law at any specific moment. This kind of reasoning is consistent with the sources thesis, but it is *not* the kind of reasoning that judges usually employ.[17] Judges usually reason *according to the law* – they usually appeal to moral principles when deciding a given case.[18] We are left to conclude that fact-based legal norms are of diminished importance in the courtroom (as compared to his earlier account). This point is underscored by the fact that Raz does not proceed to defend a two-step process of adjudication whereby both kinds of reasoning would be assured a place in their deliberations.[19] Even granting this, the key question upon which the relevance of legal sources hinges remains: what role do legal norms play in the lives of citizens outside the courtroom? Is 'reasoning about the law' something that citizens actually do, even if judges tend to reason 'according to the law'?

Recall, once again, that in *Practical Reason and Norms* we are told that fact-based legal norms are indispensable for the everyday operations of a legal system. In this early work, legal norms serve as the workhorses of the practical reasoning processes of judges and citizens alike. Citizens have a reason to defer to legal norms when deciding how to act *because* they can depend on judges to enforce the rules. The exclusionary status of norms is itself dependent on the duty of judges to apply pre-existing positive law. This link has now been severed. Once judges are thought of as moral reasoners, we can wonder whether citizens have the requisite incentive to treat legal norms as pre-emptive (or exclusionary) reasons for action. This worry is placed in sharp relief when we turn our attention to Raz's comments about the nature of legal rights. Given that the concept of a 'legal right' is not part of the stock set of Raz's theses, it is easy to overlook the way in which his thoughts on this matter

[17] Raz, *Ethics in the Public Domain*, above n 10, at 332.

[18] *Ibid*, 333.

[19] See W Lucy, 'Adjudication' in JL Coleman and S Shapiro, *The Oxford Handbook of Jurisprudence and Philosophy of Law* (Oxford, Oxford University Press, 2002) 214. See also ch 2.

change. However, the shift in his thought is necessitated by the introduction of his morally robust theory of adjudication and it takes Raz away from positivism into the world of legal realism. As I show in what follows, this shift reveals the deep instability in his current theory and mirrors the problems he faced concerning adjudication in common law traditions.[20] A more general implication can also be drawn from this elucidation; namely, that a theory of law has inescapable implications for a theory of adjudication such that they cannot be isolated from one another.

II. LEGAL RIGHTS AND LEGAL REALISM

Let us begin, once again, with *Practical Reason and Norms*. The relationship between the judicial duty to apply the law and the incentive of the citizenry to treat legal norms as reasons for action is illustrated in his discussion of legal rights. Raz explains:

> [Legal systems] contain norms determining the rights and duties of individuals. These are the very same norms that the primary institutions are bound to apply and that is the reason that they also provide guidance to individuals as to their rights and duties in litigation before the primary organs.[21]

According to Raz, law is able to guide us because judges have a duty to apply the law. Specifically, pre-existing legal norms are the locus of rights *because* judges have a duty to apply the law. Citizens look to legal norms for guidance *because* they are unambiguously understood as the locus of rights. Knowing one's legal rights is equivalent to knowing what one cannot do if one wishes to remain within the bounds of the law. Judges, as law-appliers, uphold the fact-based standards enshrined in legal norms so that they can serve as dependable fixed points that can guide action. Since positive law does all the hard practical work, the label 'legal positivism' is linked to a robust claim about how positive law helps to create and sustain order in society.

The fact that legal systems provide rights and duties to citizens is a defining feature of legality on this account. Accordingly, Raz sketches an inverse relationship between the level of discretionary activity of judges and the rights of citizens: the more discretion the judiciary is allowed, the fewer the stable rights which citizens can claim. Moreover, there is a threshold past which no rights can be found in the law at all due to the number of discretionary acts by judges. If one assumes that source-based positive law is the locus of legal rights (rather than, for instance, moral principles that are implicit in the law), then one is left with two options: judges either apply the law and reinforce these

[20] See chs 2 and 4 for similar findings.
[21] Raz, *Practical Reason and Norms*, above n 2, at 138.

rights, or judges frequently change the law and destabilize citizens' legal rights. Raz opts for the first alternative in *Practical Reason and Norms* (and in *The Authority of Law*), while he favours the second option in *Ethics in the Public Domain*. Tellingly, once judges are conceived of primarily as moral reasoners, citizens cannot look to fact-based norms in the hopes of understanding their legal rights.

In striking contradistinction to his claim that legal norms provide citizens with rights, in *Ethics in the Public Domain*, Raz argues that legal norms are *not* a stable source of rights:

> Quite often courts are called upon to fill in gaps in the law, and regularly they are called upon to continue developing the law, an activity which includes changing and revising existing legal arrangements. Consequently, quite often people do not have expectations regarding their legal rights – at least not justifiable ones – since they know, or should know, that the law is gappy or that it is liable to change on the issue in dispute.[22]

Acts of judicial discretion may become so frequent that citizens can no longer look to pre-existing norms in order to determine the content of their legal rights. If she wishes to remain within the bounds of the law, the wise citizen will try to predict what the courts will do in a given instance, rather than simply looking to ascertain the content of pre-existing positive law. Judicial creativity saps the incentive from the citizen to look to the pre-existing storehouse of fact-based norms in order to determine the content of her rights – only the naive citizen (and not the wise one) will proceed in this manner. In other words, the citizen is deprived of the requisite motivation to treat legal norms as pre-emptive reasons for action.

Raz's version of legal positivism has thus collapsed once again, only this time it has collapsed into a version of legal realism (rather than into Dworkinism). Raz now echoes Oliver Wendell Holmes, who famously argued that if you want to know what the law is and what your rights are in a given instance, you must try to predict what the judge will do: 'The primary rights and duties with which jurisprudence busies itself again are nothing but prophecies'.[23] Given such uncertainty, it would be a misguided effort to hope to find legal rights in the familiar and seemingly tangible world of rules. Law lives beyond itself, and the wise citizen should understand this.

If one cannot confidently identify one's legal rights by looking to positive law, is one still a positivist? Hart surely did not think so. He knew that if he was going to place rules at the centre of his concept of law, then the rules have to do work in the real world and not simply occupy a central place in the heaven of concepts. Hart's rule-centered theory of law was situated squarely

[22] Raz, *Ethics in the Public Domain*, above n 10, at 338.
[23] OW Holmes, 'The Path of Law' (1896–97) 10 *Harvard Law Review* 458.

in opposition to the realist position. He aimed to take our concept of law away from the shadowy world of prophesies and to refocus our attention on the idea of a rule.[24] While *Practical Reason and Norms* is, in certain key respects, continuous with Hart's project, the portions of *Ethics in the Public Domain* that we have discussed thus far signal an abandonment of it. Raz has become a positivist in name only. Insofar as these particular writings are thought to be a part of the positivist tradition, the jurisprudential debate will itself be the source of much confusion. This is not simply a point about labels; rather, it is about the need to understand which positions are possible and which ones are not. Raz's attempt to unite a positivist theory of law with a morally robust theory of adjudication is just not a viable option.

One might interject and remind readers that Holmes was also a positivist. Brian Leiter argues that Holmes viewed law as a set of positive norms, not as a set of rules and principles (as Dworkin does) and not something to be viewed through a morally robust lens (as do classical natural lawyers).[25] Leiter's point does not derail my argument, however. Rather, it helps it. Realists are identified as such because of their understanding of how law works in practice. As we move forward, it is not rules but predictions about how the judge may decide a case (or set of cases) that come to be of central importance. Legal realists are, as is often argued, disappointed positivists. We can see how Raz might fall into this category. He set out to demonstrate that judges are bound by rules, only to discover that value judgments do the real work in the decision-making process.[26] Moreover, it is unclear as to whether Holmes's positivist views can be maintained in the face of his realist commitments. In Schauer's words:

> But although the Realists differed about what 'really' mattered in judicial decision making, they were all committed to the view that what mattered was something other than, or at least much more than, positive law, legal rules, legal doctrine, and legal reasoning as traditionally conceived. The core of Legal Realism thus challenges the view that traditional legal sources and methods play a substantial role in the cause and explanation of judicial decisions.[27]

Insofar as Schauer is correct (and I believe that he is), the realists do not simply have a theory about adjudication, but they also are committed to a certain view about the nature of law, even if that view remains implicit. The arguments in this chapter (and in chapter six) will go some distance to substantiate this claim.

[24] HLA Hart, *The Concept of Law*, 2nd edn (Oxford, Oxford University Press, 1994) 80. For an excellent critique of Hart's arguments against the realists, see A Altman, 'Legal Realism, Critical Legal Studies and Dworkin' (1986) 15 *Philosophy and Public Affairs* 207.

[25] B Leiter, 'Legal Realism and Legal Positivism Reconsidered' (2001) 111 *Ethics* 278.

[26] See ch 2.

[27] F Schauer, 'Legal Realism Untamed' (2013) 1 *Texas Law Review* 769.

Ultimately, Raz is faced with the rather unpalatable choice that was offered at the beginning of the chapter: he can become a card-carrying realist or he can abandon his theory of adjudication and revert to his positivism of old. But, of course, we have already learned that his positivism of old is fatally flawed.[28] Indeed, it is now clear why the collapse of the rule-plus-exception model into a version of Dworkinian interpretation has such a devastating impact on his version of legal positivism. It exposes the fact that the common assumption about legal positivism is mistaken. Contrary to the popular view, normative positivism is not dependent on the truth of its conceptual counterpart; rather, normative positivism is all that there is.

Notice that this conclusion may also be arrived at via a slightly different path. Raz now (correctly) maintains that theories of adjudication are inherently normative:

> Clearly, a theory of adjudication is a moral theory. It concerns all the considerations affecting reasoning in the courts, both legal and non-legal. In pronouncing which extra legal considerations have force and how much weight is due them, it is engaged with moral argument. When the doctrine of the nature of law is identified with a theory of adjudication, it becomes itself a moral theory.[29]

By implication, if a theory of adjudication is normative by design, and if one's theory of adjudication has implications for one's theory of law, then one's theory of law includes an undeniable normative dimension. This is so even if one's theory of the nature of law is not 'identified' with a theory of adjudication, as Raz suggests above. The purely conceptual non-normative project dies the moment the sharp divide is breached. It is the work of the judge, and the failure to account for it in non-normative terms, that dooms the positivists' conceptual project.

As mentioned at the outset of this chapter, the current trend is to treat the distinction between a theory of law and a theory of adjudication as a matter of fact – legal theorists are expected to operate within these confines at least insofar as they hope to participate in the mainstream debate. Breaching this divide is treated as a signal that one has left the general jurisprudential debate and thus no positivist need engage with such ideas. But if the divide is one that can be breached unintentionally and with relative ease, then the argumentative burden shifts: the more effort that must be exerted to shore up this distinction, the less plausible it becomes. I would even suggest that if the distinction does not hold as a matter of fact, then treating it as such only serves to dogmatically maintain the status quo.

It is now clear why the Hartian positivist who aims at elucidating the nature of law without making any normative commitments needs the distinction

[28] See ch 2.

[29] Raz, *Ethics in the Public Domain*, above n 10, at 209.

between a theory of law and a theory of adjudication to hold. My claim, that Raz's theory of law has implications for his theory of adjudication is confirmed when we explore Raz's defence of the weak autonomy thesis against Postema's potentially devastating critique. Raz reverts back to his theory of old in order to shore up his current account – a move that is not available to him. But the fact that he makes the move is itself revealing: it is an implicit acknowledgment that he needs the rule-plus-exception model in order to shore up his positivist theory of law, which is currently defined by the sources thesis, the pre-emption thesis and the idea that law claims authority. In other words, Raz's own arguments confirm the conclusions drawn thus far.

III. BACK TO THE SETTLED CORE

Postema argues that citizens will have a reason to accord legal norms pre-emptive status in their reasoning process 'only to the extent that they believe the *courts* reliably do so'.[30] Raz does not agree. Instead, he explicitly defends the *weak autonomy thesis*: law gives citizens factually ascertainable pre-emptive reasons for action even though judges frequently create new law. That is, the aggregate of legal norms enjoy autonomy from moral reasoning outside, but not inside, the courtroom. The implication is that the motivation of citizens to accord legal norms pre-emptive status is not impacted by judicial creativity – the very point that Postema is challenging. Revealingly, in his reply to Postema, Raz eventually concedes that there is a deeper connection between the work of the judges and the incentives of citizens. He offers two distinct arguments in the hopes of diffusing Postema's complaint. I will consider each in turn.

In principle, Raz maintains, judicial creativity can have an impact on the incentive structure of the citizenry, but in practice this worry is mitigated by the fact that so few laws are challenged by judges in court. Yet, even if we agree with Raz that 'an infinitesimally small proportion of the circumstances to which the law applies *can* ever be subject to litigation in the courts', we do not have to agree with him that in 'such circumstances no problem regarding the binding force of the law arises out of the fact that it is revisable by the courts'.[31] The impact of judicial discretion on the incentives of those subject to the law is context and content dependent. The potential impact in any given case will surely depend on the nature of the law in question and the nature of the decision made by the judge. The burden is on Raz to demonstrate that

[30] GJ Postema, 'Law's Autonomy in Public Practical Reason' in R George (ed), *The Autonomy of Law* (Clarendon Press, 1996) 100.

[31] J Raz, 'Postema on Law's Autonomy and Public Practical Reason: A Critical Comment' (1998) 4 *Legal Theory* 1, 20.

there is no relation between the work of the courts and the reasoning process of citizens. He implicitly acknowledges this point when he offers an additional supporting argument.

Raz maintains that judges are conscious of their power and exercise it with self-imposed restraint. It is precisely because judges are aware of the power they have to change the normative landscape that Raz insists that 'This is a reason, well appreciated by the courts, not to make it too easy for litigants to get the law changed'.[32] Judges are reluctant to change the law even when afforded the opportunity to do so. The discretionary powers that judges have are therefore quite restricted:

> The limits on the intelligibility of the claim that a norm exists are transgressed when every occasion for its application is also an occasion for its modification or repeal. But when this is not so, when there are occasions of its application which are not occasions for its modification, there is no such problem. The case of being subject to revision by the courts is a long way from getting near the borderline of intelligibility.[33]

Judges are tasked with the job of applying the law in most instances. In a comparatively smaller number of cases judges have the power to modify the law. Judicial use of discretion is a penumbral activity, empirically speaking: the central, 'core' case is one where judges apply pre-existing law. This response signals a clear return to the traditional positivist picture of adjudication which Raz defended in *Practical Reason and Norms* and in *The Authority of Law*. Indeed, Raz even directs readers to the relevant chapter in *The Authority of Law* where he defends a rule-plus-exception model of adjudication.[34]

Not only are there serious problems with his rule-plus-exception model, which I have detailed at length in chapter two, but this model is not compatible with Raz's morally robust theory of adjudication. Raz cannot simultaneously argue that judges rarely exercise discretion *and* that 'quite commonly courts have the discretion to modify legal rules, or to make exceptions to their applications, and where they have such discretion they ought to resort to moral reasoning to decide whether to use it and how'.[35] Furthermore, by attempting to shore up the weak autonomy thesis by insisting that judges rarely exercise discretion, Raz inadvertently confirms the connection between the pre-emption thesis and the issue of motivation: if citizens are to have the requisite motivation to allocate legal norms pre-emptive status, then they must be able to anticipate that judges will rarely alter existing law by using their discretionary powers. Conversely, if judges regularly exercise discretion,

[32] *Ibid*, 20.
[33] *Ibid*, 19–20.
[34] Raz, 'Postema on Law's Autonomy', above n 31, at 18. See also ch 7.
[35] Raz, *Ethics in the Public Domain*, above n 10, at 335.

then citizens will lose at least some of the motivation to treat legal norms as pre-emptive reasons. Citizens will know that the law is 'gappy' and they will hesitate before turning to pre-existing legal norms to determine what behaviour is legal. That is, understanding what behaviour is permitted and what is prohibited is not simply a matter of knowing the positive law. Citizens must also have a sense of how positive law will be treated in the courtroom and adjust their behaviour accordingly.

In sum, instead of offering us a single coherent account, Raz vacillates unstably between two different, incompatible interpretations. The first is a positivist theory, whereby judges have very limited discretionary powers and they work to preserve the storehouse of legal norms that serve as (potential) reasons for action for law's subjects. The second account is realist: judges frequently change the law and citizens cannot expect to be guided by a set of stable rights that are located in pre-existing positive law. This account of judging requires a different account of how law guides us – one that does not have the pre-emption thesis and the sources thesis at its core.[36] Again, it has become all too clear that Raz's account of law has implications for his understanding of adjudication and his theory of adjudication has implications for his account of the nature of law.

Once the untenability of a sharp divide between a theory of law and a theory of adjudication is exposed, the repercussions for the debate in legal philosophy are profound. Philosophers who focus primarily on adjudication can no longer be dismissed as being 'outside' the jurisprudential project. Dworkin, for instance, is not engaged in a wholly different enterprise. His account cannot be easily absorbed into framework, but neither can he be easily dismissed as a normative theorist because he offers nothing more than a theory of adjudication.[37] In addition, 'rule of law' theorists who offer morally robust accounts of the nature of law suddenly have the upper hand in the debate. Such theorists self-consciously pursue a normative conception of law while Raz's theory collapses into a normative account of the nature of law (and in all likelihood, one that he will be reluctant to champion).[38]

Raz and his defenders could surely argue that this conclusion is too quick – I have not paid sufficient attention to an original thesis that is central to Razian thought, namely, that all law claims authority. That is to say, it is a conceptual truth about law that it claims authority – it claims to give citizens pre-emptive reasons for action. Whether a given norm is treated as a pre-emptive reason for action is of little moment, or so the argument goes. I will

[36] I will return to this point in ch 6.

[37] Hart makes both of these moves. See his 'Postscript to the Concept of Law'. HLA Hart, *The Concept of Law*, above n 24, at 241, 250.

[38] See D Dyzenhaus (ed), *Recrafting the Rule of Law: The Limits of Legal Order* (Oxford, Hart Publishing, 1999); NE Simmonds, *Law as a Moral Idea* (Oxford, Oxford University Press, 2007).

explore the idea that all law claims authority below, but it is worth underscoring the simple point that a significant amount of damage has already been done to the dominant framework of jurisprudence, damage that cannot be undone even if it turns out that the idea that all law claims authority proves to be a viable thesis. Raz still defends a morally robust theory of adjudication alongside this central thesis. More important still is the way in which his account of law gives shape to his account of adjudication and vise versa.

It is certainly the case that if one's attention is fixated on the idea of law's claim to authority, then the link between the incentive structure of the citizenry and the pre-emption thesis appears to be wholly irrelevant. In Raz's words, the pre-emption thesis 'merely says that if the law is morally binding then its subjects have pre-emptive reasons to comply with it'.[39] This statement seems accurate, at least insofar as one is thinking about the pre-emption thesis from the perspective of Raz's morally robust account of authority. Notice, however, that when Raz defends his account of authority, he does not discuss the work of the judiciary. Instead, he focuses on what makes a given norm or set of norms morally legitimate. The key question is not whether citizens have the requisite motivation to allocate legal norms pre-emptive force (which is important if the focus is on law's order-engendering role), but whether the content of the norm is such that the norm is morally authoritative (ie does it have the authority that it claims?). Thus, if one views law through the lens of justified authority, all the worries that are detailed in this chapter recede, but they do not wholly disappear.

Notice that the question pertaining to the motivation of the citizenry has not vanished, it has only been reconfigured: Raz offers reasons why citizens *should* treat legal norms as pre-emptive reasons for action, reasons that are disconnected from any concern about judicial discretion.[40] Citizens should accord law pre-emptive force because it will simplify their reasoning process, doing so will promote tolerance, while enabling citizens to act in accordance with 'right reason'.[41] Regardless of the persuasive power of these arguments, the fact that Raz makes them is instructive: it signals that he is aware of the fact that the pre-emptive status of norms amounts to little if citizens do not have reasons to treat legal norms as pre-emptive reasons for action. By exploring the idea that all law claims authority, not only does the inherent ambiguity come to the fore, but we find that Raz occasionally defends this idea by appealing to an account of law's order–engendering role, which itself is underpinned by a positivistic conception of rights and duties (and not the realist account that springs from his morally robust theory of adjudication).

[39] Raz, 'Postema on Law's Autonomy', above n 31, at 11–12.
[40] J Raz, *The Morality of Freedom* (Oxford, Clarendon Press, 1986) 58.
[41] *Ibid*, 58, 79.

IV. LAW'S CLAIM TO AUTHORITY: RAZ'S WAY OUT?

The uncomfortable conclusions arrived at above are hidden from view by yet another shift in Raz's position which I have already touched upon. His central thesis, which is perhaps his most popular one, is the idea that all law claims authority. The ambiguity at the heart of this thesis makes it a particularly effective screening device. Its predecessor – the judicial duty to apply the law – is notably less suitable in this respect. The duty to apply the law, which was initially at the heart of Raz's theory of law, is clear and specific: judges must apply fact-based legal norms in order to ensure that the legal system persists.[42] I have argued that Raz eventually left this thesis behind as it was too demanding.

When we work to understand what precisely Raz means when he argues that all law claims authority, things quickly become complicated. The elusive nature of this central thesis is part of the reason for its popularity – it functions like a horoscope in a newspaper in the sense that it seems to be specific and meaningful, but in fact it is sufficiently ambiguous that there is a little something for everyone. Furthermore, we discover that he cannot insulate his theory from the difficulties discussed thus far because he is unable to fully rid himself of the story about law and order which is part of his original account in *Practical Reason and Norms* (discussed at length in chapter one).

The idea that law gives us exclusionary reasons was supposed to capture an aspect of our experience that, according to Raz, was previously lost under the radar. Because we had not yet been thinking in terms of exclusionary reasons, we did not pause to identify them all around us. Once they have been identified, it becomes clear that legal norms are exclusionary in nature (or at least this is the idea). This experience is familiar enough. When walking in a field, you might notice a single spider in its web (as I once did). Once you see one, you can suddenly see all of them, scattered throughout the field, hidden in plain sight. Raz's early work was meant to elucidate the nature of law by revealing what is hidden in plain sight. The thesis that legal norms give us exclusionary reasons was not meant to capture the perspective of law (ie law's claim), but rather the perspective of practical living. It is simultaneously an account of how law works for us individually (it gives each of us exclusionary reasons) and collectively (it engenders order by providing us all with exclusionary reasons).

The idea that law *claims* authority is now held out by Raz as the universal feature that all legal systems share, replacing the idea that judges have a duty to apply the law. This idea is distinguishable from two other ideas which are related to this central thesis but remain distinct. First, whether law enjoys the

[42] See ch 1.

moral authority that it claims can only be determined after an enquiry into its content. Second, whether citizens treat a law or set of laws as authoritative is an empirical matter that is considered to be separate from the conceptual nature of law. In other words, the law's claim to authority is not dependent on whether people actually recognize that authority. The second claim (if successful) is quite ingenious. Insofar as Raz is able to insulate his thesis from empirical facts about the world, it becomes remarkably difficult to argue against. If the idea that all law claims authority is simply supposed to capture the notion that legal norms are the kind of norms that we are expected to follow, then it is a rather thin thesis that few would disagree with. If this is all Raz hopes to say, then it is compatible with a host of conceptions of law, not all of them in the positivist family.[43] For this reason, the temptation to retreat to this bare claim when the more robust versions of the thesis encounter problems should be resisted. Raz, of course, offers us more than this thin theory. He works hard to give a more substantive meaning to this central thesis, but with each attempt he creates as many problems as he solves.

To begin with, the very idea of a claim to authority introduces a rather stark and puzzling choice. Is Raz suggesting that officials claim authority on behalf of law or is he arguing that law itself claims authority? If he wishes to suggest that it is law as such, and not officials, that claims authority, then there is a simple problem: law is not the kind of thing that can make 'claims' on its own behalf. Raz acknowledges as much and this leads him to suggest that it is the officials that claim authority on behalf of law, insisting that it 'is useful to avail ourselves of the general habit of personifying the law and talking of what it requires, permits, claims, authorizes, etc'.[44] The officials tell us what the law requires, permits or claims. This clarification resolves some obvious difficulties, but it creates others. It seems plausible that officials can forgo making such claims on behalf of law and thus Raz's theory would (once again) be vulnerable to counter-examples. Kenneth Himma reminds us that the bare point that officials make claims on behalf of law is not enough to establish Raz's authority thesis. Raz does not merely have to establish that officials claim that there is a general legal obligation to obey the law; rather he must demonstrate that 'the officials claim there is a content-independent *moral* obligation to obey law'.[45] This is a difficult task; it is not self-evident that this is the kind of claim that officials are making. We have already left the thin claim far behind.

[43] A similar point is made by Waldron. See J Waldron, 'Legal and Political Philosophy' in J Coleman and S Shapiro (eds), *The Oxford Handbook of Jurisprudence and Philosophy of Law* (Oxford, Oxford University Press, 2002) 357.

[44] Raz, *The Morality of Freedom*, above n 40, at 70.

[45] K Himma, 'Law's Claim of Legitimate Authority' in J Coleman (ed), *Hart's Postscript* (Oxford, Oxford University Press, 2001) 271.

Given these worries, it is not surprising to discover that Raz frequently shifts his attention back to the features that law must have if it is to (potentially) be an authority. The emphasis is taken off the views of officials and placed on certain structural characteristics that legal systems are thought to have. In order for law to claim authority it must be capable of possessing the moral properties that authorities exhibit.[46] Law can (and often does) fail to possess the authority it claims, but significantly 'law can fail in certain ways only' and hence 'we can learn from the doctrine of authority something about the nature of law'.[47] Things like trees and volcanoes are not capable of possessing authority, so any claims to the contrary are confused: 'only those who can have authority can sincerely claim to have it'.[48] In order to shore up this point, Raz assures us that our officials cannot be systematically confused: 'For given the centrality of legal institutions in our structures of authority, their claims and conceptions are formed by and contribute to our concept of authority'.[49] In other words, the claims of officials tell us something about the nature of law: they claim to have authority and they can potentially have the authority they claim. If law was incapable of being morally legitimate – incapable of possessing the authority that is claimed – then the officials would indeed be systematically confused.

Raz proceeds to identify two features that are required if something is to be an authority First, the directive issued by the authority must be presented as someone's view about how those subject to the law ought to behave. Second, he insists that 'it must be possible to identify the directive as being issued by the alleged authority without relying on reasons or considerations on which the directive purports to adjudicate'.[50] The second condition implicates his sources thesis. Only if the sources thesis holds will it be possible for citizens to identify legal norms without revisiting any of the background reasons. If Raz is correct about this, then the views of his opponents – Dworkin and the inclusive positivists – are fatally flawed. Raz is aware of the relationship between his theses and states 'It is interesting to note that legal sources meet both conditions'.[51] Of course it is not a mere coincidence that Raz's theory of authority is consistent with his theory of law, as he seems to suggest.

When this version of the thesis is being defended, the idea of a claim to authority adds little to the proposition that legal norms offer us factually identifiable pre-emptive reasons for action. Instead of insulating his thesis from attack, this version of the thesis makes it vulnerable to the criticisms launched

[46] Raz, *Ethics in the Public Domain*, above n 10, at 215.
[47] *Ibid*, 216.
[48] *Ibid.*
[49] *Ibid*, 217.
[50] *Ibid*, 218.
[51] *Ibid*, 221.

against the pre-emption thesis. For instance, it is not clear that the common law is best captured by this model – it seems to resist both conditions. Even if legal norms are not always accorded pre-emptive status by citizens, they must be *capable* of being treated as such. Furthermore, the bare capacity is of little moment if citizens are not motivated to accord the law pre-emptive status (so we are quickly led back to the concerns explored in chapter one). After all, if the law is rarely accorded pre-emptive status, then why should Dworkin or the inclusive positivists worry about whether or not their views are consistent with Raz's conception of authority? If the claim to authority is merely about the perspective of law, saying nothing about how citizens reason with rules, then it is arid. Raz seems to understand this as he offers yet another attempt at giving this thesis determinate meaning.

In *The Morality of Freedom*, Raz looks to the idea that the law gives us rights and duties in order to give content to his central thesis concerning the authority of law. Significantly, Raz is once again locating legal rights within the confines of positive law, yielding yet another piece of evidence for the case that his new, morally robust theory of adjudication (and the account of rights that flows from it) is fundamentally incompatible with his other central theses. In addition, the notion of 'legal rights' is itself controversial, making the idea that 'all law claims authority' controversial by association. Raz, of course, insists that he is not making a controversial point; rather, he is simply making sense of *our* concept of authority. All the same, one might well wonder how he is able to make sense of legal systems that existed prior to the emergence of 'our concept'. Raz responds that in such instances, 'We say of their institutions that they claim authority because they claim to confer duties, impose rights etc'.[52] The existence or non-existence of a claim to authority now wholly depends on the presence of rights and duties. Again, this response signals a clear shift of focus away from the statements of officials onto those identifiable features that legal systems are thought to have. But what precisely does Raz mean by 'legal rights'? What precisely is the relationship between the existence of such rights in his sense and the claim to authority?

To understand what it means for claims to confer duties and impose rights we have to turn to Raz's distinction between coercive power and law. According to Raz, it is this distinction that gives content to law's claim to authority:

> I do not exercise authority over people afflicted with dangerous diseases if I knock them out and lock them up to protect the public, even though I am, in the assumed circumstances, justified in doing so. I have no more authority over them than I have over mad dogs. The exercise of coercive or any other form of power is no exercise of authority unless it includes an appeal for compliance by the person(s)

[52] *Ibid*, 217.

> subject to the authority. That is why the typical exercise of authority is through giving instructions of one kind or another. But appeal to compliance makes sense precisely because it is an invocation of the duty to obey.[53]

The appeal to compliance is a necessary feature of legal systems since this appeal is a condition for the existence of rights and duties. Raz suggests that the invocation of a duty to obey amounts to a *claim* to be a legitimate authority (whether or not a given law or a given legal system *is* legitimate is a different question). Not only have we re-opened the problem of who (if anyone) must make such claims, but another fundamental problem with Raz's argument can also be identified upon closer inspection. That is to say, the dichotomy between 'coercion without warning' and 'instructions laid down in advance which appeal for the citizen's compliance' is a false dichotomy. Coercion that amounts to treating citizens like mad dogs can take place *with* warning. Instructions can be given in advance which state, 'do this or else'. Unless Raz accounts for this point, his argument is based on a false dichotomy. Instead of accounting for this third possibility, he simply reproduces the same (false) dichotomy in a different form.

Raz argues that the creation of rights and duties endows law with certain structural features that a coercive regime lacks. In order to demonstrate this point, he asks us to imagine a society where the government fails to make this claim:

> [T]ry to imagine a situation in which the political authorities of a country do not claim that the inhabitants are bound to obey them, but in which the population does acquiesce in their rule. We are to imagine courts imprisoning people without finding them guilty of any offence; damages are ordered, but no one has a duty to pay them. The legislature never claims to impose duties of care or of contributions to common services. It merely pronounces that people who behave in certain ways will be made to suffer. And it is not merely ordinary people who are not subjected to duties by the legislature: courts, policemen, civil servants, and other public officials are not subjected by it to any duties in the exercise of their official functions either.[54]

Raz depicts a society that has a number of familiar elements (the presence of officials and governmental institutions such as courts and a legislature), but these familiar features do not function in any familiar way. The officials' behaviour is unpredictable and morally problematic. The idea is that if law fails to claim authority, then legal systems will resemble this strange conglomeration of features listed above. This passage harkens back to Raz's discussion of systems of absolute discretion, where chaos is more prevalent than order. In *Practical Reason and Norms*, the idea was that if judges did not simply apply the

[53] Raz, *The Morality of Freedom*, above n 40, at 25–26.
[54] *Ibid*, 27.

law, chaos would ensue. This is a fairly straightforward but falsifiable claim, and I argue in chapters one, two and six that it actually is false. In the later work, the argument is that if the *law did not claim authority*, then chaos would reign. Yet, the precise connection between the claim to authority and the existence of order is not immediately apparent because it is not clear what it means for all law to claim authority.

Again, the problem with this argument is that Raz suppresses the distinction between using violence *ad hoc* and using violence to enforce explicit threats. At certain points in the above quotation, the use of force by officials appears to be *ad hoc*: Raz asks us, for example, 'to imagine courts imprisoning people without finding them guilty of any offence'.[55] Power is exercised in an arbitrary manner and not in accordance with fundamental tenets of the rule of law. Citizens in this society do not enjoy basic procedural safeguards and they will live in fear of facing the coercive force of the state. The absence of a claim to authority becomes another way of expressing the idea of an absence of pre-existing norms and/or certain minimal procedural protections. Interestingly, an exploration of this point takes us beyond the austere panoply of theses championed by Raz towards a richer conception of the rule of law – I will return to this in chapter six.

Elsewhere in the above passage Raz favours the second half of the suppressed distinction: the claim to authority is juxtaposed with the use of force in the implementation of explicit threats rather than with *ad hoc* acts of violence by officials. Raz states that in coercive states, the legislature 'merely pronounces that people who behave in certain ways will be made to suffer'.[56] The violence is not random or unannounced: citizens are given advance warning about the occasions on which government force will be used. The key point is that the government issues threats instead of promulgating legal norms, which means that neither citizens nor officials are subject to duties in such a system.[57] That is to say, Raz believes that rights and duties are the product of stable legal norms and cannot originate from threats, but it is not exactly clear how threats differ from legal norms.

As Matthew Kramer notes, Raz cannot simply define away the possibility that a system can be comprised of threats rather than what we typically think of as legal norms. Consider a real-world example: the Mafia. Kramer argues that the key point when considering organizations like the Mafia is 'whether the syndicate should be designated as a legal regime'.[58] He correctly contends that 'the appropriateness of such a classification should not be denied merely

[55] *Ibid.*
[56] *Ibid.*
[57] *Ibid.*
[58] M Kramer, *In Defense of Inclusive Legal Positivism* (Oxford, Oxford University Press, 1999) 96.

because the Mafia's officials make no pretensions to moral admirability'.[59] The key questions have to do with how far-reaching their control is, how long they have control and how many people are affected. Given that criminal syndicates tend to have great difficulty coming close to establishing widespread control over all or most areas of life for an extended period of time, the oddness of giving them the title of legality should not trouble us much.[60]

This is not Raz's only attempt to explain law's order-engendering role via his account of authority. Despite his insistence that his theory has little to say about law's function, the old story about law and order re-emerges whenever Raz seeks to explain what law does in the world.[61] The pre-emption thesis is wedded to Raz's early conception of law's order-engendering role and Raz never successfully severs this link. Not only does this indicate that he can never distance himself from the worries about the incentives of citizens, but there are other consequences still. In his later works, the story of how law contributes to an orderly society is a heavily qualified one, which potentially undermines the universal aspirations of his account.

V. A STORY ABOUT LAW AND ORDER RETOLD

Raz's account of how law guides our behaviour is rule-centered: rules present us with pre-emptive (or exclusionary) reasons for action. The pre-emptive status of law allows law to serve the governed in many ways. For instance, Raz argues that one benefit of allocating legal norms pre-emptive status is that doing so saves us from having to return to the reasons that underpin the norms. Our reasoning process is simplified: we do not have to make fresh judgments about what to do in each and every case. If we do not allocate a given norm pre-emptive status, we will be left to evaluate all the competing reasons ourselves. Of course, legal norms can fail to possess the moral authority that they claim. They can also fail to reproduce the reasons for action that we have independently of the law – and in such instances we can choose to treat the law *as if* it is authoritative.

In short, individuals either follow public standards (which are of course legal norms) or they make value judgments about what ought to be done (and the fact/value dichotomy is doing work, yet again). Insofar as an individual does not arrive at the same conclusion that the law mandates, her behaviour is potentially disruptive of order. Raz understands this and he argues that according legal norms pre-emptive status promotes the value of tolerance in a pluralistic society:

59 *Ibid*, 97.
60 *Ibid*.
61 See ch 5 for a discussion of this point.

> [A]n orderly community can exist only if it shares many practices, and that in all modern pluralistic societies a great measure of toleration of vastly different outlooks is made possible by the fact that many of them enable the vast majority of the population to accept common standards of conduct.[62]

Raz is not implying that the human condition is marked by an ongoing state of perpetual disagreement (as he assumes in *Practical Reason and Norms*); instead, he is suggesting that societies marked by a diversity of beliefs are defined by the existence of deep disagreements. The unifying potential of law becomes all the more important in such contexts.

Perhaps this is so, but notice that Raz simply *assumes* that his version of the guidance function accounts for this point. That is, he leaves his readers to assume that the existence of order is evidence that law's potential has been actualized and thus legal norms are best understood as pre-emptive reasons for action. In pluralistic societies, there are seemingly two options: either we allocate legal norms pre-emptive status and thereby contribute to the maintenance of order, or we rely on our personal judgments about what we ought to do in a given instance – judgments that are potentially disruptive of the status quo. Insofar as order exists in a given society, we are left to conclude that law is working as it should – it is giving us pre-emptive reasons and saving us from returning to the reasons behind the rule. The fact that many of us do not revisit the reasons behind rules with any great frequency seems to shore up Raz's account. This conclusion may be drawn only if we presuppose the truth of Raz's account, but we should not be too hasty. There is another perfectly intelligible explanation about why we rarely return to the reasons behind rules: law does not guide conduct in the manner that Raz supposes. I will explore this possibility in chapter six.

Regardless of whether or not Raz is capable of discharging the argumentative burden needed to shore up his position (and I doubt that he is), this is the only story about law's order-engendering role that he can tell. Notice that it is connected to the idea that law necessarily claims authority via his pre-emption thesis. If Raz can insulate his core thesis from all observations we can make about law in the world, then it becomes an arid claim; if it is not insulated from his assumptions about law's function, then it is vulnerable to the litany of complaints outlined in this book.[63]

Finally, notice that in his discussion of pluralistic societies, Raz has quietly acknowledged that law orders societies in different ways. His story, which was originally a universal one about how law creates order, has now become an account of the manner in which law preserves order in some but not all societies. This places Raz in a rather curious position. It suggests that the pre-emptive

[62] Raz, *The Morality of Freedom*, above n 40, at 58.
[63] I will return to this point in ch 5.

status of legal norms is important in some societies, but not others. What about societies that are not pluralist? How does law work in those societies? Is Raz's theory, at best, an account of law in pluralistic societies? If so, it is extremely limited in reach and fails from the start to capture the existence conditions for legality, contrary to Raz's intention. I agree with Raz, however, that more than one story about the manner in which law orders society must be told. However, I will argue that we have little reason to assume, alongside Raz, that order in a pluralistic society is maintained when the pre-emptive status of legal norms is realized in full.

In sum, even though Raz appears to escape from the dilemma I have sketched above by introducing the idea of a claim to authority, he cannot shed his earlier account of law's guidance function. The moment he relies on this account, he is vulnerable to the catalogue of problems I have detailed above. I have suggested that many of these problems led Raz to abandon his early theory in the first place in favour of a morally robust theory of adjudication and a normative account of authority (while seeking to maintain his positivist commitments throughout). Although Raz's current position combines his positivist theory of law with a morally robust theory of adjudication, it proves to be incoherent and his positivism of old is no longer a viable alternative. These are but some of the perils of modern day positivism. The path becomes thornier still when we explore the internal coherence of Raz's account of authority, which is the focus of the next chapter.

4

Raz's The Morality of Freedom: *Two Models of Authority*

SEVENTEENTH-CENTURY PHILOSOPHERS WERE preoccupied with justifications for the use of coercion. Consequently, the nature and scope of the citizen's duty to obey the law was a central concern. The typical philosophical accounts that attempt to articulate the conditions under which a citizen has an obligation to obey the law tend to fall into two camps: those that ground the obligation to obey the law in consent, and those that ground it in benefits received, or possibly a combination of both.[1] More recently, however, some have argued that questions about the obligation to obey the law have been eclipsed by questions about distributive justice. The political theorist John Dunn suggests that this shift in thinking is symptomatic of modern-day overconfidence that the question of protection has been solved.[2] While this might be an accurate assessment of the status quo in certain fields of enquiry, many leading figures in modern analytic jurisprudence remain concerned with the nature of political obligation. Joseph Raz is a current-day theorist who has recognized the importance of this issue and the need for an answer that is not over-simplistic. His acclaimed book, *The Morality of Freedom*, is his most complete articulation of the nature and scope of law's authority. More recently, Raz has re-examined his account in 'The Problem of Authority: Revisiting the Service Conception', making an exploration of his theory particularly timely.[3]

The virtue of Raz's theory is that it provides a nuanced understanding of the nature and scope of law's authority. He argues that all governments claim morally legitimate authority, but not all of them actually possess it. His theory seeks to give us the tools by which to distinguish legitimate claims from those of imposters. For Raz, it is highly likely, if not guaranteed, that every legal authority will make claims of both kinds; that is, they will issue both legitimate and illegitimate directives. His test for morally justified legal norms, as I will

[1] More will be said about this distinction below.
[2] J Dunn, *The History of Political Theory* (Cambridge, Cambridge University Press, 1996) 69.
[3] J Raz, 'The Problem of Authority: Revisiting the Service Conception' in *Between Authority and Interpretation* (Oxford, Oxford University Press, 2009).

demonstrate, is highly individualistic: we look at the relationship between the individual and the authority in reference to discrete legal norms or groups of norms. The complexity and flexibility of Raz's understanding of the nature and scope of the individual's obligation to obey the law accounts for its appeal. Upon closer inspection, however, difficulties emerge.

I will argue that Raz's theory is plagued by a deep-seated tension between his two central theses: the pre-emption thesis and the normal justification thesis. While we will explore both theses in further depth, the gist of the pre-emption thesis is that it requires a pre-commitment to authority in order for the law's mediating role to be performed. Conversely, the normal justification thesis invites a case-by-case assessment of the bindingness of norms. In short, the normal justification thesis is always poised to undermine the pre-emptive status of legal norms. As we shall see, Raz recognises this tension and employs various strategies to overcome it. I will argue, however, that instead of offering us a unified conception of authority, he vacillates unstably between two models – a consent-based model and a benefits-received model. I will demonstrate that this tension is ineradicable because the theses are connected to divergent models of law and incompatible methodologies.

The chapter begins with an exposition of the conceptual elements of Raz's concept of authority: the dependence thesis, the normal justification thesis and the pre-emption thesis. I then turn to Raz's analogy with the arbitrator in order to demonstrate that the tension between the normal justification thesis and the pre-emption thesis is a product of the fact that these theses are linked to different models of authority. I will argue that, unlike the normal justification thesis, the pre-emption thesis is part of a positivist theory of law, which is at home in a consent-based model of authority. The weaknesses in Raz's attempts to overcome this tension will then be highlighted. I will argue that instead of arriving at a coherent concept of authority, he continually shifts between two incompatible models of legal authority. The problems with grounding one's conception of authority in the idea of expertise will also be explored in this section.

Finally I will explore the possibility that the tension is produced by Raz's methodological shift. The pre-emption thesis is the product of his morally bare descriptive methodology, while the normal justification thesis is the product of the morally robust focal case methodology. Implicit in my argument is the fact that one's concept of authority cannot be different in kind from one's concept of law. Moreover, even if one rejects the possibility of descriptive jurisprudence, a re-conceptualisation of Raz's project fails to unify his account of authority. In sum, he offers us two concepts of authority in the guise of one. The chapter will conclude by considering a potential solution to the issues identified – a solution that places great weight on law's ability to facilitate co-ordination and co-operation. Unfortunately, however, this solution requires significant alterations to Raz's account, which ultimately aligns him with the accounts of authority that he was seeking to discredit.

One might argue that I have, at this early stage, misunderstood Raz's concept of authority: he is able to combine a morally robust conception of authority with a descriptive account of law precisely because he argues that all law *claims* authority; he does not argue that all legal norms possess (morally) legitimate authority. It is tempting to view Raz's idea that all law claims authority as a bridge that unites his conception of justified authority and his positivist conception of law. Despite its initial plausibility, Raz's thesis that all law claims authority cannot ease the tension between the normal justification thesis and the pre-emption thesis given that the tension arises at the precise moment one attempts to assess whether a given legal norm possesses the moral authority it claims to have.[4] It is not helpful to appeal to the thesis already presupposed when difficulties emerge. Thus it is not surprising to discover that Raz offers a different, novel set of arguments to address this tension when it arises in *The Morality of Freedom.*

There is a second objection that, if successful, will blunt the force of my argument before it is articulated. One might argue that the pre-emption thesis is a practical thesis while the normal justification thesis is merely theoretical. Because the theses operate on different planes, they cannot come into conflict. There are two obstacles to this interpretation. The first is textual. Raz explicitly identifies the tension I aim to explore and offers various arguments in an attempt to diffuse it. Such arguments would not be required if the normal justification thesis was meant to be merely theoretical in nature. Indeed, Raz explicitly states that only legitimate directives give us reasons for action, thereby endowing the normal justification thesis with practical significance.[5] The second obstacle involves the implications of this view. If only the pre-emption thesis has practical force, then legal norms become binding in virtue of their status as legal norms. This is the vision of law Raz presents us with in *Practical Reason and Norms*, but it is also a vision of law he ceases to endorse in full, likely given the numerous challenges it encounters. Those who view the normal justification thesis as merely theoretical will be saddled with the various difficulties that accompany the pre-emption thesis. It is useful to begin with an understanding of Raz's central thesis before exploring the tension between them in greater depth.

[4] See ch 3.

[5] J Raz, *The Morality of Freedom* (Oxford, Clarendon Press, 1986) 46.

I. RAZ'S FOCAL CONCEPT OF AUTHORITY

In *The Morality of Freedom*, Raz 'denies the existence of a general obligation to obey the law even in a reasonably just society'.[6] Moral legitimacy is not a binary quality that authorities either possess or lack; rather he sees legitimacy as piecemeal in nature.[7] At the centre of his concept of authority is the relationship between an individual and the state – more specifically between the individual and the state as mediated through legal norms. Consequently, for Raz 'It is not good enough to say that an authoritative measure is justified because it serves the public interest. If it is binding on individuals it has to be justified by considerations which bind them'.[8] In order to give content to this statement, Raz introduces the dependence thesis and the normal justification thesis. Together, these two theses capture his normative conception of morally justified authority.

The dependence thesis tells authorities how they ought to make decisions. Ideally, authorities should make laws based on reasons that already apply to the subjects:

> *[A]ll authoritative directives should be based on reasons which already independently apply to the subjects of the directives and are relevant to their action in the circumstances covered by the directive.* (author's italics)[9]

Legal officials are not supposed to create new reasons for action. Raz communicates this idea via the analogy of the arbitrator: the arbitrator is supposed to sum up the reasons that apply to disputing parties and issue a verdict based on these reasons.[10] He is aware that authorities do not always abide by this constraint on their power and thus argues that the dependence thesis 'does not claim that authorities always act for dependent reasons, but merely that they should do so'.[11] Raz acknowledges that authorities may not even pursue this ideal.[12] He nonetheless maintains his steadfast commitment to the dependence thesis:

> It is nevertheless through their ideal functioning that they must be understood. For that is how they are supposed to function, that is how they publicly claim that they attempt to function, and, as we shall see below, that is the normal way to justify their authority.[13]

[6] *Ibid*, 70.
[7] *Ibid*, 80.
[8] *Ibid*, 72.
[9] *Ibid*, 47.
[10] *Ibid*, 41.
[11] *Ibid*, 47.
[12] *Ibid*.
[13] *Ibid*. For a critique of these claims, see K Himma, 'Revisiting Raz: Inclusive Legal Positivism and Our Concept of Authority' (2007) 6 *American Philosophical Association Newsletter on Philosophy and Law*, no 2.

Raz's reliance on a focal case methodology is clear: he is articulating an ideal of morally justified authority in order to understand the nature of authority more generally. More will be said on this point below.[14] For present purposes it is useful to turn our attention to the 'normal' way to justify authority.

According to Raz, the normal way to justify authority is captured by his normal justification thesis. While the dependence thesis tells legal officials how they ought to make decisions, the normal justification thesis determines the scope of legitimate authority in reference to a given citizen. The normal justification thesis is defined by Raz as follows:

> It claims that *the normal way to establish that a person has authority over another person involves showing that the alleged subject is likely better to comply with reasons which apply to him (other than the alleged authoritative directives) if he accepts the directives of the alleged authority as authoritatively binding and tries to follow them, rather than by trying to follow the reasons which apply to him directly*. (author's italics)[15]

A legal norm is binding on an individual if it better enables the individual to act in accordance with the reasons that apply to him independently of the law.[16]

While Raz often assumes that authorities are better able to meet the demands of the normal justification thesis than individuals relying on their own judgment,[17] he recognises that sometimes individuals can claim expertise in a certain area and that this expertise can allow the individual to rely on his own judgment rather than the judgment of legal officials. For example, if an individual is an expert on the needs of children, he 'may have no reason to acknowledge the government's authority over him regarding the conditions under which parents may leave their children unattended by adults'.[18] Legal norms are not morally binding on individuals who have the relevant expertise.[19]

Raz provides a test to capture this feature of his theory: 'does following the authority's instructions improve conformity with reason?'[20] He reminds us that 'For every person the question has to be asked afresh, and for every one it has to be asked in a manner which admits of various qualifications'.[21] In

[14] See section IV below.

[15] Raz, *Morality of Freedom*, above n 5, at 53.

[16] Raz also refers to the reasons that apply to the subjects as 'right reason' or simply 'reason'. I will use these terms interchangeably.

[17] Raz, *Morality of Freedom*, above n 5, at 61.

[18] *Ibid*, 78.

[19] The idea seems to be that citizens can 'opt out'. One may wonder what precisely 'opt out' means in the context of Raz's theory. As we have seen, Raz is clear that directives that are not morally legitimate are not binding. That is, only legitimate directives give us reasons for action. *Ibid*, 46. Raz does add that the fact that the norm is not binding on the individual does not definitively answer the question of how to act. We may have prudential reasons (ie avoiding sanctions) for acting in accordance with legal norms. *Ibid*, 103.

[20] *Ibid*, 74.

[21] *Ibid*.

short, this test for normal justification invites case-by-case assessments, which accords the normal justification thesis a degree of flexibility.[22]

The point of legal authority, from the perspective of the normal justification thesis, is to enable individuals to act in accordance with right reason. The obligation to obey the law pivots on law's point: when the law enables the individual to act in accordance with right reason, the citizen has a moral obligation to obey it; when it does not, this obligation dissolves. The obligation is linked to the benefits one receives from the authority. Given that an individual's relationship to the law can continually change, both as the law changes and as his areas of expertise change, the question of one's obligation to obey the law must be continually asked if we hope to discover whether a given norm is binding on an individual.[23]

The normal justification thesis and the dependence thesis combine to form what I have termed Raz's focal concept of authority. Raz is not merely describing law as it is (a methodology that underpins his legal positivism); rather, he is articulating an understanding of the ideal of authority. That is, he is articulating the conditions under which authoritative directives are morally justified and thus legally binding. There is, however, a third piece to Raz's conceptual puzzle: the pre-emption thesis.

The pre-emption thesis is not a product of Raz's focal case method, rather it has always been a core part of his positivist conception of law – a conception of law that was originally grounded in a theory of practical reason and not an ideal of morally legitimate authority.[24] Raz defines the pre-emption thesis as follows:

> One thesis I am arguing for claims that authoritative reasons are pre-emptive: *the fact that an authority requires performance of an action is a reason for its performance which is not to be added to all other relevant reasons when assessing what to do, but should exclude and take the place of some of them.* (author's italics)[25]

In other words, legal norms present subjects with exclusionary reasons for action. As elucidated in chapter one, this thesis is one of the defining claims of

[22] *Ibid.* Raz underscores the flexibility of this thesis in the following passage: 'On the other hand the [normal justification] thesis allows maximum flexibility in determining the scope of authority. It all depends on the person over whom authority is supposed to be exercised: his knowledge, strength of will, his reliability in various aspects of life, and on the government in question. These factors are relevant at two levels. First they determine whether an individual is better likely to conform to reason by following an authority or by following his own judgment independently of any authority. Second they determine under what circumstances he is likely to answer the first question correctly'. *Ibid*, 73.

[23] This understanding of the normal justification thesis will be qualified below in reference to Raz's suggestion that we need not apply this thesis to every norm (ie we can allocate pre-emptive status to a group of norms).

[24] J Raz, *Practical Reason and Norms* (Oxford, Oxford University Press, 1999).

[25] Raz, *Morality of Freedom*, above n 5, at 46.

Raz's legal positivist position: legal norms are factually ascertainable; it is precisely because of law's factual quality that legal norms can mediate between us and the reasons that apply to us independently of the law.[26] The law is only performing its defining role as a mediating force when citizens treat legal norms as pre-emptive reasons for action.

The tension between the pre-emption thesis and the normal justification thesis is apparent when one bears in mind that for Raz, only morally legitimate legal norms have pre-emptive force. Indeed, when explaining the pre-emptive thesis, he states that only legitimate directives provide us with reasons for action.[27] Consequently, the *very act of determining whether the norm meets the normal justification standard undermines the pre-emptive force of the norm(s) in question.* This claim is subject to a qualification: Raz is adamant that we do not have to blindly obey legal norms for his pre-emption thesis to hold. We can criticise it as long as our criticisms are not carried out with practical ends in mind.[28] When pressed, however, some perplexities emerge that help to set up my over-arching argument, namely, that Raz's two central theses are fundamentally antagonistic.

When Raz is focused on the pre-emption thesis, he insists that we must treat legal norms as exclusionary reasons for actions. We cannot treat both the norm and the underlying reason as a reason for action; if we did rely on both, we would be guilty of 'double counting'.[29] Double counting is a crime of practical reason introduced by Raz to lend support to his claim that legal norms have pre-emptive status. He needs to keep the rule separate from the reasons behind it if legal norms are to be viewed as exclusionary reasons for action rather than simply weighty reasons for action. As mentioned, Raz maintains that we can reflect on the content of legal norms, insofar as our reflections are not carried out with an eye for action: when we act, the legal norm is treated as the reason for action that excludes competing reasons, including the reasons that underpin the rule itself.[30]

But once Raz argues that legal norms only have pre-emptive (binding) status if they are morally justified,[31] maintaining the space between the rule and the reasons that underpin it becomes all the more difficult. For instance, if the norms are not morally justified then they are not binding on us and hence they lose their exclusionary status. Alternatively, if we discover that they *are* morally binding on us and act accordingly, the following question arises: are we treating the legal norm as an exclusionary reason for action, or are we

26 See J Raz, *Ethics in the Public Domain* (Oxford, Oxford University Press, 1994) 218.
27 *Ibid.*
28 Raz, *Morality of Freedom*, above n 5, at 39–40.
29 *Ibid*, 58.
30 *Ibid*, 42. See ch 1 for a lengthier exploration of these ideas.
31 *Ibid*, 46.

according some force to the reasons that underpin the rule? If the reasons underpinning the rule are accorded some weight, then legal norms become weighty reasons and the prohibition on double counting is violated. When we are focused on the normal justification thesis, such a violation is of little moment. Raz agrees.

Interestingly, but not surprisingly, when Raz explores the normal justification thesis in 'The Problem of Authority: Revisiting the Service Conception', he steps away from his prohibition against double counting:

> So when an action is rightly required by authority (ie, when there are conclusive reasons for it, independently of the authority's intervention), we may (in both senses) do as we are required either because we are so required, or for the reasons that justify the requirement, or both.[32]

Once the key factor in determining law's normative force is the content of the norm and not simply its pedigree, double counting ceases to be a crime of practical reasoning but a *requirement* of practical reasoning. Here is one sign that the two theses are like oil and water. The pre-emption thesis requires us to maintain a clear separation between the rule and the reasons that underpin it. Conversely, when law is viewed through the lens of the normal justification thesis, a norm is binding precisely because of its content.

Raz proceeds to re-cast his pre-emption thesis to accord with this account of authority by arguing that pre-emptive reasons *only exclude reasons that conflict with the directive.*[33] The difficulty with this alteration is that it conceives of legal norms as weighty reasons for action given that the reasons that underpin the rule can carry normative force.[34] Once this is understood, it becomes readily apparent that Raz's re-configuration of the pre-emption thesis is a significant concession. It reveals his awareness that the pre-emption thesis as originally conceived does not cohere with his normal justification thesis. I will argue that it also signals the sacrifice of his positivist pre-emption thesis (and the conception of law that accompanies it) to the requirements of his morally robust conception of authority.

When we read *The Morality of Freedom* with this point in mind, we discover that Raz continually rearranges his conceptual puzzle pieces in an attempt to unite his positivist pre-emption thesis with the morally robust normal justification thesis. This is an ongoing battle, but it is a losing one given the deep incompatibility between his two central theses. When we take a closer look at the animating metaphor in Raz's *The Morality of Freedom* – the metaphor of the arbitrator – we can locate the origin of the tension and then trace the

32 Raz, *Between Authority and Interpretation*, above n 3, at 144–45.

33 *Ibid*, 144.

34 A common criticism of Raz's view that legal norms are exclusionary reasons for action is that it is too strong: legal norms are weighty reasons for action, not exclusionary reasons. See MS Moore, 'Authority, Law and Razian Reasons' (1988) 62 *California Law Review* 827, 846.

movement of Raz's arguments as he continually shifts between the competing models of authority represented by each of his key theses.

II. THE ANALOGY OF THE ARBITRATOR: FROM CONSENT TO NORMAL JUSTIFICATION

In order to unravel the above argument, it is useful to examine the analogy Raz makes between the role of an arbitrator and the role of legal authorities in a little more detail. I will argue that the difficulties that plague this analogy also infect his theory as a whole. In this analogy we find implicit references to the pre-emption thesis and a direct reference to the dependence thesis. Raz does not, however, mention the normal justification thesis – an omission that is more significant than it may appear. He writes:

> Consider the case of two people who refer a dispute to an arbitrator. He has authority to settle the dispute, for they agreed to abide by his decision. Two features stand out. First, the arbitrator's decision is for the disputants a reason for action. They ought to do as he says because he says so. But this reason is related to the other reasons which apply to the case. It is not . . . just another reason to be added to the others, a reason to stand alongside the others when one reckons which way is better supported by reason. The arbitrator's decision is meant to be based on the other reasons, to sum them up and to reflect their outcome. For ease of reference I shall call both reasons of this character and the reasons they are meant to reflect dependent reasons.[35]

The arbitrator presents the disputants with pre-emptive reasons for action. The parties are supposed to treat the judge's decision as a first-order reason to act for certain considerations and a second-order reason for not acting on one's own assessment of the balance of reasons. Raz communicates this thesis best when he says that the disputing parties who are faced with the decision of an arbitrator 'ought to do as he says because he says so'.[36] To do otherwise would defeat the point of bringing their case to the arbitrator precisely because the disputing parties consented to be bound by the decision, regardless of its content.

There are limits to the consent-based authority of the arbitrator. Raz argues that the authority of the ruling is undermined if, for instance, the arbitrator is drunk, or if new reasons emerge that were not part of the set of dependent reasons considered.[37] Notice, however, that such reasons are *external* to the dependent reasons that the ruling was intended to replace.[38] The key to the

[35] Raz, *Morality of Freedom*, above n 5, at 41.
[36] *Ibid*.
[37] *Ibid*, 42.
[38] Compare this claim with his more recent argument about what reasons are excluded. See n 34 above.

pre-emptive status of norms is that we are not supposed to return to the reasons that the rule is meant to sum up and replace. In short, the pre-emption thesis requires a *pre-commitment* to act in accordance with the legal norms.[39]

At this point, one may wonder if there is potential tension between the dependence thesis and the pre-emption thesis: do rules that fail to reflect the reasons that apply to the citizens sacrifice their binding status? Raz's answer, at this point, is 'no'. He avoids any such difficulties by arguing that even mistaken directives are binding:

> Remember also that the thesis is not that authoritative determinations are binding only if they correctly reflect the reasons on which they depend. On the contrary, there is no point in having authorities unless their determinations are binding even if mistaken (though some mistakes may disqualify them).[40]

This argument preserves the pre-emptive character of norms: citizens are supposed to treat legal norms as reasons for action that exclude competing reasons. Raz underscores this point when he argues that the

> whole point and purpose of authorities . . . is to pre-empt individual judgment on the merits of a case, and this will not be achieved if, in order to establish whether the authoritative determination is binding, individuals have to rely on their own judgments of the merits.[41]

If we rely on our own judgment every time the norm in question fails to reflect what we believe to be our own dependent reasons for action, then we defeat the point of arbitration – we defeat the purpose of law. These observations keep Raz's theory of authority in line with the analogy of the arbitrator. The ideal of how authorities should behave (represented by the dependence thesis) does not undermine Raz's theory of what law is. Here the pre-emption thesis acts as a trump card.

However, this message is not the only one delivered in *The Morality of Freedom*. Raz replaces the role that consent plays in the analogy of the arbitrator with his normal justification thesis. While he does not flag this move in *The Morality of Freedom*, he does so in *Ethics in the Public Domain*.[42] This seemingly innocent move considerably alters the dynamic between the pre-emption thesis and Raz's ideal of authority. Significantly, it means that the pre-emption thesis becomes subordinate to the normal justification thesis.

Emran Mian pinpoints the manner in which the analogy of the arbitrator falters once the normal justification thesis replaces consent: each represents a

[39] This becomes clear when we remember that the key feature of the pre-emptive status of legal norms is that they exclude competing reasons: legal norms, according to Raz, are not simply weighty reasons for actions that are to be balanced against other competing reasons. Raz, *Morality of Freedom*, above n 5, at 41.

[40] *Ibid*, 47.

[41] *Ibid*, 47–48.

[42] Raz, *Ethics in the Public Domain*, above n 26, at 214.

different model of authority. Consent, which underpins the pre-emption thesis, indicates the presence of a deferral model.[43] Once an individual consents to obey the authority, he treats the authority's directives as pre-emptive reasons for action – he defers to authority. Conversely, the normal justification thesis offers us a dialogic model. When the normal justification thesis replaces consent, the individual is no longer required to make a pre-commitment to follow the law; rather, he is instructed to determine whether the said norm is binding on him (he is asked to 'dialogue' with authority).[44]

The problem is as follows: a consent-based theory exhorts citizens to treat the law as providing content-independent reasons for action (as the pre-emption thesis demands), while the normal justification thesis makes the bindingness of norms a moral matter. A moral matter is a content-dependent matter. If we must return to the reasons that underpin the rule in order to determine its bindingness, its pre-emptive status is undermined as content-dependence replaces content-independence.[45] The incoherence of the analogy with the arbitrator (once consent is replaced by normal justification) is symptomatic of the problems Raz's account of authority encounters. Given that his key theses represent different models of authority, we can wonder whether Raz can successfully unify his theory of authority.

III. PRE-EMPTION VERSUS NORMAL JUSTIFICATION: SEEKING COHERENCE

Once Raz admits that the pre-emption thesis does not trump the normal justification thesis, the tension between the two is clear: the pre-emption thesis requires a pre-commitment to authority while the normal justification thesis invites us to evaluate the reasons behind the rule. Raz anticipates this objection and attempts to address it.[46] He writes:

> [The objection] says that in every case authoritative directives can be overridden or disregarded if they deviate much from the reasons which they are meant to

[43] It is true that Raz rejects general consent-based accounts of political authority. Raz, *Morality of Freedom*, above n 5, at 80–94. Nonetheless, when we focus on his pre-emption thesis, it is clear that consent plays a central role.

[44] E Mian, 'The Curious Case of Exclusionary Reasons' (2002) 15 *Canadian Journal of Law and Jurisprudence* 99, 113.

[45] Notice that the term 'service conception', which Raz also uses to describe his theory of authority, is itself ambiguous. Raz argues that it is the law's job to 'serve the governed' and thereby officials are *supposed* to act according to dependent reasons, which aligns the idea of 'service' with the normal justification thesis. However, the word 'service' is also supposed to signal the idea that legal norms give citizens pre-emptive reasons for action. This term only superficially bridges the two models and hence it submerges the tension.

[46] The very fact that he sees a need to address this issue is evidence that he does not view the two theses as different in kind – one of mere theoretical use, the other practical.

> reflect. It would not do, the objection continues, to say that the legitimate power of every authority is limited, and that one of the limitations is that it may not err much. For such a limitation defeats the pre-emption thesis since it requires every person in every case to consider the merits of the case before he can decide to accept an authoritative instruction.[47]

Raz remarks that this objection 'does not formally challenge the pre-emptive thesis'.[48] What it does do is challenge the mediating role that Raz assigns to authoritative directives.[49] To repeat, the mediating role serves 'to save them the need to refer to the very foundations of morality and practical reasoning generally in every case'.[50] The problem is as follows: 'as the directives are binding only if they do not deviate much from right reason and as we should act on them only if they are binding, we always have to go back to fundamentals'.[51] He is aware that a return to fundamentals would undermine the pre-emptive status of legal norms.

Raz's response to this challenge is as follows: some mistakes are clear, and when such mistakes are made there is no need to go back to the fundamentals to identify them. He uses an analogy with mathematics to illustrate his point:

> Consider a long addition of, say, some thirty numbers. One can make a very small mistake which is a very clear one, as when the sum is an integer whereas one and only one of the added numbers is a decimal fraction. On the other hand, the sum may be out by several thousands without the mistake being detectable except by laboriously going over the addition step by step. Even if legitimate authority is limited by the conditions that its directives are not binding if clearly wrong, and I wish to express no opinion on whether it is so limited, it can play its mediating role. Establishing that something is clearly wrong does not require going through the underlying reasoning. It is not the case that legitimate power of authorities is generally limited by the condition that it is defeated by significant mistakes which are not clear.[52]

Raz immediately applies this example to the legal domain. He argues that the pre-emption thesis 'depends on a distinction between jurisdictional and other mistakes'.[53] He suggests that 'Mistakes which they make about factors which determine the limits of their jurisdiction render their decisions void'.[54] Directives outside the jurisdiction of the authority are not binding, while directives that are wrong but are inside the jurisdiction of the authority are binding:

[47] Raz, *Morality of Freedom*, above n 5, at 61.
[48] *Ibid.*
[49] *Ibid.*
[50] *Ibid.*
[51] *Ibid*, 61–62.
[52] *Ibid*, 62.
[53] *Ibid.*
[54] *Ibid.*

> The pre-emption thesis claims that the factors about which the authority was wrong, and which are not jurisdictional factors, are pre-empted by the directive. The thesis would be pointless if most mistakes are jurisdictional or if in most cases it was particularly controversial and difficult to establish which are and which are not. But if this were so then most other accounts of authority would come to grief.[55]

In order to avoid returning to foundational reasons, Raz urges us to group moral political reasons in the category of 'significant mistakes which are not clear', which are contrasted with jurisdictional mistakes that are 'significant and clear'.[56] He contends that 'It is not the case that legitimate power of authorities is generally limited by the condition that it is defeated by significant mistakes which are not clear'. Raz wants us to believe that the only relevant mistakes are jurisdictional mistakes. In other words, these are the only mistakes that prevent a norm from being binding on us.

Raz's appeal to the distinction between jurisdictional mistakes and non-jurisdictional mistakes serves as an attempt on his part to gloss over the serious tension adumbrated above. If he can make the connection in the reader's mind between clear and significant mistakes and jurisdictional mistakes, then the problem of revisiting the foundations of morality disappears: in order to determine whether a directive is outside the jurisdiction of an authority, we do not have to revisit the foundations of morality; we only have to revisit the rules that determine the boundaries of authority.[57] This move, if successful, will preserve the mediating role he assigns to authority while still addressing the worry about mistaken directive. Unfortunately for Raz, this argument is not convincing, given that it preserves the pre-emption thesis at the expense of the normal justification thesis.

The source of the problem can be identified once we recall that the normal justification thesis looks at legal norms with reference to their content. It seeks to determine whether a norm is binding by figuring out whether it is in accordance with right reason.[58] While Raz does not specify precisely what 'right reason' means, we can be fairly certain that it is not an allusion to jurisdictional principles.[59] After all, the normal justification thesis exists in order to determine the extent to which any regime enjoys moral legitimacy. To determine whether a directive is justified, we must return to moral and political issues, not jurisdictional rules. Conversely, in order to discover whether a jurisdictional mistake has been made, we have to consult the secondary power-conferring rules of the

[55] *Ibid.*
[56] *Ibid.*
[57] Raz believes that such rules are part of every legal system. J Raz, *The Authority of Law* (Oxford, Oxford University Press, 1979) 70, 96.
[58] Raz, *Morality of Freedom*, above n 5, at 61.
[59] Cristobal Orrego argues that Raz's under-theorised conception of right reason places him in the natural law tradition. See C Orrego, 'Joseph Raz's Service Conception of Authority and Natural Law Theory' (2005) 50 *American Journal of Jurisprudence* 317.

system (on a positivist's account) – we do not have to return to questions of political morality.

One might object that I have misinterpreted Raz's use of the word 'jurisdiction'.[60] It might be the case that 'jurisdiction' refers to expertise (ie in the sense of moral jurisdiction): if an expert on children knows that the government is obviously wrong, he does not have to return to the reasons underpinning the rules to determine this. The idea seems to be that this expert will allocate pre-emptive status to legal norms when the error is not clear. Heidi Hurd aptly draws attention to the flaw in this line of argument. She argues that it is possible for a calculator to systematically make great mistakes that are unclear. If we apply this to governments, Hurd argues that 'Raz could not think it rational to judge a government's authoritative legitimacy by its failure to make clear mistakes'.[61] She is correct to conclude that such a government is not a legitimate authority.[62]

Further evidence that Raz's response is flawed can be adduced once we recollect certain features of the normal justification thesis. Recall that the normal justification thesis provides us with an individual-based test for justification: 'For every person the question has to be asked afresh, and for everyone it has to be asked in a manner which admits of various qualifications'.[63] If the mistakes that are relevant are simply jurisdictional errors, the requisite test would reveal the same results for everyone: the individual-based assessments that the normal justification thesis allows for would be unnecessary, as the subjective characteristics of the individual would not influence the question of whether a given directive is outside the jurisdiction of the official who rendered it. This is so even if the normal justification thesis is applied to groups of norms. A jurisdictional test has to do with the powers of officials, not characteristics of individuals. Raz's appeal to jurisdictional mistakes merely masks the serious tension in his theory.

Raz has another response at his disposal. It might be the case that I do not know much about roads for instance, so I should defer to the government in reference to all norms that apply to roads. Put more generally, the idea is that individuals can apply the normal justification thesis to certain groups of norms and they can allocate pre-emptive force to other groups. This possibility seems to best capture the central thrust of the normal justification thesis which suggests that on the whole, we are more likely to act in accordance with right reason if we follow the authority's directives rather than our own judgment

[60] The careful lawyer will correctly point out that determinations of jurisdiction often involve moral and political argumentation.

[61] H Hurd, *Moral Combat* (Cambridge, Cambridge University Press, 1999) 86.

[62] *Ibid.* See also J Goldsworthy, 'The Self-Destruction of Legal Positivism' (1990) 10 *OJLS* 449, 466.

[63] Raz, *Morality of Freedom*, above n 5, at 74.

most of the time.[64] In other words, Raz expects us to treat legal norms *as if* they are justified by allocating legal norms or groups of legal norms pre-emptive status because we are not likely to do better than the authority in hitting the mark.

Notice that this approach does not eliminate the tension between the two theses, but it does (if successful) reserve a place for each. In order to achieve this end, Raz must account for the reasons why citizens would assign a given norm or set of norms pre-emptive force. Recall from chapter one that he offers two arguments on this point. First, he argues that committing to norms in advance has the advantage of simplifying our reasoning. Second, he argues that since officials get it right more often than we do, it makes sense to abide by their judgment rather than our own. Let us consider each in turn.

Raz argues that allocating law pre-emptive force enables it to play its mediating role (this is the central feature of his 'service conception of authority').[65] One of the benefits of this mediating role is that it simplifies our reasoning:

> [Law] provide[s] an intermediate level of reason to which one appeals in normal cases where a need for decision arises . . . The advantage of normally proceeding through the mediation of rules is enormous. It enables a person to consider and form an opinion on the general aspects of recurrent situations in advance of their occurrence. It enables a person to achieve results which can be achieved only through an advance commitment to a whole series of actions, rather than by case to case examination.[66]

Here Raz allows the pre-emption thesis, and its ability to simplify reasoning, to take priority over the normal justification thesis (which invites case-by-case assessments). This raises the question: should we refrain from determining whether our actions accord with right reason given that it is important that our reasoning process is simplified? In other words, does the desire or need for simplification outweigh the requirements of the normal justification thesis?

Raz explains in more detail the kind of advantages that a simplified reasoning process will yield: he argues that the mediating role of legal norms enables the 'creation of pluralistic societies'.[67] Raz contends that the allocation of pre-emptive force to legal norms 'enables people to unite in support of some "low or medium level" generalizations despite profound disagreements concerning their ultimate foundations, which some seek in religion, others in Marxism or in Liberalism, etc'.[68] The law cuts through subjective preference and produces an orderly, co-operative society by unifying judgment:

[64] See N Gur, 'Legal Directives in the Realm of Practical Reason: A Challenge to the Pre-emption Thesis' (2007) 52 *American Journal of Jurisprudence* 159, 178.
[65] Raz, *Morality of Freedom*, above n 5, at 59.
[66] *Ibid*, 58.
[67] *Ibid*.
[68] *Ibid*.

> [A]n orderly community can exist only if it shares many practices, and that in all modern pluralistic societies a great measure of toleration of vastly differing outlooks is made possible by the fact that many of them enable the vast majority of the population to accept common standards of conduct.[69]

This is the liberal twist on an old story. Law unifies judgment by offering a mid-level set of rules that citizens defer to.[70] Without legal rules, individuals will pursue their subjective preferences and order will be compromised. Ultimately, Raz's argument regarding the creation of pluralistic societies is grounded in law's order-engendering function (notice that the value of simplicity has been overtaken by the more foundational values of order and toleration). Implicit in Raz's argument is the claim that a pluralistic community cannot persist unless all members consent to obey the law regardless of whether or not the directives meet the normal justification standard. We consent to treat legal norms as pre-emptive reasons for action because we understand that if judgments about how to act are not unified, individuals will pursue their subjective preferences and disorder may ensue.[71]

In this particular argument Raz is relying on the consent-based model of authority, which signals a clear priority of the pre-emption thesis over the normal justification thesis. In fact, if we accept his arguments pertaining to the need for simplification, it becomes particularly difficult to find a role for the normal justification thesis. If a given norm is not binding on us due to our personal expertise, we will place ourselves over and above the needs of a pluralistic community. As we have seen, the normal justification thesis allows, if not encourages, individuals to opt out of law's domain if the norm(s) in question do(es) not reproduce the pre-existing reasons binding on the subject. Unlike the pre-emption thesis, the normal justification thesis does not facilitate agreement between people on any level; rather, it focuses on the relationship between the law and the individual. In his attempt to combine the two theses in his appeal to the liberal state, Raz prioritises the pre-emption thesis at the expense of the normal justification thesis.

Perhaps Raz does not have to appeal to the simplifying benefits that accompany the pre-emption thesis in order to hope to strike a balance between his two central claims. One can simply argue as follows: there are some things I know about and some things I do not, and in the latter instances it is reasonable to defer to authority. In other words, the pre-emption thesis can be relied

[69] *Ibid.*

[70] See T Hobbes, *Leviathan* (1651) (London, Penguin, 1981).

[71] Gerald Postema wonders if law can perform this particular function. He points out that when the unifying function of law is needed most, it is least effective: when the disagreements between groups are profound, they are less likely to agree to grant mid-level principles pre-emptive force. See G Postema, 'Law's Autonomy and Public Practical Reason' in R George (ed), *The Autonomy of Law* (Oxford, Clarendon Press 1996) 108–09. Also see ch 7.

on when individuals do not have the requisite expertise to evaluate the status of a given norm or group of norms. Or we can frame the assumption in stronger terms: given that the government is more likely to get it right than we are most of the time, we should defer to them, even when we have the relevant expertise.[72]

Note, however, that the assumption that the government is more likely to get it right should be made with caution. Gerald Postema cites Leslie Green's point that we have authorities on whales but no authorities on whether we should save them.[73] Mian is also sceptical about the possibility of possessing this kind of expertise:

> Of course, we may want to be extremely skeptical about the moral expertise of the rule-givers. Is their expertise reliable? Can it be rigorously evaluated? After all, in a pluralist context, from the point of view of an individual citizen, it may not be so simple to distinguish an opposing opinion from an inexpert opinion. Where is the line between moral expertise and ideology? What interests does the rule manifest? Was the rule formulated genuinely so as to enable individuals to better conform with the reasons that apply to them, or was it the product of machinations of lobbyists and sectional interests? There are some very good reasons for being skeptical of the moral expertise of modern legal authorities, or for casting aspersions on their claim that it is the moral expertise available to them that they primarily rely upon.[74]

Furthermore, even if it is possible for authorities to be experts on such matters, why should a given individual assume that the authority gets it right more often than she does?

Consider the example of the safety of pharmaceutical products – an example that relies on both scientific knowledge and moral judgment. Raz argues that 'Decisions about the safety of pharmaceutical products are not the sort of personal decisions regarding which I should decide for myself rather than follow authority'.[75] Because I lack the requisite knowledge, Raz is suggesting that I should defer to the authority (thereby preserving the pre-emptive status of norms). The decision to defer assumes that the authority has it right or, at the very least, is more likely to have it right than I am. Is this assumption justified? Just because I do not have the answer, should I assume that the government does? If my neighbour, who is a doctor, has the requisite expertise and is (on Raz's account) not morally bound by the laws that govern such matters, does it follow that my ignorance means that I am bound by the law?

The answer has to be 'no'. Even Raz is forced to acknowledge that the law 'may reflect the interests of pharmaceutical companies, and not those of

[72] Raz, *Morality of Freedom*, above n 5, at 61. Raz argues that we are 'assuming' the authority is 'more reliable'.

[73] Postema, 'Law's Autonomy', above n 71, at 107.

[74] Mian, 'Exclusionary Reasons', above n 44, at 105.

[75] Raz, *Between Authority and Interpretation*, above n 3, at 137.

consumers'.[76] In such cases, the assumption that we are better off deferring to the government is misplaced. If we are not knowledgeable, we are better off consulting someone who is. After all, if the directive in question does not meet the requirements of the normal justification thesis it does not have authority over the agent in question. We may, at times, treat a given norm *as if* it has authority, but it only has such binding authority if it is justified. In sum, we have no reason to assume that the authoritative norm is binding simply because we are not experts. When it comes to technical or scientific laws, whether or not they are binding will be a product of the correctness of the norm; it is unlikely to hinge on the relationship between the individual and the state.[77] When it comes to moral laws, it may prove to be quite difficult to determine who has identified the 'right reason', even if there is a right answer (and I am not suggesting that there is not).

Notice that we have stumbled upon another, rather serious obstacle for Raz's theory of authority that comes to light when we enquire into the application of the normal justification thesis: who gets to decide whether a given norm meets the requirements of this thesis? The answer appears to be 'the citizen'. As discussed above, the normal justification thesis allows the citizen to opt out of law's domain if he or she has the requisite expertise. The problem with the expertise-based exemptions is that they apply not simply to those who do possess the requisite expertise; they also apply to those who simply *believe* that they do, given that it is not possible for the individual who is evaluating the norm to simultaneously hold both of the following beliefs:

(1) that they are an expert in a certain area and that they know what is best; and
(2) that they are more likely to act in accordance with right reason if they comply with the government's directives in that area.

The implications of this fact are fairly serious. For instance, whether or not Raz can balance the requirements of pre-emption and normal justification hinges on the contingent beliefs of citizens, as I noted in chapter three. He cannot guarantee, on a conceptual level, that a place can be secured for each of his key theses.

Raz is aware of the precarious foundation that participants' beliefs proffer. He explicitly seeks to avoid placing too much weight on the beliefs of citizens.[78]

[76] *Ibid.*

[77] Philip Soper, in reference to the co-ordination example, explains how legal norms can apply to different people without relying on expertise: my need to get somewhere quickly combined with my safety record and the lack of traffic are all factors that can impact upon my decision as to how to act. See P Soper, *The Ethics of Deference* (Cambridge, Cambridge University Press, 2002) 42. In reference to pharmaceutical laws, one's health may be so dire that the risk that accompanies a treatment may be worth taking.

[78] Raz, *Morality of Freedom*, above n 5, at 40.

There is good reason to avoid this kind of participant-centred understanding of legal authority. As Alan Brudner argues, this move is fatal to Raz's vision of legal authority as practical authority. Brudner explains why this is so when he answers the question, who gets to decide if a given norm meets the requirements of the normal justification thesis?

> It cannot be left to the authority, since the normal justification must limit its scope as well, and we would then have to ask who decides whether its reason applies and so on *ad infinitum*. So it is left for the subject to judge whether in any particular case the authority will have authority over it, which is to say there is no practical authority and no obligation to obey the law.[79]

This is a difficulty that Raz spies when he explores the relationship between the pre-emption thesis and the dependence thesis. Recall that Raz argues that 'there is no point in having authorities unless their determinations are binding even if mistaken'.[80] Once we as participants get to decide whether a norm provides us with a morally binding reason for action, the law's practical force dissolves. When Raz grants primacy to the normal justification thesis he undermines the pre-emption thesis and law's role as a practical authority more generally.

IV. METHODOLOGY: THE SOURCE OF THE TENSION?

By exploring Raz's methodological commitments, the ineradicable nature of the tension is revealed: his positivist pre-emption thesis and his morally robust normal justification thesis are born out of methodological approaches that are fundamentally antagonistic. The central assumption underpinning Raz's positivist methodology is articulated in *The Authority of Law*. Here he explicitly states that the method he employs looks to existing legal systems in order to identify the universal and necessary features of legality. According to Raz, this approach is definitive of legal philosophy, which is a key reason why he tries so hard to reconcile his approach with the common law tradition (as I explore in chapters two, three and five). This point becomes clear when he lays bare the two assumptions that underpin his theory:

> The first is the assumption of universality according to which it is a criterion of adequacy of a legal theory that it is true of all the intuitively clear instances of municipal legal systems. Since a legal theory must be true of all legal systems the identifying features by which it characterizes them must of necessity be very general and abstract. It must disregard those functions which some legal systems fulfil in some societies because of the special social, economic, or cultural conditions of those societies. It

[79] A Brudner, *Constitutional Goods* (Oxford, Oxford University Press, 2004) 46.
[80] Raz, *Morality of Freedom*, above n 5, at 47.

> must fasten only on those features of legal systems which they must possess regardless of the special circumstances of the societies in which they are in force. This is the difference between legal philosophy and sociology of law. The latter is concerned with the contingent and with the particular, the former with the necessary and the universal. Sociology of law proves a wealth of detailed information and analysis of the functions of law in some particular societies. Legal philosophy has to be content with those few features which all legal systems necessarily possess.[81]

In order to do legal philosophy, we must look at all the existing (intuitively clear) instances of legality and identify the features that these systems all share. This is the characteristic approach to understanding law that positivists rely on. It involves a clear separation between what law is and what it ought to be. Positivists are only concerned with the 'is'. The moral evaluation of the law is a separate project altogether.[82]

In *The Morality of Freedom*, Raz takes a different approach to concept formation. Interestingly, it is an Aristotelian approach focusing on ideal instances of authority in order to get to grips with the nature of authority (and law) in general. Raz states, 'Ours is an attempt to explain the notion of legitimate authority through describing what one might call an ideal exercise of authority'.[83] The ideal of justified authority is the focal case – it serves as a lens though which authority (and hence law) may be seen. This lens organizes the data: it distinguishes between 'normal' and 'deviant' instances of a kind. Raz explains by using an analogy between authority and advice:

> The normal reason for accepting a piece of advice is that it is likely to be sound advice. The normal reason to offer advice is the same. It will be clear that these judgments of normality are normative. But the very nature of advice can only be understood if we understand in what spirit it is meant to be offered and for what reason it is meant to be taken. The explanation must leave room for deviant cases, for their existence is undeniable. But it must also draw the distinction between the deviant and the normal, for otherwise the very reason why the 'institution' exists and why deviant cases take the special form they do remains inexplicable.[84]

This method identifies central cases of a given phenomenon (friendship, citizenship, etc) in order to grasp the meaning of the concept. Once central cases are identified, so ipso facto are deviant cases: cases that resemble the central case in some ways but not others. Also notice that the 'is' and the 'ought' are no longer separate: the 'ought' allows us to understand the 'is'.[85] This fusion is

[81] Raz, *Authority of Law,* above n 57, at 104–05.

[82] See HLA Hart, *The Concept of Law,* 2nd edn (Oxford, Oxford University Press, 1994) 240.

[83] Raz, *Morality of Freedom*, above n 5, at 47.

[84] *Ibid*, 54.

[85] Deriving an 'ought' from an 'is' is often referred to as a naturalistic fallacy. Orrego points out that this is only a fallacy if there is no normative premise in the argument, Orrego, 'Service Conception of Authority', above n 59, at 322. See also J Finnis, *Natural Law and Natural Rights* (Oxford, Clarendon Press, 1980) ch II.

necessary if we are to gain an accurate understanding of the phenomena being studied, 'for otherwise the very reason why the "institution" exists and why deviant cases take the special form they do remains inexplicable'. Raz underscores this point in 'The Problem of Authority: Revisiting the Service Conception' when he disavows the possibility of treating authority as a normatively neutral concept.[86]

The incompatibility of the two methods can be seen with greater clarity when we apply them both to the concept of friendship. For instance, Aristotle identifies the focal case of friendship as existing between two individuals 'who are good, and alike in virtue' and who wish each other well for the other's sake.[87] Other types of friendship identified by Aristotle include utility-based and pleasure-based. Such friendships exist as means to different ends, and thus these types of friendship are terminated when the end sought (utility, pleasure) ceases.[88] Friendships based on utility or pleasure are secondary kinds of friendship – they can only be understood as such once we identify the focal case and compare these other cases with it. When we employ the positivist's descriptive method to arrive at an understanding of friendship we must pick out the common features shared by all intuitively clear instances of friendship. We would likely identify the fact that two people like each other and spend time together as a common feature of what we generally refer to as 'friendship'. Regardless of any other qualities that might make this list, it is clear that any other value underpinning the relationship in question should not be selected: pleasure, utility and like-mindedness would be viewed as contingent features that some friendships exhibit, not necessary features shared by all intuitively clear instances of friendship.

Likewise, if we were to build a concept of law on the assumptions set out in *The Morality of Freedom*, we would end up with a different theory from the one Raz offers us: we would not look to the common ground of all intuitively clear instances of legality; instead we would study only the healthiest systems in order to get to grips with what is 'normal' and what is 'deviant'. The healthiest systems would no doubt be morally healthy systems (just as the ideal of authority is morally justified authority).

Herein lies the key difference between the two methodologies: different features are picked out as 'significant' by each method. If focal concepts can shed light on the nature of various phenomena (such as friendship), the descriptive method obscures the true nature of these phenomena, and vice versa. These methods are inherently incompatible rather than complementary. Recall that Raz makes this point about the concept of 'advice' (and analogously with the

[86] Raz, *Between Authority and Interpretation*, above n 3, at 130. For detailed discussion of this point see B Bix, 'Raz, Authority, and Conceptual Analysis' (2006) 50 *American Journal of Jurisprudence* 311.

[87] Aristotle, *Nichomachean Ethics* (Oxford, Oxford World's Classics, 1998) 196.

[88] *Ibid*, 195.

concept of authority). He argues that our understanding of advice is obscured unless we understand the focal instance and compare it to deviant cases, which are themselves identified in reference to the focal instance.[89]

Raz might respond that he is able to combine the two approaches by focusing on law's claim to authority. He identifies this claim as clear common ground that all intuitively clear instances of legal systems share. The difference between the gunman who says 'your money or your life', and thereby exercises brute force, on the one hand, and the wicked state that enforces wicked laws, on the other, is that only the wicked state claims authority to enforce its dictates. Raz thinks that this claim to authority is what separates de facto authority from brute force, whereas the normal justification thesis lets us distinguish legitimate authority from merely de facto authority. In other words, we look to the normal justification thesis to determine whether the law's claim is morally legitimate.

As previously mentioned, Raz does not make the mistake of suggesting that all legal systems validly claim legitimate authority. Thus, the shared quality (all law claims authority) is value-neutral and hence it (potentially) serves to bridge his morally laden concept of authority with his morally bare positivist concept of law. Further, the claim to authority simply requires that a legal norm is capable of being authoritative. Capable, that is, of serving as a pre-emptive reason for action. The thesis that all law claims authority does not require that any given norm be allocated the authority it claims. At first glance, Raz seems to have the requisite conceptual tools to overcome the above critique. When pressed, however, it is clear that his argument about law's claim to authority is unable to keep the internal tension at bay. Again, the fact that *only morally justified legal norms have pre-emptive force means we have to check to see if each norm meets the requirements of the normal justification thesis*. This, as we have already seen, is a fatal move.

But one may wonder whether the descriptive method is, in fact, an option. Is it possible to make choices about what is and is not significant in the process of concept construction without relying on values?[90] This leaves open the possibility that Raz's legal positivist position is grounded in implicit value judgments, which also leaves open the possibility that his methodological commitments are not antagonistic in the way that the above argument claims. It is possible to combine the two models – the 'consent-based' model and 'benefits gained' model – into a single coherent concept of law. In Hobbes's *Leviathan*, for instance, individuals consent to be governed by the sovereign *because* the sovereign can provide the protection needed for individuals to pur-

[89] Raz, *Between Authority and Interpretation*, above n 3, at 54.

[90] Raz, *Ethics in the Public Domain*, above n 26, at 235. Raz concedes that value judgments are required, but denies that they must be moral.

sue their autonomous projects.[91] That is, they consent to allocate law pre-emptive force because of the benefits they will receive. Likewise, in Raz's discussion of pluralistic societies canvassed above, we consent to treat legal norms as pre-emptive reasons for action because of the law's ability to unify judgment and simplify our reasoning. These are the benefits promised to those who adhere to the pre-emption thesis. These are not, however, the benefits sought by the normal justification thesis.

The normal justification calculation is done in the hope of determining whether the authoritative directive is morally justified and hence binding. Reasonable action, not co-operation, is the goal. This model of authority is incompatible with one that requires individuals to make a pre-commitment to legal norms. Thus, it is clear that there are competing concepts of authority underpinning the pre-emption thesis and the normal justification thesis respectively. Instead of offering us a unified theory of the nature of legal authority, Raz vacillates unstably between two models of authority.

V. CO-ORDINATION PROBLEMS AND RAZIAN AUTHORITY

There is one final response that can potentially allow Raz to escape the criticisms launched thus far. By focusing on the law's co-ordination function, the possibility of articulating a more robust conception of dependent reasons emerges.

Consider an example Raz offers us in 'The Problem of Authority: Revisiting the Service Conception': laws that ensure safe driving meet the requirements of both the pre-emption thesis and the normal justification thesis.[92] This example works because it is clear that individuals could not, by themselves, create systems that facilitate safe driving, and thus it makes sense to defer to authority in such cases. Furthermore, it seems unreasonable not to. In other words, in such cases it is *immediately* clear that it is reasonable to defer to authority. We do not have to return to the reasons behind the rule in order to make this determination, and hence the pre-emptive status of norms is not violated by the normal justification thesis.

Upon further examination, however, we can wonder whether co-ordination problems are the best example of directives where the normal justification thesis applies. For instance, JE Penner argues that co-ordination problems are distinct from questions of normal justification.[93] The quintessential co-ordination

[91] Hobbes, *Leviathan*, above n 70.

[92] Raz, *Between Authority and Interpretation*, above n 3, at 141.

[93] JE Penner, 'Legal Reasoning and the Authority of Law' in L Meyer, S Paulson and T Pogge (eds), *Rights, Culture and the Law: Themes from the Legal and Political Philosophy of Joseph Raz* (Oxford, Oxford University Press, 2003) 72.

problem (ie driving on the right side as against the left) has certain features: the choice between the two options is arbitrary (neither is more reasonable than the other); once the decision is made, we all have good reason to abide by the decision. The law creates a reason for action in these cases and hence there was no morally correct reason for action prior to the choice being made between the options. It seems that the legitimacy of such laws is immediately apparent and there is no need to return to fundamentals, and thus the tension I have been discussing does not arise. The disconnect between such quintessential co-ordination problems and the normal justification thesis arises because it is impossible to be an expert on the creation of a rule concerning the direction of traffic flow when making the initial decision as to which side of the road cars should drive on.

But there may be another way of thinking about this example. Perhaps the very reasons we have for following traffic laws apply more generally. Consider Finnis's argument that our moral situation changes once a law is passed, even if we do not agree that the law has got it right on this occasion. So even the farmer who opposes a law prohibiting river pollution still has an obligation to obey that law, despite the fact that he may have good reason to oppose it, because of the benefits he receives from the legal system more generally. Finnis writes:

> But if and when a *law* is passed, things are changed for the farmer's practical reasoning. Now he can reason thus: 'I should comply with this law, even though this law is neither in the national interest nor in my own. I should comply because I get many benefits from "the law", from the legal system within which I live. My farm is protected from damage; my sales of farm produce are enforceable against the purchaser for the purchase price; those prices are supported by a government policy based on the laws of taxation and of market regulation; and so forth. Getting these benefits from the law, I should accept its burdens'.[94]

The law allows large numbers of people to co-exist peacefully. Because law co-ordinates our behaviour on a large scale, and in so doing we reap many benefits, we therefore have an obligation to obey it, albeit a defeasible one. The vision of law offered to us here is one of a 'seamless web' wherein 'its subjects are not permitted to pick and choose among the law's prescriptions and stipulations'.[95]

This argument dissolves the tension between the pre-emption thesis and the normal justification thesis. However, Raz explicitly rejects the claim that we have a general obligation to obey the law in a relatively just society.[96] Thus, to understand Raz's theory of authority in this way would require substantial

[94] J Finnis, 'The Authority of Law in the Predicament of Contemporary Social Theory' (1984–85) 1 *Notre Dame Journal of Law, Ethics and Public Policy* 115, 119.
[95] *Ibid*, 120.
[96] Raz, *Morality of Freedom*, above n 5, at 70.

adjustments to his position. The piecemeal nature of his theory, which accords the idea of 'expertise' a privileged place, would have to be replaced by the very theory he was trying to oppose. So while Finnis's account solves the problem I have explored in this chapter, it is not the position Raz stakes out. Unfortunately for Raz, the position that he does stake out is indeed distinctive, but it is the distinctive flavour of his theory that ultimately renders it theoretically unpalatable. He fails to offer us a unified model of authority; instead, he offers us two models of authority in the guise of one.

5

Law as Public Practical Reasons Revisited

THE SOURCES THESIS, which stands for the claim that the content of legal norms is factually ascertainable, has great intuitive appeal. In addition to conceptualizing a familiar understanding of precedent,[1] it is viewed as a key component of a popular account of how law guides us as citizens. Law, it is argued, functions as public practical reasons, unifying judgment in the face of disagreement. Political theorists, writing in the specter of Rawls, often present this story as both conceptual and normative: law can and should give us public reasons for action. Personal reasons, such as religious reasons, do not usually qualify as 'public' and thus such reasons should not become legal reasons for action binding on all.[2]

Legal philosophy (or at least a prominent strain) intersects with political theory on this point, offering us a similar account of how disagreements between citizens are managed. Unlike their political counterparts, however, legal philosophers tend not to focus on the content that makes law public; instead, they are often primarily concerned with law's form. Laws must be public in the sense of being publicly accessible to all. They must be followable and, at least potentially, serve as reasons for action for those who seek to live within law's bounds. Law, according to this general account, is a unifying force that holds together a society that would otherwise be fractured by profound and often insoluble disagreements – disagreements that can often be traced back to diverse value commitments amongst law's subjects. Law is the authoritative voice that settles such disputes and, in so doing, allows us to get on with our daily tasks. To achieve this end, it seems that the content of legal norms must be easily understood by the citizenry in order to avoid re-igniting value-laden disputes about the meaning of a law or set of laws. I will refer to this assumption as the certainty thesis, the contours of which will be explored below.

[1] See ch 3. I use the term 'positivism' to refer to Raz's version of the theory.

[2] Rawls writes: 'we are not to appeal to comprehensive religious or philosophical doctrines – to what we as individuals or members of associations see as the whole truth . . . As far as possible, the knowledge and ways of reasoning that ground our affirming the principles of justice and their application to constitutional essentials and basic justice are to rest on plain truths now widely accepted, or available, to citizens generally'. J Rawls, *Political Liberalism* (New York, Columbia University Press, 1993) 224–25.

There are many versions of this particular account of how law engenders order and of the relationship between law and political theory more generally. Raz's twist on this familiar narrative is that law gives us exclusionary (or pre-emptory) reasons for action. Legal norms are first-order reasons to act in a certain way and second-order reasons for excluding competing reasons for action. In *The Authority of Law* we find that Raz's main argument in support of his sources thesis appeals directly to this familiar account of law's function. The sources thesis, Raz argues, 'captures and highlights a fundamental insight into the function of law':

> It is a commonplace that social life requires and is facilitated by various patterns of forbearances, co-operation, and co-ordination between members of the society or some of them. The same is true of the pursuits of goals which the society or sections in it may set themselves. Different members and different sections of a society may have different views as to which schemes of co-operation, co-ordination, or for-bearance are appropriate. It is an essential part of the function of law in society to mark the point at which a private view of members of the society, or of the influen-tial sections or powerful groups in it, ceases to be their private view and becomes (i.e. lays a claim to be) a view binding on all members notwithstanding their dis-agreement with it. It does so and can only do so by providing publicly ascertainable ways of guiding behaviour and regulating aspects of social life . . . It helps to secure social co-operation not only through its sanctions providing motivation for confor-mity but also through designating in an accessible way the patterns of behaviour required for such co-operation.[3]

On this account, factually ascertainable legal norms play an important role in society. Legal norms facilitate co-ordination and co-operation, and they are able to do so because they offer citizens factually ascertainable reasons for action. Raz's sources thesis is presented as a significant jurisprudential posi-tion precisely because it is a key part of an accurate understanding of how law works. Raz grounds his account of what law *is* in an account of what law *does*.

Tying the sources thesis to this popular view of law's function is both a blessing and a curse. Insofar as Raz is successful in connecting his theory of public practical reasons with this account of law, the relevance of the sources thesis moves out of the domain of legal theory and into broader debates in political philosophy, extending its reach. However, there is a noteworthy risk that accompanies this argumentative strategy. The idea that law offers us public practical reasons is a theoretical account of how law works in the world and not merely a description of a brute fact. By grounding his sources thesis in a contestable (albeit popular) understanding of law's function, the sources the-sis becomes dependent on the outcome of a debate in political philosophy.

[3] J Raz, *The Authority of Law: Essays on Law and Morality* (New York, Oxford University Press, 1979) 50–51.

Questions about the value-neutrality of both the method and the viability of the substance of his position are immediately raised. If, in the process of figuring out what law *is*, theorists commit themselves to contestable philosophical claims about the nature of our political order, then the strict divide between legal theory and normative political philosophy is compromised. That is to say, a description of what the law is (such as that presented by positivists) presupposes a normative standpoint about how the law should function, as I show in what follows. It is not surprising to discover that Raz attempts to distance himself from this function-based account – a point I will explore at the end of this chapter. The methodological challenges posed by a function-based account are significant, but there are also a number of substantive issues that are equally difficult to overcome.

I will argue that the view of law's function which Raz defends above commits him to a simple positivist picture of law – but it is too simple to be viable. It is not clear, for instance, that the common law and customary law offer us a set of discrete reasons for action, as this model supposes. Insofar as these kinds of law cannot be accommodated, they emerge as counter-examples to this account. There is a second, related problem. If legal norms are going to work as Raz suggests, then citizens must be capable of determining the meaning of these norms with minimal effort. This is a difficult requirement given the fact that laws are often written in technical legal language using terms that are vague and value-laden. Thus, there appears to be a gap between Raz's theory and actual practice, as Raz himself recognizes. In response to this worry, Raz redefines the sources thesis so as to better account for the complexity of legal practice. This move gives the appearance that Raz's positivist position is subtle and responsive insofar as it combines a host of seemingly incompatible elements into a single concept. Like a camera lens moving between the close-up shots and the distant horizon, Raz's argument shifts focus, presenting a picture of intuitive simplicity and intricate complexity as if it were a single shot. But in fact, this reading is deceptive. By tracing the movement between the simple picture, which has intuitive appeal, and the complex defence of the position that is offered in certain contexts, we find that the two pictures never form a coherent whole.

I will argue that the complex definition of 'legal source' is little more than a distraction that makes his position appear more subtle than it is. Raz cannot simply absorb all the relevant interpretative practices into the idea of 'legal source', a point that he inadvertently concedes in his exchange with Gerald Postema. When pressed by Postema about the threat posed to the sources thesis by the need to interpret the law, Raz's simple story about social facts quickly transforms into a search for facts. If legal sources are going to be found, values must be actively kept out. In the course of his response to Postema, Raz presents the sources thesis as an ideal of legal reasoning.

There are further problems still. Once the sources thesis becomes an ideal of adjudicative reasoning, we must then enquire into the reasons that drive the ideal. Judges are not interested in preserving the sources thesis for the mere sake of it. If the ideal is going to tell us something about law, judges must have their own reasons for seeking fact-based legal sources. I will illustrate that Raz's theory (in its current form) lacks the ability to explain why judges would seek to interpret law in a manner consistent with the sources thesis. The reasons proffered by other normative positivists – legitimacy, certainty and predictability – are not available to Raz due to his commitment to a morally robust theory of adjudication. The deep tension in Raz's account is evident once again.[4]

I. THE SOURCES THESIS: DEFINED AND REDEFINED

Raz does not, of course, present the account of law's function as a controversial theoretical commitment. Instead it is offered to readers as an observation about legal practice: law simply operates as a set of public practical reasons that unify judgment. The thought that this account of law's function is relatively uncontestable seems plausible because of the way in which he characterises his sources thesis. The sources thesis *appears* to have a very low threshold which must be crossed in order to establish its truth. The legal status of a given norm or set of norms simply depends on whether it has the proper pedigree. In Hartian terms, if we are able to trace the norm back to the Queen or Parliament, then we can rightly declare that the norm in question is, in fact, a legal norm.[5]

At times Raz echoes Hart, suggesting that meeting the criteria set out by his sources thesis is not a particularly demanding process. When taking on his interpretive-based opponent Ronald Dworkin, Raz attempts to shore up his own theory by arguing that it takes very little effort to figure out what law is:

> An income-tax statute is meant to decide what is the fair contribution of public funds to be borne out of income. To establish the content of the statute, all one need do is to establish that the enactment took place, and what it says. To do this one needs little more than knowledge of English (including technical legal English), and of the events which took place in Parliament on a few occasions. One need not come to any view on the fair contribution to public funds.[6]

When set against this Dworkinian backdrop, Raz's theory is bolstered. Surely when a citizen seeks to determine what the law is, she is not simultaneously

[4] This argument presupposes that the distinction between a theory of law and a theory of adjudication does not hold. See ch 3.

[5] HLA Hart, *The Concept of Law*, 2nd edn (Oxford, Oxford University Press, 1994) 102.

[6] J Raz, *Ethics in the Public Domain: Essays in the Morality of Law and Politics* (New York, Oxford University Press, 1994) 221.

determining what it ought to be. For instance, if I want to know what the tax law is in Canada, I do not set out to calculate the amount of money that I think I should owe in an ideal world. Instead I will attempt to figure out the precise sum that I do, in fact, owe under the current tax scheme. If the choice is between these two options, then Raz's is clearly preferable. The alternative (as he presents it) is barely plausible. If we understand the sources thesis in these terms, this core positivist thesis lends effortless support to the idea of law as a set of public practical reasons. We can all be guided by law with relative ease because we only have to know a few basic things about the norm in order for it to serve as an authoritative reason for action that unifies our collective judgment, thereby facilitating co-operation and co-ordination.

This example does not hold up to scrutiny, however. Notice that Raz has presented his sources thesis as the default option. If a citizen is not actively trying to figure out what ought to be the case, then she is ascertaining facts. This is a false dichotomy. Those seeking to understand a given legal provision are not confronted with the bald choice of acting as a starry-eyed version of Bentham's censor or his plain-thinking expositor. Values do not simply enter when we offer moral judgments about what ought to be; values can also enter through normal interpretive processes where the goal of the process is to understand what the content of a given norms *is*.

When we turn our attention to the work of officials, it is not clear that law is simply a matter of social fact. Complex practices of interpretation and argumentation inform the work of judges and legislators. Even with the requisite training, the content of any given law may be the subject of deep controversy – a point that Raz acknowledges. Accordingly, he attempts to accommodate the complex nature of legal practice by incorporating interpretative materials into his definition of the sources thesis:

> This sense of 'source' is wider than that of 'formal sources' which are those establishing the validity of a law (one or more Acts of Parliament together with one or more precedents may be the formal source of one rule of law). 'Source' as used here includes also 'interpretative sources', namely all the relevant interpretative materials. The sources of a law thus understood are never a single act (of legislation, etc.) alone, but a whole range of facts of a variety of kinds.[7]

While this definition is more nuanced than the simple version (which only requires us to be literate and to grasp some basic facts about the origin of the norm), we can wonder whether interpretative sources can be captured by Raz's broad definition of 'legal source' without sacrificing the central notion that underpins the sources thesis: namely, that law offers us a set of public practical reasons for action, which seems to presuppose that we can all identify the content of a given law or set of laws with relative ease.

[7] Raz, *The Authority of Law*, above n 3, at 48.

Notice, also, that this second, more complex definition is very different from the first. The first 'simple' definition sought to deflect interpretation-based challenges by characterizing Dworkin's position in a manner that made it untenable as it runs up against settled features of our shared experience (ie citizens do not tend to read tax laws through rose-tinted glasses when they are simply seeking an understanding of tax law as it currently exists). Conversely, the complex definition does not define away the competition; instead it absorbs the very features of law that Dworkin's theory focuses on ('interpretive materials') into the definition of source. Of course, a key difference remains: contra Dworkin, Raz insists that the act of ascertaining the content of a legal norm might be complex, but it is not an exercise in moral argumentation. I am now in a position to sharpen the question. Again, is there a third option whereby value judgments enter into the decision-making process in an implicit way? If so, then the sources thesis ceases to be the default option; rather, the burden shifts to the positivist to establish that values are kept out of the interpretive process. As we shall see below (in section IV), this is a remarkably challenging task.

When we have the complex definition of 'legal source' before our minds, additional questions can be asked. Is this definition compatible with the simple one? Can this complicated account of legal sources still furnish citizens with a set of public practical reasons that unify judgment? Once all of the complex practices are absorbed by the very idea of 'source', it is difficult to see how legal sources can perform the function Raz assigns to them via his function-based argument. After all, the more complex the interpretive task becomes in a given instance, our faith in the ability of law to generate consensus is surely weakened (hence so is the persuasiveness of this particular account). It seems reasonable to assume that any interpretive complexities that officials may encounter would be magnified outside the courtroom. Most of us have not been trained to think like lawyers. In order for legal norms to function as public practical reasons it must be assumed that the content of these norms is fairly certain. It is this assumption that I will now explore.

II. SOURCES, CERTAINTY, AND PUBLIC PRACTICAL REASONS

The certainty thesis is not a thesis Raz explicitly endorses. Instead, he actively denies that the sources thesis is wedded to the certainty thesis. His denial appears plausible because of another argumentative strategy that makes his position appear far more nimble than it actually is. In an attempt to deflect the certainty thesis (and the simple picture of law), Raz considers the contours of his sources thesis in isolation. When the focus is on the sources thesis alone, it seems malleable enough to accommodate all the subtleties of our shared experience. This positivist thesis is itself silent about the practical role fact-based norms play in our lives as it is wholly backwards looking (it merely tells us something about how to identify the content of legal norms). However, once Raz situates the sources thesis within his broader theory of law – specifically when it is viewed alongside his pre-emption thesis and his understanding of law's order-engendering role – it becomes markedly less flexible.

If legal norms are going to serve as reasons for action that unify judgment as Raz suggests, then citizens must be able to understand and follow law's directives. In jurisprudential terms, this simple idea is encapsulated by the certainty thesis.[8] The certainty thesis (as its name suggests) captures the claim that the content of law is ascertainable with relative ease. A number of prominent theorists have argued that Raz is committed to the certainty thesis.[9] Positivists, by way of response, often accuse their detractors of saddling them with a caricature of their position. Raz, for instance, adamantly denies that he is committed to the certainty thesis. He asks: 'Has the sources thesis much to do with certainty?' And then replies: 'I do not think so'.[10] The reason it is not immediately apparent that Raz's sources thesis commits him to the certainty thesis is that the sources thesis is itself silent about law's function. Raz explains that 'the sources thesis does not rest on an assumption that law cannot be controversial', instead it merely signals that 'the existence and content of the law is a matter of social fact which can be established without resort to moral argument'.[11] This position 'does not presuppose nor does it entail the false proposition that all factual matters are non-controversial, nor the equally false view that all moral propositions are controversial'.[12]

One of the reasons Raz is anxious to distance himself from the certainty thesis is that he needs to accommodate features of practice that seem to suggest a more complicated picture. In the same breath that he downplays the importance of certainty, he argues that, 'both customary law and common law are sources of law, recognized by the sources thesis'.[13] Laws that emerge from these particular sources do not fit easily into the simple positivist picture. Neither the common law nor customary law come pre-packaged as a discrete set of norms ready to be followed.[14] Raz's account has to be nuanced in order

[8] The reverse need not hold: one can be committed to the certainty thesis without being committed to the sources thesis.

[9] See, eg D Lyons, 'Moral Aspects of Legal Theory' (1982) 7 *Midwest Studies in Philosophy* 223, 238. See also R M Dworkin, *Taking Rights Seriously* (Cambridge, MA, Harvard University Press, 1977) 347.

[10] J Raz, 'Postema on Law's Autonomy and Public Practical Reason: A Critical Commentary' (1998) 4 *Legal Theory* 1, 13.

[11] Raz, *Ethics in the Public Domain,* above n 6, at 234.

[12] *Ibid.*

[13] *Ibid.*

[14] AWB Simpson, 'The Common Law and Legal Theory' in AWB Simpson (ed), *Oxford Essays in Jurisprudence,* Second Series (Oxford, Clarendon Press, 1973).

to reflect this aspect of legal experience. His sources thesis seems to have enough built-in flexibility to allow for the needed subtleties to be incorporated into the positivist position. I will suggest, however, that the flexibility that Raz reads into the sources thesis is deceptive. When Raz deflects the charge that he is committed to the certainty thesis above, he does so by considering the definition of this thesis in isolation. Strictly speaking, Raz is correct to argue that facts can be controversial and complex. The important question is not about the nature of facts but about the qualities that legal norms must have if Raz's account is going to be viable. If legal norms are going to operate as public practical reasons that serve to unify judgment in society, then they must enjoy a degree of certainty that allows this task to be carried out.

Once the bare definition of legal source is placed aside his understanding of how law works in the world, the degree of flexibility enjoyed by the sources thesis contracts and what emerges is a commitment to the certainty thesis. When Raz reflects on the sources thesis alongside the function he expects legal norms to play, he admits that the need for certainty is relevant to his position:

> The sources thesis is based on the mediating role of the law. It is true that the law fails in the role if it is not, in general, easier to establish and less controversial than the underlying considerations it reflects. But this generalization is exaggerated and distorted when it turns into the universal, conceptual dogmas of the explicit content or the non-controversiality theses.[15]

Raz acknowledges that he needs a degree of certainty to accompany legal norms – the argument is for *relative certainty*. It must be easier for citizens to identify the content of the norm than it would be for them to figure out what to do in the absence of the norm. Here he is concerned with accounting for the reason *why* citizens may turn to legal norms to guide their conduct: if it is easier to follow the law's instructions than to figure out what they should do on their own, then citizens will still have the requisite motivation to look to the law for guidance. This echoes his claim that treating laws as pre-emptive reasons for action is often desirable as our reasoning process is thereby simplified.[16]

One problem is immediately apparent. The above argument considers the reasoning process of the isolated individual. This is not enough. It is true that the motivation of the individual citizen to treat the law as a reason for action is relevant,[17] but it is only part of the conceptual puzzle. The collective aspect of rules, whereby legal rules are understood to play a unifying role in society, requires more. If law is going to perform this important job, all citizens must

[15] Raz, *Ethics in the Public Domain,* above n 6, at 234.

[16] J Raz, *The Morality of Freedom* (Oxford, Clarendon Press, 1986) 58.

[17] Contrary to what Raz now maintains. See Raz, 'Postema on Law's Autonomy', above n 10, at 12.

interpret the law in the same way, or at least most of us must do so most of the time. The more interpretive work that has to be carried out in order to ascertain the content of a given norm (or set of norms), the less likely this outcome will be.

Let us step back for but a moment here and notice that while issues of interpretation are prevalent in law (to such an extent that this is a point barely worth making), the weight that positivist theories (Raz's included) place on the need for interpretation is striking. If we think of law as a set of norms that serve (potentially) as reasons for action, then the legal norms (and the possibility of interpreting them in a uniform way) end up bearing a lot of the weight in the explanation of how law is able to generate order. If the law is going to be successful to this end, then surely legal norms must be communicated to a potentially diverse populace with relative ease. Conversely, if law's ability to guide conduct is viewed, at least in part, as a complex and ongoing process of socialization whereby the understandings of what is and what is not permissible for anyone to do in society are transmitted through familiar and rather mundane methods (like education and socialization), then much pressure is taken off the interpretative resources.[18] Given that Raz maintains that law is a set of reasons for action, it is hardly surprising to discover that an implicit commitment to legal certainty reappears frequently in his writings.

Consider, for instance, one of the central arguments that Raz offers in defence of his sources thesis in *The Authority of Law*. The sources thesis, Raz argues, makes sense of a series of familiar distinctions: settled versus unsettled law, applying existing law versus creating new law, and a judge's legal skill versus his or her moral character.[19] Judges either use their legal skill to apply settled law or they use their moral sense to create new law. The law is either settled or it is unsettled. Raz insists that the law does not exist in the realm of principle, waiting to be discovered by a skilful lawyer or judge. He does, however, acknowledge that the language judges occasionally use when adjudicating may make it seem as if 'no one knows what the law is – as if there is law on the question which is very difficult to discover'.[20] He contends that this language is misleading. Happily, most of the time lawyers 'express themselves more accurately, saying that this is an open question, that the law is unsettled, etc'.[21] Here the idea is that disputes about the content of law do not point to the controversial nature of existing law, but to the fact that *the law is unsettled* in reference to this particular issue. When the law is not clear on a particular issue, Raz urges us to conclude that there is no law on that issue.[22] In such

[18] This point will be explored in ch 6.
[19] Raz, *The Authority of Law*, above n 3, at 48–50.
[20] *Ibid*, 49.
[21] *Ibid*.
[22] *Ibid*.

cases, judges can employ moral arguments to create law anew. The law, by definition, is certain and the certainty of its content is signalled by consensus about meaning.

This assumption that the content of law is usually relatively certain resurfaces whenever Raz discusses the practical aspect of legal norms – the very aspect that the sources thesis is initially supposed to capture. He assumes that citizens can potentially treat any given legal norm as a reason for action. For this to be a possibility, citizens must know what is being asked of them. Consider, by way of illustration, Raz's discussion of mandatory norms in *Practical Reason and Norms*. He argues that when we are dealing with mandatory norms, such as legal norms, 'for the most part the presence of a norm is decisive'.[23] Mandatory norms answer the question of what ought to be done. The scope of the rule or competition from reasons not excluded by the rule are complicating factors that may prevent the norm from being determinative; however, he adds that these complicating factors only arise in a *minority of cases*.[24] In most instances the legal norm, and the legal norm alone, does the practical work in our lives. Significantly, the complicating factors listed by Raz do not cast doubt on the content of the norm in question – he never suggests that the content of the norm may be too complex, controversial or vague to perform the exclusionary role he assigns to it.

Is there another way out? Raz, as I mentioned earlier, now denies that his theory has anything to do with an account of law's function.[25] As an historical claim about his theory, this is simply false. As a solution to the particular set of worries that is occupying us at the moment, we can ask whether this argument presents him with the much needed escape route. At first glance, it appears to be a plausible tactic. One of the more popular readings of Raz's position is that he is primarily concerned with the question of normative authority: only legitimate legal norms give us pre-emptive reasons for action. In *The Morality of Freedom* Raz does not repeat the view that the presence of legal norms is 'usually decisive'; instead we are given a specific set of standards that allow us to determine whether a norm or a set of norms *should* be treated as decisive.[26] The question of law's role in engendering order is now subordinate to the question of the legitimacy of law. This subtle shift in thought lends plausibility to the idea that Raz's account is not wedded to any particular view of law's guidance function.

Contrary to appearances, Raz cannot completely excise the account of law's guidance function that he relies on so heavily in his early works (namely, *Practical Reason and Norms* and *The Authority of Law*). Like a shadow, the vision of

[23] J Raz, *Practical Reason and Norms* (Oxford, Oxford University Press, 1999) 79.
[24] *Ibid.*
[25] Raz, 'Postema on Law's Autonomy', above n 10, at 2–4.
[26] Raz, *The Morality of Freedom,* above n 16, at 58.

law's function (and the certainty thesis) follows the pre-emption thesis wherever it goes. Recall that in *The Morality of Freedom*, one of the defining features of legal norms is their capacity to be legitimate. As mentioned, this translates into the claim that legal norms must be *capable* of serving as pre-emptive reasons for action. To do so, the content of a given law must be such that citizens can figure out what is expected of them with relative ease. Even if citizens do not allocate law this kind of priority in their daily lives, they must have the option of doing so. Thus, Raz is left to explain why citizens should allocate legal norms such a pre-emptive status in their practical reasoning process. One of the answers offered has quite a familiar ring:

> [A]n orderly community can exist only if it shares many practices, and that in all modern pluralistic societies a great measure of toleration of vastly differing outlooks is made possible by the fact that many of them enable the vast majority of the population to accept common standards of conduct.[27]

The narrative of law as public practical reason is never far behind the pre-emption thesis. Unlike the sources thesis, the pre-emption thesis has both a forward-looking and a backward-looking aspect making it far less flexible than the sources thesis. Legal norms must be both factually ascertainable (as the sources thesis suggests) *and followable* by those to whom the laws are directed. The practical reasoning process moves us from the present into the future whilst relying on norms that emerge from the past. Moreover, legal norms move us collectively as well as individually. The existence of an 'orderly community' that is pluralist in composition depends on the 'vast majority of the population' accepting 'common standards of conduct'. Thus, if Raz's theory is going to work, the content of these norms must be clear to most of us most of the time.

As we have seen above, Raz concedes that certainty is relevant to the mediating role he assigns to law, with the following qualification: we do not need certainty per se, but only *relative* certainty. The reasoning process must be easier to engage in than a fresh balancing of reasons for action. I have suggested that relative certainty is not enough if law is going to guide us as Raz supposes. Upon further scrutiny, it becomes clear that 'relative certainty' is not something he can argue for in the abstract, and thus this argument fails on its own terms.

Once the interpretive gates are opened, Raz cannot guarantee that the process of law ascertainment will be simpler than the process of practical deliberation that a citizen would undertake in the absence of that law. Such judgments will be context-sensitive and dependent on numerous variables over which theorists have no control: variables that include the complexity of

[27] *Ibid.* For a critical evaluation of this position, see chs 2 and 4.

the law in question and the ease with which the citizen could make practical decisions in the absence of the norm in question. Once we take such factors into consideration, we are left to conclude that Raz cannot guarantee that the content of the law is 'in general, easier to establish and less controversial than the underlying considerations it reflects'. This is a judgment that can only be made on a case-by-case basis, after the fact.[28] Moreover, such judgments remain speculative in character as they will always rely on counter-factual claims about how citizens may have deliberated in the absence of law. Raz cannot rely on this particular argument to create distance between his positivist account and the certainty thesis (even though he has implicitly conceded that this must be done if his account is going to be plausible).

In sum, the certainty thesis only appears to be shakeable when the sources thesis is considered in isolation; once placed in the larger context of his account of law's practical role in the world, legal norms need certainty. The implications for his theory are significant. If customary law and the common law are too uncertain to perform the practical role Raz assigns to legal norms, then they emerge as counter-examples to a theory of public practical reason.[29] His theory, which has revealed itself to be little more than a model of rules, is too simple to be viable. To be clear, my point is not that legal norms have content that is certain; the point is that Raz's positivist position relies too heavily on this assumption. Indeed, it is the gap between his theory and certain features that law exhibits – features that a good theory must account for – that renders his account untenable.

Raz needs the complex definition of 'legal source' (whereby all the interpretive materials are included in the definition of 'source'), but he cannot have it. After all, if Raz cannot eliminate the certainty thesis, it is difficult to see how he can champion the complex definition of legal source into which all of the interpretive problems are absorbed. If the complex definition of legal sources is not available to Raz, then his version of positivism only *appears* to be subtle and complex – it appears to be a subtle and complex position precisely because Raz shifts between the two accounts of the sources thesis depending on which portion of the story they need to shore up.

[28] One can only make this general claim in advance if one is committed to a certain kind of political theory. See D Priel, 'Are Jurisprudential Debates Conceptual? Some Lessons from Democratic Theory' (2012) 50 *Osgoode Hall Law Journal* 359.

[29] Recall that this is the conclusion drawn at the end of chs 1 and 2. Scott Shapiro also has difficulty dealing with customary law. He views law as plans, but acknowledges that customary norms are 'plan-like'; such laws are not the product of intentional design and hence they fit uneasily (if at all) in his positivist theory. See S Shapiro, *Legality* (Cambridge, MA, Harvard University Press, 2011) 140.

III. THE WEAK AUTONOMY THESIS

One might argue that I have overlooked a key thesis in the positivist's arsenal: the weak autonomy thesis. The weak autonomy thesis circumscribes the role of both the simple and complex definitions of 'legal source'. Positivists may point out that they can have both definitions insofar as each definition is put in its proper place. The simple definition holds for citizens who need to know what the law *is*, while the complex definition animates the juridical sphere where judges must decide how we *ought* to move forward. Raz now champions a morally robust theory of adjudication whereby judges are conceived of as moral reasoners.[30] The difference between the job of the judge (to reason morally) and that of the citizen (to figure out what the law requires of them) accounts for why interpretive problems often enter into the courtroom but do not tend to impair law's ability to guide us.

The weak autonomy thesis assumes that the relationship between the judge and the law is very different than the relationship between that of a citizen and the law. The judge is closer to performing the role of Bentham's censor, who is tasked with the job of determining what law ought to be and not simply what law is. By contrast, citizens are concerned only with what law is, at least insofar as they hope to abide by its demands. In short, the idea is that law is a set of autonomous norms that potentially guide the conduct of the citizenry. However, law is not autonomous from the perspective of the judge given that morality informs the work of judges to some degree. Is this account of legal reasoning accurate?

One sign of trouble is that it is inconsistent with the ideas of legal reasoning that Raz champions elsewhere. In *Ethics and the Public Domain,* Raz makes the opposite claim. He is adamant that there is only one kind of legal reasoning that is equally available to judges and citizens alike. While it is true that only a judge's decision is legally binding, 'it does not follow that the courts reason in some special way'.[31] Raz adds that 'People and the courts alike attempt to establish the law, or to establish how – according to the law – cases should be settled'.[32] Legal reasoning, on this view, is a kind of reasoning that we can all undertake. It is not the specialist domain of lawyers and other legal practitioners. When we engage in legal reasoning we are not simply mimicking judges, or trying to predict what they will say in a courtroom. It is simply reasoning with rules and we can all do it. The key difference, of course, is that judges have the power to change the law. Nonetheless, the idea that legal reasoning

[30] Raz, *Ethics in the Public Domain,* above n 6, at 340.
[31] *Ibid,* 327.
[32] *Ibid.*

is a public kind of reasoning is not a superficial claim, but one that has a long history amongst those who view law as public reasons for action.[33]

In order to determine whether there are problems with regard to the weak autonomy thesis that are of a fundamental nature, let us sharpen the enquiry. Instead of considering the adjudicative process as a whole, I will focus exclusively on the sources thesis, exploring the possibility that judges can be expositors of the law in the Razian sense. Can judges ascertain fact-based legal sources with relative ease? I am, of course, assuming that judges can look up the relevant cases and statutes. The question is an interpretive one and the central worry that gives rise to this line of questioning is as follows: if it is difficult for those who are trained to understand law to ascertain the content of law without allowing any judgments of value to enter implicitly or explicitly, then it will be equally difficult for citizens to do the same. The way that judges interpret the content of the law cannot be wholly different from the way in which citizens do – both are concerned with the content of the same norms. If interpreting law in accordance with the sources thesis proves to be challenging, then there are serious implications: the common view of law as public practical reasons becomes less plausible, at least insofar as this narrative is linked with the sources thesis. That is to say, people cannot live in harmony with others if they cannot understand the laws that are supposed to make such harmony possible.

A closer look at the issue reveals that Raz's inclusion of 'interpretative sources' in his definition of 'legal source' glosses over what turns out to be a deep problem for his account. Once we press on the issue of interpretation, we discover that the path to legal facts is a narrow one that is difficult to traverse. Facts do not emerge, but are actively sought. Or more accurately, in the words of Raz, they *should* be actively sought. In an attempt to shore up the sources thesis against a challenge launched by Postema, Raz transforms the sources thesis into an *ideal* of legal reasoning, confirming yet again the deep instability of conceptual positivism; it is an ideal that is particularly puzzling when situated within his theory as a whole, because he cannot explain why judges may actually be moved to pursue his positivist ideal. The dichotomy between finding facts and offering moral judgments about what ought to be thus proves to be a false one. Values can (and do) enter the interpretive process, explicitly and implicitly, and Raz does not account for the latter possibility. This third possibility is explored further in the next section in relation to the idea of reasonableness.

[33] Thomas Hobbes, *Dialogue*, 62.

IV. THE SOURCES THESIS AND INTERPRETATION: NUANCE OR NUISANCE?

Postema's challenge to Raz is as follows: he argues that in the process of reconstructing a previous decision, the judge usually relies on his or her own understanding of reasonableness.[34] If this occurs, then what was initially a fact-finding mission becomes an interpretive one that potentially displaces the 'original' meaning of the legal norm in question. The sources thesis is thereby threatened, alongside the view of law as public practical reasons. The first problem with importing one's own understanding of reasonableness is that determining the content of a given norm will involve implicit value judgments, which violates the value-neutral requirement of the sources thesis. The second related worry is that if judges tend to impart their own understanding of reasonableness, then citizens would surely do the same. Unless citizens share an understanding of reasonableness, the law will become the locus of interpretive dispute rather than a unifying force (especially if we assume, as Raz does, that law unifies an otherwise discordant population).

Raz admits that interpretative issues pose a potential threat to the facticity of legal norms and thus to the cogency of the sources thesis. If the core idea that underpins his positivism is to hold – the idea that law is a set of discrete norms, the content of which are identifiable as a matter of fact and not as a matter of value-laden interpretation – he must deal with this particular worry. In short, the possibility of meeting this demand must be there, even if in practice judges appeal to moral norms with some frequency. In response to Postema, Raz acknowledges that the interpretative process may interfere with the judge's ability to accurately identify legal sources:

> I agree, of course, that in fact we often rely on our ideas of what is reasonable when reconstructing other people's thoughts. But if we are any good at the task, we do so only when we have reason to think those others share our view of what is a reasonable opinion, or a plausible argument.[35]

In order to figure out what the law 'is' we must reconstruct the arguments put forth by previous judges. This is an intellectual skill a judge must be adept at if she hopes to arrive at fact-based sources. It is also a skill that she must consciously exercise. Distancing ourselves from our own understanding of reasonableness is an important part of this process, but this is not something we do 'naturally' or without effort (the force of Postema's point turns on the fact

[34] GJ Postema, 'Law's Autonomy and Public Practical Reason' in R George (ed), *The Autonomy of Law: Essays on Legal Positivism* (Oxford, Clarendon Press, 1996) 96–97. Note that I also discuss this particular exchange in ch 7.

[35] Raz, 'Postema on Law's Autonomy', above n 10, at 15.

that conceptions of reasonableness inform our judgments often without our conscious awareness). Consequently, it is not sensible to assume that judges already reason as Raz suggests.

Raz concurs. He argues that 'When assessing Postema's objection, the crucial test is not how we reason, but how we *should* reason, what we do when we reason *correctly*' (my italics).[36] He is no longer grounding the sources thesis in a claim about the way in which judges do reason (as a matter of statistical regularity); instead, the sources thesis is held out as an ideal. It represents the reasoning process that judges *should* undertake if they are interested in reasoning 'correctly'. If we rely on our own understanding of reasonableness when figuring out the meaning of a law, and we are not sure if the previous judge shares our understanding of reasonableness, then we may well have breached the strict demands of the sources thesis. Note that contrary to the Benthamite dichotomy between the censor and the expositor, the interpreter in such a case is not interested in figuring out what the law ought to be; rather, such value judgments enter implicitly and covertly into the interpretive process. Raz now has the difficult task of policing the fact/value boundary against such subtle threats – he must work to ensure that value judgments of all kinds are kept out.

Notice, also, that the sources thesis is no longer occupying the default position. The argumentative burden is firmly on the positivist's shoulders and the bar is set very high (and not low, as the simple picture suggests). Once the sources thesis becomes an ideal of legal reasoning, it becomes more elusive and its significance ceases to be transparent. Judges need to know *why* they must seek to reproduce the understanding of reasonableness that the previous judge relied upon. It is not obvious that this is something judges currently do, nor is it obvious that it is something that they should try to do. Why, after all, should judges seek to emulate Raz, rather than, say Hercules?[37]

One answer is that we must figure out what the law is so we can apply it.[38] If a stable body of norms can be maintained, citizens can understand in advance what is required of them. This is a vision of the judicial role that echoes the one offered to us in *Practical Reason and Norms*. The ability of judges to factually ascertain the law before applying it to the case at hand is essential to this model. It means the difference between order and chaos.[39] Yet, this story about law's role in the world becomes implausible when it is told in the context of the Raz/Postema exchange. Once it is apparent that interpretive effort must be exerted if facts are to be arrived at, then it is hard to believe that judges and citizens are actively seeking sources. In other words, unless judges

[36] *Ibid*, 16.

[37] R Dworkin, *Law's Empire* (Cambridge, MA, Harvard University Press, 1986) 239.

[38] This is, of course, the very point that Dworkin denies. For a brief discussion of Dworkin's views, see ch 2.

[39] See ch 2.

already reason like Raz, we need another account of how law contributes to order. The onus is on Raz to explain why judges should try to ascertain fact-based norms. Without a convincing argument on this point, his response to Postema merely captures a self-serving attempt to preserve positivism, whilst obscuring the nature of adjudicatory practice in the process.

V. WHY REASON LIKE RAZ?

In his most recent works, Raz champions a morally robust theory of adjudication in addition to his positivist theory of law. He now argues that 'quite commonly courts have the discretion to modify legal rules, or to make exceptions to their applications, and where they have such discretion they ought to resort to moral reasoning to decide whether to use it and how'.[40] However, once judges are thought of primarily as moral reasoners, it becomes rather puzzling to try to determine why a judge would undertake the interpretive hunt for intentions. If judges are going to make moral decisions about what a given case requires, why would they exert the intellectual effort required to ensure that they are finding facts? Again the answer to this question is not transparent. What is clear is that Raz needs an answer. There is simply no point in seeking facts for the mere sake of it.

In his attempt to shore up the viability of his sources thesis, Raz finds himself on the horns of a dilemma. He is either going to have to go back to supporting a rather awkward version of a two-step account of the adjudicative process (wherein judges must first find facts before deciding what ought to be done from a moral point of view) *or* Raz must champion a fully-fledged normative positivist theory wherein judges are expected to apply the fact-based norms that they find. Only the former is consistent with his theory of adjudication, but only the latter is plausible in the context of the Raz/Postema exchange. Indeed, I will demonstrate that only a normative positivist theory of adjudication can explain why a judge would want to reason like Raz. The pressure to apply fact-based sources need not be absolute, but it must be there.

Let us consider the first option: the two-step vision of the adjudicative process. At times, this account of the adjudicative process seems to flow naturally from Raz's writing, even if he does not explicitly endorse it. Consider yet another distinction in Raz's repertoire:

> I expect that it is now clear why we need to distinguish reasoning *to* the conclusion that the law as it exists at a certain time has a certain content, from reasoning *from* premises that the law, as it exists at a certain time, has a certain content.[41]

[40] Raz, *Ethics in the Public Domain*, above n 6, at 335.
[41] Raz, 'Postema on Law's Autonomy', above n 10, at 6.

It is certainly the case that we can aim to reason in these two distinct ways. We need not query Raz on this point. But he needs more for his argument to work. Raz must establish that the process of reasoning to the conclusion that the law exists at a certain time and has a certain content is a fact-finding exercise. In his response to Postema, Raz admits that things are more complex. The two-step account of judging is a plausible one only if positivists can demonstrate that factually ascertaining the content of the law is always easy – just a matter of reading what is written. Once placed in the context of the Raz/Postema exchange, the two-step process of adjudication loses much of its initial promise.

If the two-step vision of adjudication is to hold, judges must be prepared to distance themselves from their own understanding of reasonableness when necessary. If judges have to work hard to distance themselves from their own (often implicit) understanding of reasonableness in order to arrive (hopefully) at facts, then there must be a reason for them to carry out this intellectual exercise. If we are looking to make the morally best decision, or at the very least not a morally bad one, it is more sensible to expect judges to interpret the previous law in a reasonable manner, disregarding the first step altogether. This does not mean that judges can never arrive at interpretations of the current law that they deem to be unreasonable; nor am I assuming that determining the content of the law is always a value-laden exercise. I am simply suggesting that if judges are thought of as moral reasoners there is little impetus for them to *consciously* work to distance themselves from their own understanding of reasonableness in the hopes of excising all value judgments from the interpretive process (thereby meeting the demands of the sources thesis). Absent some pressure to apply unreasonable norms, it seems more sensible to expect that judges interpret the law in a reasonable way, bypassing the first step altogether.

The only adjudicatory theory that is able to provide Raz the support he needs at this juncture is normative positivism. The link between 'conceptual' positivism and normative positivism has been argued before, but the connection is staunchly denied by many prominent positivists. John Gardner, for example, argues that connecting these two versions of positivism is an error that students commonly make, but that this 'myth' is easily corrected by highlighting the weaknesses inherent in both 'textualism' and 'originalism',[42] or by pointing out that sometimes cases arise that were unanticipated by lawmakers, rendering 'law application' an impossibility.[43] While these are valid concerns, they do not do the work that positivists require in reference to Raz's version of legal positivism. I have not argued that 'intentionalism' or 'textualism' are

[42] J Gardner, 'Legal Positivism: 5 1/2 Myths' (2001) 46 *American Journal of Jurisprudence* 199, 218–19.

[43] *Ibid*, 212.

sound positions, I have only argued that Raz's sources thesis needs them. Further, Raz does not need judges to meet the requirements of these two theories all of the time (consequently, it does not matter if intentions are not available all of the time). The point is that if fact-based legal norms are going to prove to be a valuable part of the adjudicative process (so much so that we place them at the centre of our theory), then judges must be able to identify fact-based norms and there must also be some normative pressure to apply the norms found. The turn to normative positivism comes at a price. If the relevance of the sources thesis depends on normative positivism, the Hartian project has, once again, revealed itself to be the impossible dream (or at the very least, a dream deferred).

Traditionally, theorists who champion a version of normative positivism are motivated by worries about law's legitimacy, or by more general rule of law concerns about certainty and predictability. The first option – an appeal to legitimacy – involves a familiar argument. The job of judges is to apply the law as they find it and thus they should not alter it as they see fit. Such 'activism' would take them beyond the bounds of their job, at least insofar as they are working in a democracy. The difficulty with this argument is that it is usually forwarded in reference to legislation enacted in a democratic regime. When placed in the context of common law adjudication, which positivists must also account for, this particular version of normative positivism loses much of its punch.

There is another well-trodden pathway that aims at explaining why judges should seek to apply the law. On this account, the application of legal norms is important because it serves the twin virtues of certainty and predictability, which in turn are thought to serve overarching goals of co-ordination and co-operation. The idea is that judges should seek to ascertain and apply fact-based law in order to ensure that a stable body of norms is maintained. If the conduct of citizens is to be guided by norms, then citizens have to know what is expected of them. The best way to ensure this is to apply positive law, avoiding frequent appeals to contentious values such as justice and fairness. In *The Authority of Law* Raz has yet to abandon his claim that judges have a duty to apply the law. Consequently, it is not surprising to discover that he defends a familiar argument pertaining to the value of judicial restraint. He argues that generally, the benefits of applying the law outweigh the defects:

> It may be better to cause hardship in a few cases than to lead to great uncertainty in many. Uncertainty frustrates expectations, prevents planning, encourages abuses of the law by encouraging attempts to exploit its vague margins, and very often policing such laws involves prying into the private affairs of individuals.[44]

[44] Raz, *The Authority of Law*, above n 3, at 31.

In this argument, Raz forwards a version of rule utilitarianism rather than act utilitarianism: in the long run, the benefits of applying the law outweigh the costs of appealing directly to values such as justice, even though in a given case justice may be better served if the law is not applied in a given instance and instead, judges exercise discretion. Judges, according to this argument, must apply unreasonable norms some of the time in order to ensure that citizens know what is expected of them over time. This is a normative claim about the priority that certain principles should have in a well-ordered society and not a descriptive claim about law.[45] Judges can do otherwise, but they should seek to apply the law for the sake of these principles.

The argument that judges should work to apply pre-existing law, in order to ensure that the law is certain, presupposes that pre-existing fact-based norms do most of the work when it comes to guiding conduct and that shared conceptions of reasonableness do little. Yet, on the occasions when upholding the law involves arriving at absurd, unreasonable, or unjust results, it is not clear that the values of 'certainty' and 'predictability' are being served. Such judgments are contextual and contestable.[46] Despite these complications, this argument offers Raz some of the support he needs if his response to Postema is going to succeed. However, if Raz wishes to rely on this argument, his morally robust theory of adjudication must be abandoned. Once again we learn that Raz's theory of law is not wholly distinct from his theory of adjudication.

The lessons learned are the opposite of the tenets commonly preached by legal positivists. Not only is the sources thesis transformed into an ideal of legal reasoning in the course of Raz's response to Postema, but it is also clear that an additional argument is required to give this ideal a place in the world. The sources thesis needs normative positivism. It cannot exist as a freestanding 'descriptive' or 'conceptual' claim about the world.

Raz's response to Postema inadvertently calls into question the value of the sources thesis as such. Upon closer scrutiny, it becomes clear that the sources thesis needs normative positivism, but normative positivism does not need the sources thesis. Normative positivists do not have to establish that legal norms meet the requirements of the sources thesis in order to distinguish their position from competitors. Judges who are positivistic in their approach will be less willing to turn to self-conscious appeals to ideals such as justice or fairness when absurd or unjust results emerge from the application of their chosen method. They will be more rule-bound or formalistic in their approach than

[45] Raz proceeds to argue that 'In matters these considerations are important and where serious hardship and injustice is rare, certainty is at a premium and the courts are justifiably denied exceptive power'.

[46] See ch 6.

their colleagues, prizing certainty over other juridical values.[47] Normative positivism is not dependent on the truth of its conceptual counterpart (as is commonly thought).[48]

The conclusions drawn during the Raz/Postema exchange cannot remain quarantined in the judicial sphere. Recall that in *The Authority of Law*, Raz seeks to convince us to see the importance of the sources thesis by arguing that fact-based legal norms play an important role in ordering our collective lives by giving us public reasons for action that serve to unify judgment. We are now in a position to question the role of the sources thesis in illuminating the practical role of legal norms in our lives (and thus we can also question the feasibility of the weak autonomy thesis). Or more precisely, we can wonder if Raz's specific version of law's role is viable. If interpreters have to work hard to keep values out, then it is quite probable that citizens will have difficulty meeting the demands of the sources thesis, at least some of the time. If it is hard for officials to find legal facts, then it will surely be all the more difficult for citizens to do the same. It is unlikely that citizens will have access to the understanding of reasonableness that the previous judge relied upon. And, of course, all parties would have to rely on their own understanding of reasonableness when making judgments about a particular judge's understanding of reasonableness (or that of a set of judges), raising only more interpretive quandaries for Raz to grapple with.

In sum, if source-based legal norms are performing the unifying function Raz assigns to them, then it must be easy to meet the requirements of the sources thesis. If it is not easy to meet those requirements, a point which Raz concedes above, then we must revisit the understanding of *how* law guides us. Undoubtedly, positive law will likely play a substantial role in any viable account of how law works in the world; the above argument has merely cast doubt on Raz's particular account, which is underpinned by the sources thesis and the weak autonomy thesis.

Defenders of positivism might argue that the features of our world offer us evidence that law is successful in carrying out the task Raz assigns. Citizens tend not to engage in the same kind of interpretive disputes as judges and lawyers and, if they do, such disputes are far less frequent outside the courtroom. One might be tempted to point to this simple fact about the world in order to deflect this problem: because the law works, we can conclude that citizens do not need to distance themselves from their own understanding of reasonableness in order for legal norms to perform the mediating role. This

[47] See P Sankoff, 'The Search for a Better Understanding of Discretionary Power in Evidence Law' (2007) 32 *Queens Law Journal* 487. I return to this general theme in ch 6.

[48] *Cf* Shapiro, *Legality*, above n 29, at 24. For a thorough defence of normative positivism, see TD Campbell, *The Legal Theory of Ethical Positivism* (Dartmouth, 1996).

argument echoes the one that Hart offers in *The Concept of Law,* where he gives short shrift to interpretive worries:

> In any large group general standards, rules and principles must be the main instrument of social control, and not particular directions given to each individual separately. If it were not possible to communicate general standards of conduct, which multitudes of individuals could understand, without further direction, as requiring from them certain conduct when occasion arose, nothing that we now recognize as law could exist.[49]

This argument is too quick. Hart assumes that his 'minimal' claim – that law guides conduct by giving the population rules that are communicated to the population – is itself a matter of fact. Although order may prevail in a given instance, this does not prove that Hart is correct. The existence of order is the shared starting point from which competing theories take root; it is not a feature of our experience that can be appealed to in order to shore up one's own position. In other words, the fact that the interpretative problems do not seem to impede the ability of citizens to obey the law does not necessarily mean that the interpretive problems I have been discussing are of little moment. The more accurate reading of the situation is that the positivist account of the manner in which law functions is itself inadequate.

The outcome of the Raz/Postema debate points us down a different theoretical path of enquiry – one where we must consider the role that shared values play in allowing law to guide conduct. The existence of a degree of certainty on the part of the population regarding the kinds of behaviour that are prohibited and permitted does not mean that the law can be interpreted uniformly by all. The story may be more complicated, and unlike the story offered by Raz, it does not rely on a sharp distinction between fact and value. This is a point that will be explored further in the final chapter.

VI. LAW AND ORDER: SOME REFLECTIONS ON METHOD

In a recent work, Raz has reversed the order of his claims, eschewing any possibility that his core theses, including the sources thesis, have anything to do with law's function. He maintains that 'even if we assume that it is a good thing for a society to enjoy unity in its political judgment, it is not obviously the law's task to secure it, or even to contribute to that goal'.[50] Methodologically, he now insists that what law does (or does not do) is not relevant for a determination of what law is: 'But while no one would doubt the importance of knowing why we should have law, if indeed we should have law, this cannot

[49] Hart, *The Concept of Law,* above n 5, at 124.
[50] Raz, 'Postema on Law's Autonomy', above n 10, at 3.

be an argument for the thesis that the law is one way or another'.[51] Raz has clearly changed his position without fully acknowledging it. The interesting questions pertain to his motivation and to the potential success of this move. Why does he seek to conceptualise law without reflecting on what law does in the world? Can he successfully separate his understanding about what law is from a view of what law does, given that his core theses are the product of a certain understanding of law's function?

A sharper picture of the nature of jurisprudential enquiry and the relationship between method and substance emerges from this particular line of questioning. It is clear from the above arguments that Raz has difficulty distancing himself from his function-based account unless he is willing to discard his pre-emption thesis, although he has good methodological reasons to do so. One reason why positivists have grown weary about functional accounts is that it is unclear if this kind of account can live up to its universal aspirations, as understood through Hart's eyes. Leslie Green voices this worry, insisting that the 'hypothesis of a generic end for law is not needed to explain why all legal systems have certain common features', noting that nonetheless he has 'not shown the hypothesis to be false'.[52] He proceeds to limit his thoughts on the issue of allocating an overarching function to law to the following terse comments:

> [I]t is perhaps a warning sign that many of the candidates that have been offered for law's generic end (eg protecting human rights, securing respect for persons, keeping the peace) are attractive ideals for law and are neither common to all legal systems nor unique to them, while others (eg maintaining order, coordinating activity) are so vague as to be useless to jurisprudence and, when specified more precisely, quickly lose their claims to universality.[53]

There is much truth in what Green argues. Protecting human rights is not a 'generic end'. His observation that the more precision one gives their account of law's order-engendering role, the less plausible its claim to universality becomes, is also sound.

It may not be particularly controversial, for instance, to argue that one of law's functions is to guide the conduct of the citizenry. To take a paradigmatic example, if one argues that the main function of law is to guide conduct, it would seem fairly easy to generate a substantial amount of consensus around this claim. However, once a philosopher has to explain *precisely how* law guides us, the account becomes more contestable, especially if it is offered as an account of how all legal systems work (rather, than an ideal to which all legal systems should aspire). Montesquieu helpfully draws our attention to two familiar mechanisms that a government can use to maintain order:

[51] *Ibid*, 11.

[52] L Green, 'Law as a Means' in P Cane (ed), *The Hart-Fuller Debate in the Twenty-First Century* (Oxford, Hart Publishing, 2010) 184.

[53] *Ibid.*

> A moderate government can, as much as it wants and without peril, relax its springs. It maintains itself by its laws, and even by its force. But when in despotic government the prince ceases for a moment to raise his arm, when he cannot instantly destroy those in the highest places, all is lost, for when the spring of the government, which is fear, no longer exists, the people no longer have a protector.[54]

Those who rule with the sword are less powerful than those who win the hearts and minds of the citizenry. Fear is a mighty weapon, but it is also labour-intensive. The general point is simply that there are (at least) two mechanisms for maintaining order. Green is correct. While we might all agree on the abstract formulation that law guides conduct, this claim is too abstract to be useful. When we give it the needed specificity, the quest for a single 'universal' account becomes far less promising. Legal philosophers are faced with a rather stark choice. They can choose to follow Hart in a search for the features that all existing systems exhibit and avoid this line of enquiry.[55] Alternatively, legal philosophers may choose to reflect on law's relationship with order and abandon the positivist enterprise as Green conceives of it. Is the first option the only path to the most fundamental jurisprudential insight as many positivists assume?

The fact that a positivist must refuse to ask questions about the relationship between law and order is worrisome. With each question that is put aside for this reason, the legal theorist signals that the goals of 'value-neutrality' and 'universality' (as they understand it) are paramount. The positivist may only ask and answer questions that do not rely on contestable values, including but not restricted to contestable conceptions of the nature of the political order. The list of questions that meet this criteria is likely to be quite short, and the list of available answers is (I suspect) even shorter.[56] The remarkably elusive nature of the goal methodological neutrality – should give us pause. Just as it is difficult for positivists to establish that value is kept out of judgments about what law *is* at the practical level, it is equally difficult to keep value out at the methodological level. Notice that this point does not draw upon the distinction between the 'is' and the 'ought' as it is commonly construed by positivists. In other words, a legal philosopher need not be interested in trying to determine how law *should* guide (although she might be); rather, they can explore the various ways in which law works which can lead easily to the articulation

[54] AM Cohler, BC Miller and HS Stone (trs and eds), *Charles de Second at Montesquieu, The Spirit of the Laws* (Cambridge, Cambridge University Press, 1992) 28.

[55] A third option would involve discussing any and all relevant issue under the rubric of normative philosophy which is relevant, but distinct from the Hartian project. Leslie Green maintains that positivism can only be a partial theory. See Green, 'Legal Positivism' in *The Stanford Encyclopedia of Philosophy*, Spring 2003 edn: plato.stanford.edu/archives/spr2003/entries/legal-positivism. For a powerful critique of partial positivism, see J Finnis, 'The Truth about Legal Positivism' in, *The Collected Essays of John Finnis*, vol IV (Oxford, Oxford University Press, 2011) 182–86.

[56] See also, J Finnis, *Natural Law and Natural Rights* (Oxford, Clarendon Press, 1980) ch II.

of a legal ideal.[57] Values can enter covertly into the analysis when legal philosophers offer arguments that rely on contestable assumptions from political philosophy. Raz's account of how law guides conduct, quoted at length at the start of this chapter, is but one potential example. Any account of the way in which law works in the world will likely invoke various assumptions from the broader debates in political philosophy. Such assumptions can enter in a covert manner and may prove to be quite difficult to excise.

Consider, for instance, Raz's assertion that it is unclear if we should have law at all.[58] He is (I believe) trying to attempt to remain neutral between competing normative conceptions of the social order. When the positivist wonders whether it is good to have law at all, she inadvertently betrays an affinity with the utilitarians (and any others who share a certain view of the world). The deep assumptions that are at work become visible when it is made clear that different philosophical visions of the world give rise to different questions and that not all philosophical visions of the world give rise to this particular question.

Consider the debate about the relationship between law and human freedom, for example. Utilitarian thinkers conceive of the coercive aspect of law as a limit on human liberty. The conception of freedom is an abstraction which flows from an isolated individual who serves as the basic political unit from which all philosophical reflections take root. Conversely, if one views the human condition through the lens of Thomistic philosophy, the picture that emerges is markedly different. For St Thomas Aquinas, law is not viewed as a limitation of freedom, but as a condition of it. Stanley Parry explains:

> Law, insofar as it puts into concrete terms the general imperatives of nature, is not adventitious. Rather it is a conscious recognition and corporate specification of the natural boundaries of action in the real conditions of life. Thus law is perfectly compatible to the freedom proper to man.[59]

Freedom is always embodied and always constrained by the 'real conditions of life'. The content of the legal constraints, not the mere existence of them, can signal the loss of freedom. In other words, law is not considered to be an enemy of freedom, but is instead a pre-condition of it. It does not follow from this position that law cannot exist alongside oppression.[60] The point is simply that there is no fundamental antagonism between freedom and the existence of law. Parry explains that the 'problem for the Thomist is to work out a system of government that will realize in fact the theoretical harmony between law and freedom'.[61] One would not be led to ask whether it would be good to

[57] See ch 6.
[58] Raz, 'Postema on Law's Autonomy', above at n 10, at 11.
[59] S Parry, 'Introduction' in St Thomas Aquinas, *Treatise of Law*, 5th edn (Chicago, Henry Regnery Co, 1965) x.
[60] *Ibid*, x.
[61] *Ibid*, x.

have law at all (it is); rather one would always work to realize law's potential to enable us to enjoy freedom as Thomists conceive of it.

The problem of how best to organize political society is conceived of in remarkably different terms if one is a utilitarian. The goal for the utilitarian is to work out a system that will sacrifice as little freedom as is compatible with the preservation of order.[62] Law is always a constraint on freedom for the utilitarian and so it is easy to see why the utilitarian might wonder whether we should have law at all. Law may prove to be too much of a constraint on human liberty. The utilitarian may certainly wonder whether it is good to have law at all. Thus when Raz wonders whether it is good to have law at all, he inadvertently signals that his foundational assumptions are more closely aligned with utilitarians and not classical natural lawyers.[63] Serious questions can be asked about the extent to which positivists can avoid relying on contestable assumptions and ideas from political philosophy.[64]

In sum, it is very difficult to achieve the kind of methodological neutrality that many positivists covet. A legal philosopher's fundamental assumptions may not even be consciously recognized or defended, but such assumptions nonetheless give shape to both the nature of the enquiry and the range of conclusions that can be drawn. There is no view from nowhere. A neutral position that hovers above and does invoke, or in some part depend on, fundamental assumptions about the nature of the human condition is remarkably elusive.

One of the worries that motivates theorists to partake in value-neutral analysis is the same worry that underpins the conception of law as public reasons for action.[65] Recall that according to this popular philosophical account of law, legal norms unify judgment by providing a set of facts that we can all treat as reasons for action. Without law, disagreements about how we ought to behave would permeate society, threatening to disrupt the order. Values, from the perspective of this theory of law's function, are the troublemakers. A similar fear permeates jurisprudential debate. If we cannot establish a baseline of consensus, we will continually talk past each other or we will become distracted by debates about value.[66] In other words, if we allow individual value-judgments to drive the analysis, then we will spend our time locked in a perpetual insoluble debate

62 *Ibid*, x–xi.

63 This is not a superficial point about positivism. See M J Stone, 'Planning Positivism and Planning Natural Law' 25 *Canadian Journal of Law and Jurisprudence* 232.

64 See also D Priel, 'Evaluating Descriptive Jurisprudence' (2007) 52 *American Journal of Jurisprudence* 13; S Coyle, 'The Intellectual Commitments of Modern Juridical Thought' (2010) 23 *Canadian Journal of Law and Jurisprudence* 461.

65 J Waldron, 'Legal and Political Philosophy' in J Coleman and S Shapiro (eds), *The Oxford Handbook of Jurisprudence and Philosophy of Law* (Oxford, Oxford University Press, 2002) 366–68.

66 See J Pojanowski, 'Review Essay: Legal Thought in Enlightenment's Wake' (2013) 4 *Jurisprudence* 158, 170.

about morals, thwarting all hope of making progress in legal philosophy. Progress, it is believed, is only possible if we can generate consensus about some basic truths. Once this constellation of worries is made explicit, the pull of legal positivism, and the sources thesis in particular, is intelligible.

I have argued that the hope that Hart's promise – to allow theorists to make a clean break from broader debates in legal theory – is misplaced (or at the very least the attempt to realise it comes at a great cost). After all, even if the path is pursued, disagreements do not disappear. This fact has led to another jurisprudential puzzle and the subsequent turn to metatheory: how do we crown a victor in the debate? Instead of examining first principles and reflecting on the nature of the law as it is manifest in the world (which is the only place for traditional political philosophers to return to), there has been a turn, as of late, to meta-theoretical values. The values like simplicity and coherence are supposed to be used to evaluate competing conceptions of law. Such reflections have the effect of taking the philosopher's eye off the world, leaving her to reflect on her own reflections, ad infinitum and with little pay-off insofar as the hope is this kind of introspection will anoint a champion.[67] The failure to find a single, uncontroversial answer to the question 'what is law?' is only dismaying to those who think that these matters can be settled definitively and permanently. For those of us who think that philosophy requires constant reflection, in the hopes of articulating a truth, even if it is partial and never wholly captured with the words we have at our disposal, the failure to achieve complete consensus is not a moment for despair. Consensus, after all, is not always a sign that truth has been reached; it can also signal the triumph of dogmatism over curiosity.

At first glance, legal positivism may seem like an obvious position that few could or should disagree with. It offers us a simple thesis: all law is factually ascertainable. This basic point is often thought to be the cornerstone of legal theory – the starting point for our reflections that can generate widespread consensus before theorists splinter on more minor points, often shading into normative disagreements about ideals. On this view, positivism represents the minimal claim that launches us forward into all kinds of rich theoretical debates. If the domimant framework does not hold, this is good news for many. The dominant view has resulted in a quick (and sometimes hostile) dismissal of opponents who are not adhering to the strict methodological principles advocated by many of the prominent legal theorists of our day.[68] If the dominant view does not hold, the debate can be re-invigorated. Long-lost friends of old, from Plato and Aquinas to Montesquieu and Mill, can rejoin

[67] Disagreements tend to reproduce themselves at the meta-theoretical level. See B Bix, 'John Austin and Constructing Theories of Law' (2011) 24 *Canadian Journal of Law and Jurisprudence* 431. For an alternative view see J Dickson, *Evaluation and Legal Theory* (Oxford, Hart Publishing, 2001).

[68] A Halpin, 'Austin's Methodology? His Bequest to Jurisprudence' (2011) 70 *CLJ* 175, 201.

the conversation. Students, once released from the strict confines of the dominant framework, can let their curiosity lead the way. The world, in all its complexity, becomes central to jurisprudence once again.

6

The Path Not Taken

RAZ, I HAVE argued, was faced with a choice once the rule-plus-exception theory collapsed. Two rather obvious paths reveal themselves as clear possibilities. Raz could revisit the question regarding how law and the work of officials contribute to an orderly society, or he could recast his positivist theses in the hopes of preserving them in a new context. It is the second of these two paths that Raz opted to travel down, introducing readers to his morally robust theory of adjudication and re-orienting his theory around a normative account of authority. I have argued that both moves create deep incoherencies and inconsistencies in his account. In what follows, I will travel down the path not taken. I will revisit the central question that informs his early works, namely I will reflect upon the relationship between law and order. By asking the same questions, but arriving at better answers, an ideal (or focal) conception of the rule of law emerges from these rather pedestrian roots.

As argued in the previous chapter, an account of how law works requires us to reflect on at least two kinds of regimes. Recall Montesquieu's words:

> A moderate government can, as much as it wants and without peril, relax its springs. It maintains itself by its laws, and even by its force. But when in despotic government the prince ceases for a moment to raise his arm, when he cannot instantly destroy those in the highest places, all is lost, for when the spring of the government, which is fear, no longer exists, the people no longer have a protector.[1]

Following Montesquieu, fear-based regimes work in a different way than their moderate counterparts. By attending to this difference, rather than suppressing it, a clearer understanding of law materializes. As I indicated in chapter four, this simple shift supports a focal case conception of law, at least insofar as one hopes to preserve the thought that moderate regimes are morally preferable to despotic ones. By exploring the similarities and differences between these two types of regimes we are led into the territory of natural law. I will not move into the territory, I will only suggest that it cannot be avoided.

Despite claims to the contrary, positivist theories (specifically those offered by Hart and Raz) are not 'neutral' between the two modes of operation that

[1] AM Cohler, BC Miller and HS Stone (trs and eds), *Charles de Secondat Montesquieu, The Spirit of the Laws* (Cambridge, Cambridge University Press, 1992).

are highlighted in Montesquieu's discussion; rather, by suppressing the distinction between wicked and benevolent systems, they conceptualize law in a manner that subtly prioritizes wicked legal systems where law operates in a top-down fashion wherein officials' relationship with legal norms is dispositive. This preference becomes visible when we turn our attention to the relationship between Hart's discussion of the internal attitude and his chosen methodological commitments. If one wishes to take the idea of the internal aspect of rules seriously it leads us to a very different understanding of law, an understanding that is competitive with the theories offered by Hart and Raz.

On this point, Oliver Wendell Holmes's reflections are invaluable. His brief remarks about the 'bad man' contain the seeds for a more precise explanation of the manner in which law guides conduct in moderate regimes. It is surprising, therefore, that many legal philosophers find little of value in this particular passage in 'The Path of the Law', complaining that he focuses too much on sanctions and not enough on the reason-giving nature of legal norms.[2] This criticism presupposes the very point at issue. If Holmes is right, it is profoundly unhelpful to think of law divorced from the forces of coercion and conscience. It is not Holmes's realist beliefs that are of primary interest in this regard, but his more realistic characterization of the perspective of the citizen and the work of the lawyer. Indeed, not only does he provide the resources for an account of law's work in the world that is competitive with the narrative of law as a set of public practical reasons, Holmes also offers a more accurate account of legal reasoning as a kind of specialized art and not, as Raz insists, a kind of 'public reasoning'. These subtle changes allow us to take the mystery out of Holmes's claim that law is about predictions. This idea is only mysterious if one assumes, as Raz does, that law is best understood as a discrete set of reasons for action.

It is not simply the distinction between benevolent regimes and their wicked counter-parts that is of significance. The distinction between societies wracked by uncertainty and those where citizens generally know how the power of the state will be used is also crucial. This distinction underpins Raz's account in *Practical Reason and Norms*, but Raz misdiagnoses the causes of uncertainty and thus he misrepresents the nature of law. With Fuller's assistance (particularly his parable about the hapless King Rex), I will offer a more accurate account of the variables that contribute to uncertainty, which in turn produces a more accurate conception of law. By exploring a series of concrete examples, the dichotomy of law application (in the service of certainty) and law creation (in the service of justice) is pierced. It also becomes evident that the idea that laws are general and public are ideals to which legal systems aspire, rather than mere facts that accompany the existence of positive law.

[2] For a version of this line of critique, see HLA Hart, *The Concept of Law*, 2nd edn (Oxford, Oxford University Press, 1994) 90.

It will become clear that law is not best understood as a discrete set of public practical reasons, but as a public system of norms. While a slight shift, I will suggest that it is a significant one. Thinking about the content of norms is important if law is to work as a system; likewise we must consider the ways in which the public dimension of law is impacted by the work of officials and the shared understandings of law's subjects. Note that my point is not that any given law is incapable of serving as a reason for action (or even a pre-emptive reason), but rather that a more complex account must be given and it is one that does not lead us to place the idea of a pre-emptive reason at the centre.

When these aspects of legality come into view, it also becomes clear that understanding law requires us to grasp an ideal rather than a value-neutral concept. The ideal grows from the seeds planted by Raz: the same questions are asked, but better answers are given, ones that better capture basic features of our shared experience. This shift in perspective also illuminates the precise manner in which reflections on the nature of law can be at once of both philosophical and practical importance.

I. HART AND THE INTERNAL ASPECT OF RULES

Hart is often viewed as offering knockdown arguments against his positivist predecessor, John Austin. Austin defines law as commands of the sovereign which the populace habitually obeys.[3] This definition, Hart argues, is inadequate for a host of reasons. One of those reasons is that it wholly overlooks a familiar way in which rules operate. Citizens do not obey laws out of mere habit; rather, they often internalize law's demands, holding them up as standards of behaviour by which to assess their own behaviour and the behaviour of others.[4] Hart refers to this as a 'critical reflective attitude' (or the attitude of acceptance): 'These views are manifested in the criticisms of others and demands for conformity made upon others when deviation is actual or threatened, and in the acknowledgment of the legitimacy of such criticism and demands when received from others'.[5] It is the widespread presence of this attitude that distinguishes social rules (which have a normative dimension) from mere habits of obedience. And it is this aspect of life under law that can account for law's continuity through time – something that the mere idea of a habit is unable to do according to Hart.

The force of Hart's argument can be understood with greater clarity when we have before our minds Montesquieu's distinction between despotic regimes

[3] *Ibid*, ch 2.
[4] HLA Hart, *The Concept of Law*, above n 2, at 55.
[5] *Ibid*, 57.

and moderate regimes. Austin's model better captures life in a despotic regime, where power is centralized and sanctions act as the primary mechanism used to maintain law and order. Hart, by way of contrast, focuses readers' minds on certain familiar features of life in a moderate regime where the fear of sanctions fades into the backdrop of daily life and legal norms are often internalized by the populace. Nevertheless, Hart does not keep the readers' minds fixed on this familiar feature of life under law. His chosen methodology necessitates the shift away from this aspect of our lived experience towards a consideration of darker examples of existing legal systems.

Like Austin before him, Hart is interested in identifying the features that all legal systems share.[6] This methodological principle of selection informs the content of his concept of law and supports the conclusion that the 'attitude of acceptance' is not an essential feature of law.[7] In other words, legal norms need not be internalized by a given population in order for a legal system to exist. The mere existence of a legal order does not demand it. When Hart finally articulates the content of his concept of law, the attitude of acceptance is conspicuous in its absence. Law, he argues, is best understood as a union of primary and secondary rules that are generally obeyed by the populace. Significantly, citizens can obey the law for *any* reason (fear or acceptance, habit, etc); only legal officials must adopt the internal attitude towards the norms that govern them.[8]

The different regimes of law identified by Montesquieu (and implicitly by Hart) do not vanish, they are merely submerged in Hart's account. By seeking the common ground between legal systems, Hart subtly prioritizes despotic regimes. Law is conceptualized as a top-down projection of power that echoes Austin's theory. Instead of offering an account that is neutral between types of legal orders, he better accounts for despotic ones at the expense of making sense of life under law in moderate regimes.[9] If Hart opted to take the internal aspect of rules seriously he would be led to consider the way in which law works in moderate regimes. Such reflections lead him quickly into the territory of the ideal of the rule of law and away from a consideration of the features shared by all existing legal systems. In what follows, I will suggest this is a more fruitful path for the legal philosopher to travel down. Not only is there practical value in this approach, but the practical value is itself wholly dependent on the ability of this method to serve truth. Moreover, there is nothing

[6] For a discussion of method, see F Schauer, 'Positivism before Hart' (2011) 24 *Canadian Journal of Law and Jurisprudence* 2.

[7] For a well-know and excellent criticism of this move, see J Finnis, *Natural Law and Natural Rights* (Oxford, Clarendon Press, 1980) 11–18.

[8] Hart, *The Concept of Law,* above n 2, at 16.

[9] J Finnis's famous critique of Hart and Raz on this point is on point. J Finnis, *Natural Law and Natural Rights,* above n 7, at 13–14.

inherent in the approach that I am advocating that means that one would be left without the resources to identify existing legal systems.[10]

Holmes offers us an excellent entrance point into a consideration of the internal aspect of rules – his discussion of the 'bad man' situates readers within a moderate regime (that of the United States). This famous example will serve as a platform from which a more nuanced account of the internal attitude can quickly develop alongside a conception of law's guidance function that is competitive with Raz's account. This discussion will enable me to tie up another dangling end: in chapter three I suggest that a realist account of adjudication will require an account of the nature of law that is different from the one that Raz offers readers. The Holmes inspired reflections to follow will go some distance in substantiating this claim.

II. A LITTLE HELP FROM HOLMES

Similarly to Hart, Holmes is worried about the 'the confusion of legal and moral ideas'.[11] Holmes's antidote is slightly different from Hart's, however. For Hart, what the law *is* is a matter of fact; evaluative standards are appealed to in order to determine what the law *ought* to be. Conversely, one might characterize Holmes as trying to isolate the legal 'ought' as it is manifest in daily life. This task is not particularly easy given the overlap in linguistic usage of moral and legal terms, combined with the complexity of human motivations. Accordingly, in order to identify what one might call the 'pure legal ought', Holmes asks us to consider the practical reasoning process of the 'bad man':

> If you want to know the law and nothing else, you must look at it as a bad man, who cares only for the material consequences which such knowledge enables him to predict, not as a good one, who finds his reason for conduct, whether inside the law or outside it, in the vaguer sanctions of conscience.[12]

The din of complex motivations that is frequently encountered in experience is distilled down to its bare components in the reasoning of the criminally-inclined. The legal reasons for action and the moral reasons for action come apart, allowing the reason-giving potential of law to be realized in full. Notice, however, that the reason for action that the law provides is not 'exclusionary' in the Razian sense, but prudential in nature. The potential lawbreaker does

[10] It is worth bearing in mind that the Hartian method requires legal philosophers to identify the features that all legal systems share. So the line between existing legal systems and non-systems is drawn at the outset. The theory that I am advocating will not undermine our ability to identify existing systems, but rather (following Fuller) it will provide a finer lens through which to understand the phenomena.

[11] OW Holmes, 'The Path of the Law' (1896–97) 10 *Harvard Law Review* 457, 458.

[12] *Ibid*, 459.

not wish to face state sanctions and thus his obedience is motivated by this sole desire. Since the 'bad man's' misadventures know no bounds, any given norm or set of norms can motivate his choices.

If we turn our attention to the average citizen, once again we discover that Holmes's brief remarks ring true. Citizens often obey the law for reasons of conscience rather than out of deference to the force of public reasons. For instance, most people refrain from committing murder because they believe it is wrong. If this particular law were struck down, then even though more murders would surely occur, many would still decide not to kill because of the widespread belief that it is wrong. Conversely, if the prohibition against cannibalism were to be struck down, then it is unlikely that many people would change their behaviour as the impetus to engage in this act is rare and remains largely unaffected by the kinds of conflicts that emerge in the crowded conditions of social life. In order to understand the way in which legal norms impact on our practical reasoning, these are the kind of variables that must be considered.

To think of legal norms as a discrete set of content-independent reasons for action also fails to capture another common way that law can, and often does, impact on our lives on a daily basis: legal norms can operate as background considerations that are constitutive, or partially constitutive, of our ideas of right and wrong. In some instances, the practical impact of legal norms may be invisible. The law may mark the boundaries as to what is permissible and what is not, but the general understanding of these boundaries is learned through quite ordinary mechanisms. When I ask my students how they knew what was lawful behaviour before they entered law school, it takes but a moment for the words 'mom and dad', 'school' and 'church' to be uttered. These familiar processes of socialization are often the means by which the citizenry comes to learn what is permitted in society and what is not, without knowing the content of particular laws. One sign that a moderate legal system is working well is when citizens who hope to be law-abiding can achieve this end with relative ease. Individuals tend to become better acquainted with certain areas of law when the need arises, but in such instances they usually seek out the assistance of lawyers.

The temptation, of course, is to massage the positivist picture to absorb these observations into the theory on an *ad hoc* basis. It is, however, difficult to get around the basic fact that these observations concerning background beliefs and socialization processes are not represented in Raz's picture of law, explored in the preceding chapters. It is not a coincidence that those who defend the claim that law gives us public practical reasons for action rely so heavily on the laws that regulate traffic, as such examples reinforce their conception of law's guidance function while remaining at a safe level of abstraction. Consider, for instance, the legal rules that regulate parking. Signs are posted in public places in order to signal to us where we can park and for how long. Conscience plays little role, at least in the sense that if all the 'no parking' signs were removed, few of us would think twice about parking in the spaces that were previously deemed off-limits. Accordingly, these particular laws give us a discrete set of autonomous public practical reasons that unify judgment and facilitate co-ordination and co-operation by directly influencing the reasoning process. An important qualification is required, however: the possibility of getting a ticket also helps to motivate compliance. The normative power of law rarely works on its own, removed from the forces of coercion or conscience.

This set of observations and reflections about the relationship between citizens and the law – points which can be qualified and classified, corrected or elaborated on at length – can, and should, re-orient our theoretical reflections. The aim is to arrive at a theoretical account that is as accurate as possible. Regrettably, this project has largely been displaced by a stalwart determination to preserve positivism. Once the complexity of legal experience is in view, it becomes apparent that Raz's conceptualization of the role of law in our lives is not as helpful as it may seem. Citizens are not usually faced with the stark choice between treating legal reasons as pre-emptory reasons for action or returning to the reasons behind the rules (see chapter four). Raz's account pays little attention to the constitutive nature of law and ignores the diffuse and multifaceted ways in which legal norms can enter into our reasoning process. Nor does it account for the complex motivations individuals might have for complying with the law.[13]

Recall that Raz tells us that 'double counting' – treating both the legal norm and the underlying reasons as a reason for action – is prohibited.[14] Now it is all too clear that the only reason why this would be so is that Raz needs it to be so. If his pre-emption thesis is going to be the cornerstone of a distinctive account of law, legal reasons must not collapse into weighty reasons. When we shift our focus away from what his position requires to how law is manifest in the world, the lesson is quickly reversed. In benevolent regimes double counting is often a very good thing because it is a sign that legal norms have been internalized. The system becomes more resilient (as Montesquieu notes) and people have the added benefit of living in a society where fear is not a part of daily life for most.

When we move from benevolent regimes to wicked ones, the narrative about the way in which law orders the world must be adjusted. For law-abiding citizens in a benevolent legal system, legal norms usually operate as weighty

[13] Some may attempt to absorb these features into a Razian account. My question is: if we begin with this complex account, do we end up thinking about law as a set of content-independent pre-emptory reasons for action? Any such observations must be *ad hoc* and this is by design: recall that the philosophically relevant features are those that are shared by all existing legal systems. The features which I am considering are prominent in moderate regimes, but may be less prominent (or absent) in other kinds of regimes.

[14] See chs 1 and 4.

reasons for action or as invisible constraints woven into the social fabric which we self-consciously or habitually operate within every day. Only in wicked systems would we expect the reason-giving ability of law to work in isolation from other reasons, such as reasons of conscience. The average citizen in a wicked regime is likely to adopt a posture similar to that of the 'bad man' in a good regime: she is more likely to treat legal norms as reasons for action because she fears what may happen if she fails to obey. Again, we discover that Hart and Raz do a much better job capturing the top-down structure present in wicked systems than the role law plays in the healthier counterparts.

Insofar as double counting is a feature in wicked regimes, this may serve as a sign that the citizen has internalized morally questionable norms in wicked societies. Two unfortunate consequences follow from this: the citizen can either become part of the machinery by which the government achieves its morally questionable ends or citizens may themselves be led like sheep to the slaughterhouse.[15] Hart's famous warning is powerful in wicked regimes, but less so in good ones. Hart implicitly acknowledges this. When he introduces readers to the idea of the critical reflective attitude he does not warn us that this attitude may prove to be a dangerous one in certain contexts. One can easily get the impression that Hart views the critical reflective attitude as an important and even a laudable feature of life under law. Unlike the legal sceptics, Hart does not argue that all citizens should always be wary of law's demands in all contexts. In other words, the posture of detachment that Hart encourages at some moments (we must identify the law before we evaluate its moral worth) is at odds with his discussion of the internalization of legal norms near the outset of *The Concept of Law*. To explain the difference in tone, I wish to suggest that Hart has simply shifted focus.

Above, I contend that when Hart introduces the attitude of acceptance, he directs readers' minds to certain features of healthy legal regimes such as his own. When he advocates that citizens maintain a sceptical distance from the powerful pull of law, he is surely worried about the way in which law is used in wicked regimes. The intuition that the widespread adoption of the attitude of acceptance on the part of the general population may prove to be good in good systems but problematic in wicked ones, can only be adequately explained if we attend to, rather than suppress the distinction between moderate and despotic regimes. Again, this leads us into the territory of natural law as one must explain why those who accept legal norms in moderate regimes are not simply 'singing in their chains' so to speak. What makes a good system good? I will not aim to answer this question in the remaining pages of this book, but I will gesture towards some of the lines of enquiry that may prove to be relevant.

[15] Hart, *The Concept of Law,* above n 2, at 117.

Given the complexity of social life and legal practice in particular, it should be evident that thinking of law as a set of legal norms that offer us reasons for action provides a distorted picture of how law guides conduct. Living within law's bounds is not simply a matter of choosing to treat legal norms as reasons for action: it is often a matter of education and socialization. Ideas of what is right and wrong, polite and impolite, etc do far more practical work than the positivist theory indicates. The boundary between legal norms and social norms is fuzzy and to suggest otherwise is to simply impose a crisp line onto the world, creating an artificial overlay onto the practice.[16] Once we aim to understand the way in which law works in different contexts (which is an intellectual endeavour that is surely unending), ideas that are rarely discussed by positivists such as custom, tradition and habit re-enter the picture alongside law's coercive dimension.

An alternative account of law's nature is presented by Sean Coyle, who combines the background features of social life with law's authoritative dimension, offering us both a more accurate and a more complicated understanding of law:

> A vision of law as a set of 'external' rules within which individuals freely move can be seen as illusory. Most aspects of social life are grounded to a greater extent in habit and tradition than in rule. To bring social relationships within the scope of formal rules, the law must perform its reflective function, seeking to give more precision and stability to those modes of interaction which exist socially and independently of it. But in carrying out this important function, the law also gives definite expression and authoritative shape to those modes of interaction. In imposing a fixed (or relatively fixed) form upon the conditions of social engagement, the law inevitably supplants and modifies what it attempts to pin down. Viewed in this way, the question of how law can be both reflective *and* constitutive of social order becomes more clear. Reflection, creation and modification are not *separate* processes undertaken by the legal order, but aspects of the same process.[17]

Coyle argues that law is not an all-powerful force that emanates from above, but is itself heavily dependent on the broader normative landscape for its meaning and its practical force. Law relies on traditions, customs, practices and the beliefs of the community to carry out its work. Officials can, of course, intentionally transform this very same landscape, making it seem to be infinitely adjustable – the product of an aggregate of acts of will. Positivist concepts capture this facet of legality, but they take it out of the context that gives it meaning. The authoritative dimensions of legality can only be properly understood when they are viewed as one part of a more complicated story. By

[16] Here I am challenging the autonomy thesis (in both its forms). See also ch 2. I return to this point below.

[17] S Coyle, *Dimensions of Politics and English Jurisprudence* (Cambridge, Cambridge University Press, 2013) 171 (footnote omitted).

contrast, Raz's conception of law as a set of content-independent reasons for action is an abstraction that tells us little about how law actually works in the world. The value-laden fabric which gives law its life is abstracted away only at great cost.

Once the 'bottom up' aspect of law is considered, the sources of certainty become more diffuse, and thus the decision that best promotes certainty may turn out to be a principled decision. Expectations that are generated about what ought to happen are not the product of positive law alone. A complex network of expectations (social and legal, often indistinguishable) is a part of daily life, but sometimes the expectations are only identified once they are breached. The point is not (as Raz suggests) that discretionary activities are so minimal that their impact can be contained;[18] rather, we learn that such practices can actually reinforce law's ability to guide conduct because such decisions track common understandings of what is fair – a point I will return to in the next section.

For now, let us consider one more aspect of Holmes's position in order to cast light on another conceptual puzzle piece awaiting consideration. I have suggested that thinking about law as a set of public practical reasons is wedded to the idea that legal reasoning is itself 'public reasoning': there is no real difference between the way in which citizens and legal professionals reason with rules, outside the obvious point that only judges can make rulings that are binding (ie backed by the force of the state). In short, if law is going to function as Raz assumes, the way in which citizens interpret legal norms must be (for the most part) in accordance with the way in which officials and other citizens interpret them.[19]

However, if we examine the particulars of the profession we find a technical practice where familiar words become terms of art and other words and phrases have meaning only within the legal sphere – meanings that are familiar to lawyers, but often not to the average citizen. According to Holmes, the need to predict what the judge will do is not a mystery, but a familiar part of the lawyerly craft:

> When we study law we are not studying a mystery but a well known profession. We are studying what we shall want in order to appear before judges, or to advise people in such a way as to keep them out of court. The reason why it is a profession, why people will pay lawyers to argue for them or to advise them, is that in societies like ours the command of the public force is entrusted to the judges in certain cases, and the whole power of the state will be put forth, if necessary, to carry out their judgments and decrees. People want to know under what circumstances and how far they will run the risk of coming against what is so much

[18] J Raz, 'Postema on Law's Autonomy and Public Practical Reason: A Critical Comment' (1998) 4 *Legal Theory* 12, 19–20.

[19] See ch 5.

> stronger than themselves, and hence it becomes a business to find out when this danger is to be feared. The object of our study, then, is prediction, the prediction of the incidence of the public force through the instrumentality of the courts.[20]

The idea that legal reasoning is a specialized kind of reasoning is a feature of legal practice that students become acquainted with very early in law school. They learn how rules, principles, statutes and precedents tend to be interpreted in the courtroom. They also learn how familiar words take on a precise meaning in the courtroom. Students learn to think like lawyers.[21]

Representing law as a technical discipline appears to be a rather basic observation that few would dispute. The problem is that this is not an observation that is adequately represented by the positivists. If specialized training is required in order to accurately interpret the law, then how can we expect citizens to treat legal norms as reasons for action as Raz supposes?[22] The answer is simple: we do not have to expect citizens to know the precise content of legal norms because law does not guide their conduct as he presupposes. Legal norms are but one element in a complex set of norms and practices that together, enable us to understand how we can live within law's bounds if we so desire.

The idea that legal rights are nothing but prophesies of what the courts will do is only mysterious if one presupposes that legal norms guide conduct primarily by offering the citizenry reasons for action. But, as Fuller notes, we can make sense of Holmes's idea of prophesies when we take into account the resources that are available to lawyers:

> If we are to predict intelligently what the courts will do in fact, we must ask what they are trying to do. We must indeed go further and participate vicariously in the whole purposive effort that goes into creating and maintaining a system for directing human conduct by rules.[23]

The purposes of a given law or set of law's (which are not necessarily the purposes of lawmakers), combined with an understanding of the social context in which a given law is operating are but some of the resources at the lawyer's disposal.[24] Again, the assumption that the application of pre-existing norms is itself a source of stability stands in need of qualification. It is to this issue that I now turn.

[20] Holmes, 'The Path of Law', above n 11, at 457.

[21] I borrow this term from Frederick Schauer. See F Schauer, *Thinking Like a Lawyer* (Cambridge, MA, Harvard University Press, 2009).

[22] See ch 5, specifically my discussion of the certainty thesis.

[23] L Fuller, *The Morality of Law*, revised edn (New Haven, Yale University Press, 1969) 106–07. See ch 2.

[24] See ch 2.

III. BETWEEN CHAOS AND LEGALITY: THE SOURCES OF CERTAINTY

If we return for a final time to *Practical Reason and Norms*, and specifically to the distinction between legal systems and systems of absolute discretion, we find another feature of functioning legal regimes identified by Raz that is worthy of further consideration. Despite the good intentions of judges in discretionary systems, Raz asserts that the end result is chaos. By taking each case on its own terms rather than applying pre-existing norms, the settled expectations of the population become unhinged, leaving the good citizens of Raz's imaginary society with insufficient resources to determine how the power of the state will be exercised in the future.

Significantly, a functioning legal system allows citizens to do something that is vitally important for them individually and for society collectively: they can choose to live within law's bounds. In other words, a functioning legal system creates a space for self-directed action.[25] The key contrast at this juncture is not between wicked legal systems and their benevolent counterparts, but between legality and a Kafkaesque reality where power is exercised in a manner that is arbitrary and unpredictable from the perspective of the citizen. The possibility of being able to choose to be a law-abiding citizen is important at an individual level and at an institutional level. Something is wrong when people who are trying to abide by law's demands find themselves on the wrong side of the divide.

Raz's implicit message – that there is a link between law and rational agency – is an important one, but his explanation of this link is marred by two errors. First, he assumes that judicial discretion is the source of this crippling uncertainty. However, once it becomes clear that discretionary activities are not only exercised by imaginary judges, but are instead a common feature of functioning legal systems, then a new explanation of the link between law and order is required. Second, while a system of absolute discretion only exists in a fictitious world of Raz's own invention, the Kafkaesque state of confusion is a very real problem that societies exhibit to varying degrees. When we begin to reflect on the actual sources of confusion we are quickly led into the territory of the ideal of the rule of law.

Lon Fuller helps us to articulate that ideal and offers readers a more accurate assessment of the variables that can contribute to the state of uncertainty. Writing on the heels of the rise and fall of National Socialism, Fuller was concerned about the abuses of law that transpired under the Nazi regime. He was not, of course, only interested in the particulars of Nazi rule; he also wanted to

[25] See NE Simmonds, *Law as a Moral Idea* (New York, Oxford University Press, 2007); K Rundle, *Forms Liberate: Reclaiming the Legal Philosophy of Lon L Fuller* (Oxford, Hart Publishing, 2012).

say something about the nature of law more generally. Such an exploration of the ways in which the Nazis used (and misused) law highlights the inherent limits of law, limits that are beyond the control of legal officials. To illustrate this point, Fuller introduces us to the fictional King Rex. Like Raz's well-intentioned judge who works in his hypothetical system of absolute discretion, Rex also has noble aims – he simply happens to be thoroughly incompetent. His eight attempts to implement legal rules are marked by eight glaring mistakes: Rex enacts a secret code; a retroactive code; a set of rules that are impossible to follow; a set of rules that are radically uncertain; a set of rules that lack generality; a set of rules that is enforced in an incongruent manner; an ever-changing set of rules; and finally, a set of conflicting directives. These mistakes manifest themselves in a failure on his part to rule via law and in most cases a failure to rule full stop.

The extreme nature of Rex's failures has an unintended consequence for Fuller: it appears to saddle him with a positivistic understanding of law, despite the fact he is one of Hart's famous adversaries. The model is positivistic in the sense that law is presented as a set of norms laid down by a ruler that guides the conduct of the population. This point seems to be confirmed by Fuller's own words:

> Surely the very essence of the Rule of Law is that in acting upon the citizen . . . a government will faithfully apply rules previously declared as those to be followed by the citizen and as being determinative of his rights and duties. If the Rule of Law does not mean this, it means nothing.[26]

Despite appearances, Fuller's understanding of the rule of law as it is presented in his parable of Rex is agnostic between competing conceptions of law on at least two fronts: first, whether the eight desiderata mean that law has inherent moral value or whether the eight principles are merely principles of efficient rule; and second, whether law is best understood as a set of factually ascertainable norms or as an ideal of the rule of law. It is the second point that I will focus on.[27] In so doing, I show that although Fuller's story about Rex is wholly silent on the function of the judge, a more complete account of law emerges when Fuller's other writings are mined for insights. The requirement that law is public is itself an aspirational principle and not simply an aspect of law's positive existence. This aspect of legality comes to light when we explore a number of examples – examples that also point to a myriad of sources of certainty.

[26] L Fuller, *The Morality of Law*, above n 23, at 209–10.

[27] For insight into the first issue, see the most recent exchange between NE Simmonds and M Kramer. M Kramer, 'For the Record: A Final Reply to NE Simmonds' (2011) 56 *Am J Juris* 115: NE Simmonds 'Kramer's High Noon' (2011) 56 *Am J Juris* 135.

The requirements that the law must be public, general and certain (to some degree) are not features of law that stand or fall with the existence (or non-existence) of positive law, as is often assumed.[28] Rather they are best understood as principles of legality as such. In order to ensure that law is a public institution, the demand that the law must be general may have to be breached; at other times, a principled decision (rather than one wherein the positive law is applied as written) re-enforces the idea that law is public. To illustrate this point, I will consider certain examples that Fuller explores in his writings – scenarios in which the positive law is shown to have a limited effect on the determination as to what the best legal outcome should be. Not only do I wish to suggest that the idea that law is public is an ideal of legality that can be pursued in the courtroom and understood by legal philosophers. This discussion seeks to pierce the sharp dichotomy, often appealed to, between the certainty that the positive law can engender and the justice that can be brought about by offering a ruling that appeals to principles like justice and fairness.

Consider Fuller's example of a judge who accepted bribes in a number of cases involving patents, a breach of his legal duties that was only discovered seven years after the fact. Fuller insists that it is not the job of the judge to rectify this wrong, but lawmakers could and did respond. The United States Congress enacted special legislation extending the life of the patents by seven years.[29] Fuller notes that although this is an imperfect solution, given that advances in technology would decrease the amount of profit incurred, all things considered it is still a desirable outcome. [30] This is because this particular statute reaffirms rather than detracts from the public nature of law, notwithstanding the fact that the statute under consideration was directed at specific individuals and thus it lacked the generality that is usually a hallmark of law.

Although the corrupt judge had given greater weight to his private ends over those of his public office, the statute acted as a mechanism by which to re-affirm the idea that legal norms apply equally to all. Once again it is clear that law's public nature is an idea: more precisely, it is an ideal. The realization of this ideal is of great practical importance in this instance, since the threat of official corruption is one of the real-world instances in which power is wielded in an arbitrary manner from the perspective of the citizen. If the corruption is widespread, then the citizens may be tossed into a Kafkaesque reality where they may find themselves on the wrong side of the law, but by no fault of their own.

[28] J Raz, *The Authority of the Law: Essays on Law and Morality* (New York, Oxford University Press, 1979) 31.

[29] L Fuller, *The Anatomy of the Law* (Harmondsworth, Penguin Books, 1971) 25.

[30] *Ibid*, 24.

Not only might the generality of law be sacrificed in order to uphold the public nature of law, we might find that the application of the positive law may detract from the public and general nature of law. For instance, judicial decisions in which judges fail to apply the law in a given instance do not necessarily mean that the public nature of legal norms is being sacrificed to the values of justice and fairness, as is often thought. Yet another example from Fuller's writings illustrates this point. Fuller introduces us to Mr X, a house-to-house canvasser who 'claims that on 10 February he slipped and sprained his ankle on Mr Y's sidewalk because it was covered with ice'.[31] Mr Y is unaware of the incident until Mr X calls him threatening to sue. The relevant statute states that one has to give notice of such intentions no more than 12 days after the incident, but Mr X is late. Now, as Fuller, notes, if Mr X argues that he is late because he was too busy to take the necessary actions – few of us would have sympathy because we are all busy to some degree or other. Insofar as we wish to take legal action, we must follow the same rules that hold for everyone. The system is a public system that is not supposed to bend to accommodate all our personal activities and preferences.

Fuller then asks us to consider another possibility. What if the accident is the reason for the delay? Let us imagine the very real possibility that when Mr X fell he was rendered unconscious for a period that was greater than 12 days.[32] Here Mr X seems to have an excellent excuse: he could not have been in contact sooner precisely for the reason that the legal action was necessary. In other words, but for Y's slippery walk, the need for legal action would not have arisen, nor would the delay in notice (and the breach of that statute). The reasonable limits of the law can only be seen when the purpose of the norm is considered and held up against the fact scenario.

When the principled limits of the law come into view, we can see how we are constantly taken beyond the confines of positive law without sacrificing the public nature of law. The official recognition of exceptions can serve as a way to preserve, and not undermine, the public nature of law. Furthermore, to accuse the judge of acting as a quasi-legislator would be misplaced in this instance. The claim that the legislature should have drafted a better law is unpersuasive: lawmakers chose 12 days, but they could have chosen any other number and the same scenario could arise. A coma can, after all, last for an indefinite period of time. It seems absurd to allow Mr Y to escape from the reach of the law because of the severity of Mr X's injury. The result would be absurd precisely because of what we expect the law to do in this case: protect us from unnecessary risks imposed by others. It is an understanding of the underlying purpose of this area of law which may (and should) lead a judge to carve out a principled exception.

[31] *Ibid*, 57–58.
[32] *Ibid*, 58.

Moreover, once it becomes apparent that the expectations of the citizenry need not (and likely will not in this instance) stand and fall with the positive law (eg with regard to the stipulated 12-day limitation period), then it quickly becomes clear that judges are not always faced with the stark choice between making a principled decision in the pursuit of justice in the case before them and preserving certainty by applying pre-existing legal norms. After all, it is unlikely that Mr X will have organized his life around this particular law – he will surely become aware of its presence if he is forced to hire a lawyer (who will then argue that this law should be applied). But the thought that failing to apply this law would thwart the populations' ability to plan is unconvincing on this occasion.[33]

Consider another much discussed case that illustrates this same point: *Riggs v Palmer*.[34] The defendant, Elmer E Palmer, was set to inherit money upon the event of his grandfather's death. Elmer knew this and he proceeded to murder his grandfather in order to get this money – a crime for which he was convicted. The question before the court was whether Elmer was entitled to inherit despite his conviction. The law governing inheritance was clear: there was no provision prohibiting a murderer from inheriting. The dissent insisted that this fact should be determinative.[35] The majority, however, held that Elmer should not be able to inherit, citing the principle that 'no man should profit from his own wrong'.[36]

Dworkin points to this case to shore up his view that law is about principles in addition to rules.[37] Yet, there is another lesson to be learned. We can ask, for instance, what the general population would have expected the outcome

[33] Fuller does not draw out all of the implications implicit in this example. He uses this example to make a slightly different point. He wishes to use this case to demonstrate how two conceptions of justice can come into conflict in any given case. What he terms 'legal justice' involves a commitment to applying pre-existing legal rules (the preservation of certainty, discussed above, can be viewed as an element of this kind of justice). Conversely, the justice of dispensation is 'a justice ready to bend the letter of the law to accomplish a just result'. In the background of Fuller's distinction is yet another familiar contrast between the collective and the individual. Legal justice, as defined by Fuller, captures the idea that 'the law must be the same for all'; while the justice of dispensation stands for the principle that 'the law must not itself become an instrument of injustice'. In order to ensure that this does not happen, judges must bend the letter of the law in order to ensure that justice is done in an individual instance (often ensuring that an individual is taken care of) even if this means that the collective vision of legal justice must be compromised in a given instance. What I am suggesting is that such a contrast is too strong. In Fuller's example of Mr X and Mr Y we do not find an instance where a judge must sacrifice what is best for the collective in order to do what is best for the individual. Instead, I have argued that enabling Mr X to recover will serve both the collective and the individual even though the decision would not be based on pre-existing positive rules, but on a conception of the purpose of those rules.

[34] *Riggs v Palmer* [1889] 115 NY 506.

[35] *Ibid.* The dissent argued that, 'one should not be punished beyond the ways specified in the statute'.

[36] *Ibid.*

[37] R Dworkin, *Law's Empire* (Cambridge, MA, Harvard University Press, 1986) 15–20.

of the case to be. It is likely that most people would expect Elmer to lose his share in the inheritance for the fairly obvious reason that he murdered his grandfather. The expectations of the public are easily traced to a more foundational norm – the prohibition against murder. The power of the principle that 'no one should profit from their own wrong' is, in this instance, parasitic on this normative force of the prohibition against murder. The principle is particularly powerful in this context because the profit aimed at in this case was the very thing that motivated Elmer to commit the murder.[38] Given that it is likely that many citizens in the wider population will side with the majority on this matter, a principled decision can reinforce, rather than detract from, the expectations of the populace. In this instance, certainty has not been sacrificed on the altar of justice.

Notice, also, that the ruling in *Riggs* reinforces the idea that law is a public system of norms. While the accused might have been disappointed that his clever crime did not produce the anticipated windfall, he was likely not to have been surprised by the outcome. If Elmer had been successful in court, he would have been taking advantage of a loophole in the law. His private interest in attaining money would have successfully trumped the public dimension of norms. Moreover, had the court ruled in his favour, the legislature would surely have enacted a law to ensure that this perverse incentive was eliminated. While there may not be a single answer to every legal problem, there is but one answer to this particular legal problem. The value of the judiciary (rather than Parliament) rendering this particular judgment is also clear: it prevents an act of injustice from being realized in this case while simultaneously affirming the expectations of the population at large. Since all loopholes cannot be identified in advance, it is reasonable to expect judges to close such avenues of abuse when the opportunity arises.[39] The expectations of the citizenry are generated by the interconnected matrix of norms, and thus so-called 'activist' decisions may work to preserve law's public dimension and indeed, may work to promote rather than undermine certainty. In sum, *Riggs* does not stand on the side of justice, over and against the value of legal certainty, stability and predictability that would result with the strict application of black letter law.[40]

Notice that the reflections above are at once of philosophical and practical significance.[41] An understanding of how law works on the ground can (and

[38] Compare this with instances when the convicted criminal profits from his wrong by writing a book about his life.

[39] Note that I am not supposing that there is always a sharp line between what I have called 'loopholes' and 'judicial activism'. Moreover, what counts as judicial activism is theory dependent. For an illuminating discussion of this point in the American context, see R Kozel, 'Settled Verses Right: Constitutional Method and the Path of Precedent' (2013) 91 *Texas Law Review* 7.

[40] Compare with Schauer, *Thinking Like a Lawyer,* above n 21, at 229.

[41] See ch 2 for a defence of this line of thought.

should) inform our theoretical understanding of law; a good theory can, in turn, help practitioners better understand the nature of the problems and potential solutions that they grapple with on a daily basis. A careful analysis of real-world scenarios can both deepen our philosophical understanding of law whilst providing assistance to practitioners who may wish to reflect upon the values at stake in the decision-making process. Under what conditions might the value of certainty stand in competition with that of justice? When must one sacrifice the generality of legal norms in order to ensure that the public nature of law is upheld? I have suggested that one can only answer this question by considering a host of factors, thereby necessitating the abandonment of the assumption that applying positive law promotes certainty.[42] A misdiagnosis of any given problem can easily generate potential solutions that will hinder rather than help bring about the desired result.[43]

IV. CONTENT MATTERS

Fuller's reflections bring into the picture two things that certain modern positivist theories tend to overlook: the relationship between legal norms and law's subjects and the relationship between norms themselves. In other words, Fuller explores law's efficacy and law's systematic nature – aspects of legality that require the legal philosopher to pay close attention to the content of norms and to the social (and legal) environment in which they are meant to operate. It is not surprising to discover that both of these aspects of legality are rarely discussed by positivists, who tend to focus on the existence conditions of legal systems and the validity of individual norms.[44]

Consider the basic idea that the rules that are communicated to the population are capable of being followed. To achieve this end, the lawmaker must respect both the limits of what is possible for humans to do and the limits of what law is capable of achieving in any given social context. A lawmaker cannot, for instance, demand that people fly under their own power when travelling in public spaces and expect compliance. A law that takes this shape would be little more than an excuse to arrest anyone and everyone who ventures outside their respective places of residence. We can rephrase this point. While the law can, in principle, have any content, it cannot insofar as it is

[42] For a discussion of the variables that contribute to certainty see M Martin, a book review of Peter Cane (ed), *The Hart-Fuller debate in the Twenty-first Century* (July 2012) 4 *Ethics* 801. P Yowell, 'Legislation, Common Law and the Virtue of Clarity' in R Ekins (ed), *Modern Challenges to the Rule of Law* (Wellington, LexisNexis, 2011).

[43] Fuller, *Anatomy of the Law*, above n 29, at 59.

[44] Raz, *Authority of the Law*, above n 28, 88. Raz argues that the very task of the legal philosopher is to articulate the existence conditions for legal systems. His comments about efficacy are remarkably terse.

expected to do work. It is the work that law is expected to do which places limits on it.

Lawmakers who rely on acceptance rather than fear must pay heed to the context in which the law is meant to operate insofar as they hope that the new law will be internalized by the population, ensuring the continued efficacy of the system. Jeremy Waldron explains that 'legislation is not just the addition of a rule to the heap of laws; it is a modification of the corpus juris', adding that 'each bill must be framed in a way that pays attention to the juridical (as well as the social) environment in which it is to operate'.[45] If a new law is going to do the important practical work that it is crafted to do, then it must fit within a system of laws that have a certain relationship to the broader social landscape and to other relevant norms.

The limits that must be understood and respected by lawmakers are of at least two sorts – those imposed by the legal form itself (Fuller's eight desiderata) and those determined by variables of the cultural and social sort. In despotic regimes, such limits will likely prove to be less important. As Simmonds rightly explains, there may be good reasons for self-interested rulers to breach any one of the eight constraints.[46] Likewise with the socio-cultural variables: when the sword is the primary mechanism through which peace is secured, rulers will not have to think as much about the social context in which any new norms will have to operate: when fear rather than acceptance is the primary mode of operation, the law becomes a more flexible tool of power.[47] When we focus on this point, the idea of law as a set of content-independent reasons for action becomes all the more plausible in such systems. But what is obscured in the process is the way that law works in moderate regimes. Again, (at least) two accounts of law's ability to guide conduct must be articulated, not one.

The deeply obscuring effect of the positivist lens can be seen if we reflect on Raz's idea of 'directed powers'. As I noted in chapter two, the idea is introduced to account for the existence of value-laden terms in the positive law. Such values, Raz argues, are not part of the law, but rather lawmakers are directing judges to appeal to extra-legal considerations. The idea of a 'directed power' captures the notion that those who make law can intentionally direct those who apply the law (ie judges) to appeal to moral norms. Not only do the intentions of legislators become extremely important, but the legislature, from this perspective, appears to have unlimited power – they can direct judges to apply the law *or* to make moral judgments. Power is exercised in a top-down fashion, with the legislature at the top of the hierarchy. The shadow of Austin's

[45] J Waldron, 'The Concept and the Rule of Law' (2008) 43 *Georgia Law Review* 1, 34.

[46] Simmonds, *Law as a Moral Idea*, above n 25, at 85–88.

[47] This does not mean that law is equally serviceable for good ends and evil ones. See NE Simmonds, *Law as a Moral Idea*, above n 25.

command theory looms behind the technical language here. The result is a misleading representation of the practice as it suggests that the only constraints on the judiciary are placed there by the legislature and that there are no constraints on legislators that are built into the practice of law-making itself.

Consider another basic insight that Fuller offers us into how legal systems function: legal systems should be free of contradictions to the extent that it is possible. The reason for this is straightforward, as it is impossible for citizens to abide by contradictory instructions. As the King Rex example illustrates, conflicts of this kind are a problem because law is supposed to be able to guide conduct. If citizens are supposed to abide by the law, then the law must not instruct them to act in incompatible ways. Here we have come across another real-world variable that has the potential to lead us from a state of legality to one of Kafkaesque uncertainty. The principle of non-contradiction that underlies such functioning points us to a consideration of the systematic nature of law (specifically the relationship between legal norms and law's subjects), which is fundamentally different from the consideration of individual norms in isolation in reference to either a master rule or the reasoning process of an individual. This is an important shift, as it moves us away from the ground on which positivists are most comfortable. Notice that a consideration of Fuller's eight desiderata also threatens the value neutrality coveted by Hartian positivists. It is not the case that legal norms, by the sheer fact that they were enacted, are public, prospective, or conflict-free. Rather these requirements are ideals that can be realized or undermined by officials. Pavlos Eleftheriadis is correct to suggest that if one's concept of law is going to be 'normatively inert', positivists should include within the rubric 'law' an idea of a secretive and unpredictable order; a point, he notes, that some modern-day positivists happily admit.[48] Gardner, for instance, contends that

> a legal norm that is retroactive, radically uncertain, and devoid of all generality, and hence dramatically deficient relative to the ideal of the rule of law, is no less valid *qua* legal, than one that is prospective, admirably certain, and perfectly general.[49]

If we are concerned with the validity of a single norm, we can concede Gardner's point. However, it is hard to imagine a legal system that exists in which most or all of the norms are retroactive, radically uncertain, or secretive. The intelligibility of such systems is wholly dependent on our understanding of functioning legal systems. In other words, it is by interpreting a healthy legal order using the focal case method that enables us to identify

[48] P Eleftheriadis, 'Austin and the Electors' (2011) 24 *Canadian Journal of Law and Jurisprudence* 450.

[49] J Gardner, '5 1/2 Myths about Legal Positivism' (2001) 46 *American Journal of Jurisprudence* 199, 209.

dysfunctional instances of a kind.[50] Ironically, positivist theories are attractive to many precisely because they promise to conceptualize all of our shared intuitions about law, but by the end of the analysis we are being asked to step away from all that is familiar.

Fuller understands what positivism struggles to make sense of: that law is always in the process of becoming. However, it is not simply becoming what we make it by serving our chosen ends. It has its own limits: limits which must be understood if we are to understand law; limits that must be respected if we are to live under law's rule.

The parable of Rex is instructive in yet another sense. Rex is completely incompetent, but often the real concern is not radical incompetence (although this is also a worry), but intentional abuse. This is a real-world worry, and it is one of the variables that can undermine the rule of law and replace it with unilateral exercises of arbitrary power. Consider once again the example of a corrupt judge. If accepting bribes becomes a normal occurrence in a given society, then it is clear that citizens cannot expect a fair outcome, which in turn will likely undermine public trust. When trust is undermined in a significant way, people will be wary about relying on the legal system to sort out any of the conflicts they might have. The probable outcome of widespread corruption is, in all likelihood, going to be an increase in acts of extra-legal violence between citizens.[51]

If we compare healthy legal systems where trust is present to failed or failing systems, we can identify another aspect of legality: namely, a functioning legal system can cut through and thus transcend the friend/enemy dichotomy. Fuller argues that legal systems create a new category of person: the friendly adversary.[52] This term captures the legal relationship between people and points to something vitally important that a functioning legal system achieves, even if it is not an end aimed at by officials. When the dispute-resolution mechanism is working as it should, it is able to help facilitate smooth interactions between people. In particular, the instinct for revenge is channelled and transformed in the process. Conversely, if corruption is rampant, the friend/enemy divide is not transcended, only reshaped. Your friend is any official who will take your money and deliver the result you ask for. Your enemy is the opposing party in the dispute as well as the official who took money from your opponent. The idea that there is a link between legality and civilization therefore contains at least a grain of truth – a truth wholly hidden by the positivist account.[53]

[50] Finnis, *Natural Law and Natural Rights*, above n 7, at 9.
[51] Consider the case of Bolivia: www.economist.com/node/21542421.
[52] Fuller, *The Morality of Law*, above n 29, at 112.
[53] Contra Raz, the rule of law is more than a negative virtue. See Raz, *The Authority of Law*, above n 28, at 224. The possibility that law (in a healthy legal regime) is *more than a sum of its parts* is

Once this aspect of living under law comes into view, so too do the precise ways in which law can fail. For instance, even in so-called healthy legal regimes, the friend/enemy distinction may not be transcended in full. Lawmakers may use the law as a tool of discrimination or subjugation. Slavery in the United States and apartheid in South Africa are examples of this kind of failure. Law can also be used as an instrument of revenge. When procedural safeguards are loosened, even in the service of justice, the outcome threatens to look more like revenge than the distinct form of justice that law is uniquely positioned to offer. Any given system can fall short of the ideal of the rule of law, but it is the ideal as such that allows us to understand law's potential and the risk of failure. Moreover, when attention is focused on the real-world causes of uncertainty, a theorist's gaze is directed at the very same issues that lawyers, politicians and citizens face.

Notice that I did not set out to craft a theory about the ideal of the rule of law; rather, I simply set out to offer some answers to the question that animates Raz's early work. Nevertheless, the close connection between the rule of law considered as an ideal and the actual existence of a functioning legal system now comes into view, as do some of the additional shortcomings of the positivist's method. For instance, we can ask, does corruption undermine the rule of law, or the governance of law full stop? If one sets out in search of the common ground between legal systems, we would not identify this particular question as relevant to our enquiry as it is not fully realized in all societies that might qualify as having legal systems. This feature only comes into focus when we consider the differences between flourishing systems and their dysfunctional counterparts. A study of good order must itself inform our study of order.

Likewise, a study of order can inform our understanding of good order, but many lessons are left unlearned if we accept the assumptions that structure the current debate. For instance, if we return to the way in which law works in the world, the coercive dimension of law calls for further exploration. The fact that legally impermissible behaviour is often met with some form of coercion is one of the reasons that reflecting on the nature of law is a markedly important task. Modern day jurisprudes tend to treat the coercive dimension of law as a contingent and not a necessary feature of law. The mere mention of the term 'coercion' is usually met with at least one of the following arguments. First, it is asserted that a society of angels would need norms to co-ordinate their behaviour, but they would not require coercive sanctions to ensure that the law's aims were achieved. Second, it is possible to conceive of a system in

hidden from view if one conceives of law at the outset as nothing more than an aggregate of norms. It is not clear whether corruption (which can take many forms) undermines the ideal of the rule of law, or whether it also undermines the claim that a full-fledged legal system exists. I contend that it does both. As Rundle notes, Fuller was also critical of Hart for failing to make sense of legal pathology within his framework. See Rundle, *Forms Liberate*, above n 25, at 29.

which our rights and duties are delineated in a court of law, but the state does not then proceed to enforce these rights.[54]

These thought experiments are relied upon to determine what is 'conceptually possible'. It is at this moment that philosophical reflections enter the realm of the imagination, revealing the unbounded nature of the project of 'conceptual analysis' as currently construed. While imagined examples can be of great use, it depends upon how they are utilized. They can, for instance, bring into view the principled limits of the law, or (as with good utopian literature) they can cast light on features of the human condition that are often overlooked or misunderstood.[55] But the example of a society of angels is used in this instance to achieve the opposite: it is used to circumscribe the sphere of jurisprudential enquiry and effectively erase the very possibility of reflecting on what is surely a key aspect of *human* life under law. Moreover, the mere fact that some laws 'enable' us to do certain things and seem to exist without the support of traditional coercive mechanisms, does not mean that the systems can exist without the support of coercive force. While each individual norm need not be backed by coercion, coercion is certainly a necessary element of human legal *systems*. The system as a whole requires it.

If we press on the idea of coercion, what is quickly revealed is the value-laden foundation of law. As Raymond Plant illustrates, we view the quintessential legal sanctions as coercive precisely because they involve the denial of goods that the vast majority of us hold dear: life, liberty or property.[56] (Monty Python's comic take on the Spanish Inquisition plays with this very theme). Law lives upon a foundation of shared values, the extent to which any given society is permeated by disagreement remains a question worth exploring rather than presupposition made about the nature of modern society, or society in general. Disagreement is present, no doubt, but the nature of and extent of this disagreement must be explored.[57] The creation myth outlined in the opening pages of this chapter which presupposes that law is the force that binds us and prevents us from descending into chaos must be rethought. The way that traditions, habits, practices, and shared values contribute to the creation and maintenance of order must be part of the story told, at least when we are thinking about moderate regimes. Discussions of human nature and law are parsed at great expense.

[54] J Raz, *Practical Reason and Norms* (Oxford, Oxford University Press, 1999) 158–59. Fred Schauer's forthcoming book is a welcome departure from the norm. See F Schauer, *The Force of Law* (Cambridge, MA, Harvard University Press, forthcoming 2014).

[55] See Book Four of Swift's *Gulliver's Travels* prompts us to think about what we mean by 'reason'. J Swift, *Gulliver's Travels* (New York, Knopf, 1991).

[56] R Plant, 'Freedom, Coercion, Necessary Goods and the Rule of Law' (comments) (2011) 2 *Jurisprudence* 1, 10.

[57] Coyle, *Dimensions of Politics and English Jurisprudence*, above n 17, at 55.

It is also by attending to the way in which coercive force is exercised that we can begin to evaluate certain jurisprudential propositions about the nature of law. Raz argues that law is fundamentally a tool that is equally serviceable for good ends and wicked ones.[58] Against this view, Nigel Simmonds offers a powerful argument grounded in actualities and not conceptual possibilities. While his argument is lengthy and involved, one of his central points is that rulers who wish to realize their wicked ends have good reason to employ extra-legal violence.[59] When coercion is used by the rulers in accordance with law rather than in extra-legal ways, citizens enjoy freedom from the power of another. Simmonds gives voice to the commonly held view that

> a moral ideal, representing the very antithesis of force and arbitrary power, even while we are uneasily aware that legal systems can sometimes appear to be no more than complex institutional systems wherein the rule of force is made more perfect . . .[60]

While this is but a snap-shot of a Simmonds's position, it is immediately apparent how a consideration of the coercive force in real-world contexts helps to identify key questions that must be grappled with if one hopes to understand the nature of law. Only if we begin to reflect on the coercive aspect of law can we begin to make sense of the shape of, and potential value of, life under law.

Getting the philosophical account right can have significant practical consequences. If we follow the positivists and conceive of law as a tool that is capable of serving both good ends and wicked ones, then we will fear its force in certain contexts but we may also be led to place our hopes in its emancipatory power. While many positivists deny that law has any inherent connection with justice, to think of law as a tool suggests that we only need to select the correct ends if we wish to use law's power for good. However, if we overestimate law's ability to change the world, we may exacerbate rather than eradicate the very inequalities and injustices that we set out to correct.[61]

There is yet another unintended consequence of thinking about law through a Hartian lens. Notice, also that the evaluations that Hart's theory facilitates are remarkably blunt. Recall that Hart urges us to separate the question of what law is from the moral evaluation of what it ought to be. We are left to point to Nazi regimes as examples of bad law, and uphold modern Western legal systems as examples of morally good law. The worry, which is a real one,

[58] Raz, *The Authority of Law*, above n 28, at 226.
[59] Simmonds, *Law as a Moral Idea,* above n 25, at 85–88.
[60] *Ibid*, 5.
[61] For a discussion of a similar point in the context of international law, see M Martin, 'International Criminal Law: Between Utopian Dreams and Political Realities' in *Rethinking Criminal Law Theory: New Canadian Perspectives in the Philosophy of Domestic, Transnational, and International Criminal Law* (Oxford, Hart Publishing, 2011) 249–66.

is that the positivist approach reifies the status quo, both by crystallizing current forms of social organizing by labelling them as fully-fledged legal systems, and by generating (albeit unintentionally) such blunt assessments.[62] Conversely, Fuller's approach casts a light on the variables that stand in need of consideration if we are going to begin to understand law, thereby offering us a fine lens through which to reflect on and evaluate life under law in all regimes. The line between illumination and distortion may prove to be a thin one and hence legal philosophers must be vigilant.

The version of focal case method that I have been employing takes us directly to the doorstep of the natural lawyer – the territory that positivists work so hard to avoid.[63] As we have seen through the analysis of Raz's work, it can only be avoided by excluding certain questions or by offering incomplete answers. For their part, positivists characterize natural law theory as standing for the claim that moral values are included in the criteria for validity for law. Even if this is an accurate representation of a strain of natural law thinking, which is itself doubtful, it is now clear that the questions that natural lawyers grapple with are manifold and extremely difficult to evade. The alternative is to artificially halt enquiries in the hopes of maintaining the status quo.[64] However, the goal of articulating a value-neutral conception of law is a remarkably arduous one to meet. Consider, for instance, the commonly held view that law is conventional, a view supported by positivists of all stripes, is not a mere fact about law – it reflects a fundamental value commitment. Once this becomes clear, the nature of the challenge facing the modern-day positivist becomes evident.

V. IS LAW MERELY CONVENTIONAL?

It is commonly assumed (and asserted) that all law is conventional. This is presented as a bare fact, and it is one that coexists quite comfortably alongside positivism. However, this is a claim that cannot be assumed; it must be argued for, and this takes us back into the territory of the natural lawyer. It is a path that cannot be avoided. The reason why the conventional status of law requires argument becomes clearer when we explore the meaning of the word 'positive'. This term has two meanings that pervade the history of jurisprudential thought but are rarely discussed by modern legal positivists. In part,

[62] Moreover, as Finnis correctly notes, circumscribing the terrain of jurisprudential enquiry in this way is artificial. See Finnis, *Natural Law and Natural Rights,* above n 7, at 357–58. Finnis also eloquently explains the connection between legal theory and moral and political theory.

[63] For another (more well-known) version, see Finnis, *Natural Law and Natural Rights,* above n 7, at 15. Finnis places the practically reasonable person at the centre.

[64] See ch 5.

this is because modern-day positivists view law through the lens of their seemingly proprietary interpretation of the term 'positive'.

JB Murphy identifies a deep ambiguity in the term 'positive'. In one sense, it is sometimes used to capture the idea that the norm was 'deliberately laid down' or 'posited'. Law that is posited is opposed to law that 'grows up' over time, such as customary law. When one states that a given norm is positive in this sense, it is a descriptive claim about the origin of the norm. The second meaning of 'positive' is very different from the first: the term may also mean 'arbitrary', in the sense that it could have been otherwise. When used in this manner, law that is 'positive' stands in contrast to law that is 'natural'. To state that a given norm is 'positive' in this sense is not merely a descriptive claim about the source of the norm, but rather it is a *normative* claim about its content.[65] This poses a problem for certain legal positivists. We can see precisely why this is so when we recast these ideas in reference to the claim that law is conventional.

There is a distinction between what is merely conventional (arbitrary) and what is natural within the category of positive (posited) law. By way of illustration, consider Hart's discussion of the minimum moral content of natural law. Here he is distinguishing between laws that are natural (must be present) and those that are merely conventional (in the sense of 'arbitrary', or could have been otherwise). According to Hart, laws prohibiting murder and theft (for instance) are 'natural'.[66] Hart implicitly acknowledges that the argument he is making is not descriptive in nature as he proceeds to support his position by appealing to the value of survival.[67] Whether the dividing line is best drawn here (encompassing only the value of survival) or elsewhere is up for debate, but the debate is inherently normative. In addition, even laws that deal with murder and theft may have different content in different societies, this does not mean the laws in question are *merely* conventional, it simply means that natural laws can have a conventional dimension. Thus, even if all laws have a conventional dimension this does not establish the claim that all law is conventional.

The deep ambiguity at the heart of the claim that all law is conventional is now visible. If one uses the term 'conventional' to signal the idea that all law is positive law (ie posited), then this thesis is vulnerable to counter-examples: common law and customary law are sources of law that grew up over time (consequently the claim that all law is conventional is demonstrably false insofar as it is forwarded to be a descriptor). Conversely, if the term 'conventional' is used to indicate that the content of law is arbitrary and not natural, then

[65] JB Murphy, *The Philosophy of Positive Law: Foundations of Jurisprudence* (New Haven, Yale University Press, 2005) 5.
[66] Hart, *The Concept of Law,* above n 2, at 194.
[67] *Ibid*, 191.

this is a normative claim and not a descriptive statement. Any pretentions that one's theory is non-normative, or merely conceptual are sacrificed. Indeed, to work to establish that law is conventional in this second (normative) sense requires the legal philosopher to wade into waters that have been travelled down before – the history of philosophy teaches us that claims of this sort must be supported by an understanding of the human condition more generally. The Hartian project is thought to prescind from these earlier debates, setting out a theoretical path whereby legal philosophers can focus on making sense of law without becoming ensnarled in the morally charged debates that have pre-occupied philosophers for thousands of years. But the status of law in general (or any given laws in particular) as merely conventional or natural (or having dimensions of both) is one that cannot be permanently excised.

It is apparent that a legal philosopher who declares that law is conventional has found herself on the horns of a dilemma. The dilemma is a familiar one: the positivist can opt for the descriptive version of the claim, but this version is vulnerable to counter-examples (eg the common law); alternatively, she can opt for the version of the claim that is not vulnerable to counter-examples, but in this form the claim is inherently normative. Once again we discover that the Hartian method has betrayed its devoted adherents. The third option is silence, but silence for the sake of the preservation of a (contestable) methodology is to subvert the philosophic spirit before it can take flight.

While modern-day positivism held out a promise to learn about law, the tract of land that forms the positivists' kingdom is far smaller than was once believed, and the set of questions compatible with its method is far narrower than Hart would have hoped. We do not learn about law by reflecting on our own reflections, hoping to crown the illusive victor, or by creating imaginary societies where conceptual possibilities take our attention away from real-world problems. Nor does law reveal her many secrets to those who spend their time patrolling the boundaries of value-neutral concepts – expelling questions, theories, philosophical traditions or thinkers that threaten to bring in values. Instead, the legal philosopher should keep a steady gaze on the world and work to make sense of what she sees. This task quickly reconnects the work of the philosopher with the work of legal practitioners and the worries of the layman. It also places her in conversation with the great thinkers of yesteryear. Legal philosophy, on this understanding, does not pursue truth *or* practical benefits – these options appear to be mutually exclusive only if we see law through the prism of positivism. Rather, a better understanding of the nature of law can provide a bit of light for those living and working in the trenches.

7

Conclusion: The Raz–Postema Debate Deconstructed

BY LOOKING AT the problems raised by Gerald Postema in 'Law's Autonomy and Public Practical Reason', and Raz's reply, we are able to gain an understanding of Raz's thinking on the relationship between the various elements of his theory. This exegetical task is invaluable in discharging the argumentative burden that the main theses of this book set forth. The central claims I have forwarded are as follows: (a) Raz's theory has changed over time, and (b) the resulting theory is not fully coherent. I am well aware that many jurisprudes (both defenders and critics of Raz) will resist the second, stronger claim.

While some readers might not object to the idea that Raz's thinking has developed over time (as this usually happens with any theorist), few would be inclined to accept that his theory has changed in so significant a way as to render it untenable. Indeed, Raz's defenders tend to argue that his theory does not actually contain serious tensions, but rather demonstrates his ability to combine so many seemingly disparate elements, thereby revealing Raz's great subtlety of mind. Raz's critics tend to be less generous with their accolades than his supporters, but they often agree with his supporters that his theory fits together coherently. Given the resistance that my argument will surely encounter from these defenders and critics alike, it is important to make readers aware of Raz's statements about the relationship between his various theses. A detailed summary of Raz's response to Postema will achieve this end.

Raz's views tend to be thought of as a series of theses that have become familiar ideas in the debate. What Postema is exploring and challenging, as we will see, is the foundation of these ideas. The detail with which both theorists discuss these issues speaks to the complexity and controversial nature of Raz's core theses. One of the central issues at the centre of the debate between Postema and Raz is whether or not Raz allocates a central function to law. Most of Postema's criticisms of Raz are valid only if Raz allocates law such an underpinning function. Raz's main strategy is to deflect Postema's complaints by denying that he defends the view that law has a central function, or that he is (or has even been) committed to the theses that Postema discusses.

Unfortunately for Raz, answering Postema's charges is not this simple. The problem is that the elements of Raz's theory in its original form in *Practical Reason and Norms* are interconnected in such a way that they cannot easily be individually altered. Thus, Raz cannot simply deflect Postema's complaints in the above manner – if he is to overcome them, he must respond at length by reconfiguring his entire theory. Suspicion is warranted as to whether this task is achievable: one of the central messages of this book is that Raz will be hard-pressed to reconfigure his theory to account for the nature of common law adjudication while still maintaining his exclusive legal positivist commitments.

LAW AS PUBLIC PRACTICAL REASON: RAZ VERSUS POSTEMA

Recall the vision of law that Postema believes Raz champions. It is a vision that sees the function of law as providing a public framework of practical reasons – practical reasons which enjoy autonomy. Such reasons are autonomous because citizens do not have to enter into political debate about the parameters of acceptable behaviour in order to determine the content of existing law. Postema begins by outlining a 'creation myth' which seeks to explain law and its role in society:

> Political authority and laws, Cicero tells us, were invented for the same reason: to establish and secure justice and equality of rights. When people were satisfied that this task could be accomplished by a single man, they accepted the rule of a king. However, they were forced to invent laws when they realized that they could not count on their kings being just. The special virtue of law, says Cicero, is that it is able to speak on matters of justice and rights to all citizens at all times with a single voice. In Pufendorf's version of this creation myth, royal faithlessness exposed not only the lack of royal accountability, but also, and more troubling, the people's inability to agree on standards by which to judge the king's justice. As their numbers increased, so too did the jarring dissonance of social life. People needed standards more dependable than the king's faulty sense of justice and more public than their particular and often dissonant judgments. The faithlessness of the king may have been the immediate problem, but the deeper need was to unify the judgment of the people, to enable them to speak the language of justice to each other in a single voice. Law taught them this language.[1]

Postema adds that such myths 'are told more to teach us about the nature of things than to teach us about their history'.[2] He then argues that this particular myth unites a host of philosophers who have written about law over the

[1] GJ Postema, 'Law's Autonomy and Public Practical Reason' in R George (ed), *The Autonomy of Law: Essays on Legal Positivism* (Oxford, Clarendon Press, 1996) 79 (footnote omitted). I quote this passage in ch 1 as well.

[2] *Ibid.*

centuries. The list stretches 'from Cicero to the present day, counting in its membership theorists as different as Aquinas and Bentham, Hobbes, Pufendorf, Locke and Hume, Hart, Raz, MacCormick, and John Finnis'.[3] He claims that,

> [a]ccording to this tradition, while the law's ultimate aspiration may be justice, its proximate aim and defining task is to supply a framework of practical reasoning designed to unify public political judgment and co-ordinate social interaction; and in this view of law's fundamental task lies a key to understanding its nature.[4]

Postema states that the aim of his article 'is not to defend an account of jurisprudential history, but rather to examine one perennially attractive thesis about the nature of law that is debated and defended within this tradition'.[5] He calls this the 'Autonomy Thesis' and he defines it as follows:

> According to the Autonomy Thesis, legal reasoning is a viable and vital form of public practical reasoning that is able to serve the task assigned to it because of its autonomy from moral and political reasoning. The autonomy consists, roughly, in the fact that the existence, content, and practical force of the norms from which legal reasoning proceeds are determined by criteria that make no essential reference to considerations of political morality, and so legal reasoning can proceed entirely without engaging in arguments of political morality.[6]

Any understanding of law based on the autonomy thesis has various elements that hang together in a certain way because this approach as a whole is underpinned by a core methodological assumption. The core methodological assumption is that, in order to explain the nature of law, we must explain *how it functions*. Law engenders order by offering the populace a set of factually ascertainable public practical reasons. This assumption necessitates a certain interconnectedness between the pieces of one's jurisprudential theory: the question of what law *is* is grounded in an understanding of what law does (or should do) and how it does it. According to the vision of law mentioned above, law is a system of norms whose content can be identified without engaging in moral/political argumentation. In a world fraught with disagreement, law is an organizing force that engenders co-operation and facilitates co-ordination.

The autonomy thesis comes in weak and strong versions. The weak version states that the law is an autonomous domain of practical reasons for citizens to utilize. The strong version of the autonomy thesis adds an additional claim to the weak version: judges also treat the law as an autonomous domain by

[3] *Ibid*, 80.

[4] *Ibid.*

[5] *Ibid.*

[6] *Ibid.* This is so despite the many other differences in both content and method that can be readily identified amongst the theorists in this disparate group who, according to Postema, are united by their support, perhaps unknowingly, of the autonomy thesis.

applying existing laws whenever possible. In other words, the weak version claims that law is autonomous in its identification, whilst the strong version claims that law is autonomous in its identification *and* its application. The problem with the strong version is that the phenomenology of judicial decision-making does not support it: common law adjudication is a counter-example to this account (a point that I argue for in chapters one and two). I have detailed Raz's unsuccessful attempts to deal with this feature of the practice throughout this book, but especially in chapters one, two, and five.

The obvious defect in the strong autonomy thesis may lead many (including Raz) to view the weaker version of the autonomy thesis as the more plausible one. Postema is not convinced, however. His main complaint is that the autonomy thesis is trivial unless it applies to judges as well as citizens. Indeed, he wonders 'whether law's autonomy can be maintained, and whether the point of insisting upon this autonomy can be sustained in the face of extensive, non-autonomous judicial reasoning'.[7] Raz responds to Postema by denying that his theory of law is another instance of this creation myth. More specifically, he rejects the following claims:

A. the law's ultimate aspiration is justice;
B. that he (Raz) allocates an overarching function to law;
C. that he is committed to the strong version of the autonomy thesis;
D. that he is committed to the strong version of the limited domain thesis;
E. that he grounds his theory of law in a need for co-operation;
F. that he endorses the method of explaining why and how law functions;
G. that the relationship between the pre-emption thesis and the sources thesis that Postema articulates is correct;
H. that he is committed to the certainty thesis;
I. that Postema understands the role of the sources thesis;
J. that Postema understands the role of the pre-emption thesis.

By considering each claim in turn, we are led to confront a series of difficult questions about the relationship between Raz's various theses. In short, Postema's critique of Raz is based on a certain understanding of how the elements of Raz's theory hang together. Raz attempts to deflect Postema's attacks by insisting on the radical separability of what he regards as distinct theses. While this strategy makes it easier for Raz to defend himself against Postema's charges, it runs into the trap of making each thesis seem increasingly arbitrary. Each thesis has significance when it is considered in the context of Raz's theoretical account as a whole, but we can wonder how much insight they can provide once they are detached from this larger picture of law. Many admirers of Raz's work may have admired precisely the apparently interlocking nature of

[7] Postema, 'Law's Autonomy', above n 1, at 88.

his different claims. Without such interdependence, the reasons for adopting each thesis in isolation are much weaker.

A. Law's Ultimate Aspiration is Justice

As we have seen, Postema argues that a specific creation myth informs Raz's theory of law (just as it does many other theories).The vision of law presented by this myth maintains that 'law's aspiration may be justice' but its 'proximate aim is to supply a framework of practical reasoning designed to unify public political judgment and coordinate social interaction'.[8] Raz begins his defensive manoeuvres by denying that the law's ultimate aspiration is justice:

> Justice, I believe, is not the law's ultimate aspiration, for there is no one moral virtue that all law by its nature aspires to, other than to be good: that is to be as it should be. This means that it should be just, and generous and compassionate and many other things. It is important to remember that the law has no specific function (though it, or parts of it, have many such functions). Being good is but a formal function: everything should be good i.e., should be as it ought to be. That does not tell us anything of substance about how it should be. It merely says that that thing is subject to normative evaluation.[9]

This passage is curious given that it has undertones of natural law rather than legal positivism: legal positivists tend to deny that law aims to be good.[10] References to justice are conspicuously absent from Raz's account of the moral underpinnings of legal authority. Raz's belief that law's ultimate aim is to be good makes law an aspirational or 'focal' concept, rather than a descriptive one. The difference (and the incompatibility) between these two kinds of concepts was explored in chapters four and six. Note that in *The Morality of Freedom*, Raz argues that *authority* is a focal concept, not law. However, given that law is an instance of authority, I argue in chapter four that Raz has great difficulty in combining a positivist descriptive concept of law, based on the sources thesis, with a focal concept of authority.

Whether or not Raz sees justice as law's ultimate aim is less important for our purposes than the second half of Postema's charge, which refers to law's proximate aim. Postema argues that those who endorse the autonomy thesis understand law's proximate aim as supplying 'a framework of practical reasoning designed to unify public political judgment and coordinate social interaction'.[11] The remainder of this discussion will confirm the link between Raz's theory and

[8] J Raz, 'Postema on Law's Autonomy and Public Practical Reason: A Critical Commentary' (1998) 4 *Legal Theory* 1, 2 (footnote omitted).

[9] *Ibid*, 2.

[10] But see S Shapiro, *Legality* (Cambridge, MA, Harvard University Press, 2011) 213.

[11] Postema, 'Law's Autonomy', above n 1, at 80.

the strong autonomy thesis before drawing out (with Postema's help) the myriad of challenges that arise as a result. The key question is: does Raz assign law the overarching function of facilitating co-ordination by providing a set of public norms that citizens can rely on in their practical reasoning?

B. Law's Overarching Function

Raz denies that he grounds his theory of law in this particular function – indeed, Raz denies that he allocates *any* central function to law. He identifies three possible interpretations of Postema's claim that law has one central function and ultimately rejects all three. The first interpretation Raz considers is to understand law's central function as law's 'umbrella task' – 'that is, the task of which all other tasks the law has are instances'.[12] Raz rejects this possibility, arguing that a 'good law fulfils many tasks' and that 'Not all good laws fulfil the same tasks'.[13]As for legal systems more generally, Raz contends that the 'tasks that good systems fulfil depend on the circumstances of their countries'.[14] He proceeds to provide us with an example to illustrate this point: some countries regulate air traffic efficiency while others do not; however, most countries regulate air traffic safety in some manner. Despite the existence of this kind of common ground between countries, Raz sees 'no reason to think that there is any abstract description of their function which applies to all of them and of which all other functions are instances'; he sees 'no reason to think that the law has an umbrella task'.[15] This example does not address Postema's main charge: it is not particular functions (like controlling air traffic) that inform the view that law offers us a set of public practical reasons for action. Perhaps this is why Raz offers us two additional interpretations of Postema's complaint.

Raz then considers a second interpretation of Postema's charge. He ponders the possibility that 'a framework of practical reasoning designed to unify public political judgment and coordinate social interaction' could be 'a necessary condition for the law's achieving any useful purpose, or at least that it is a necessary condition for the law's legitimacy'.[16] Raz quickly rejects this possibility as mistaken.[17] The problem is that 'law can achieve many important goods, which cannot otherwise be achieved, by measures that do not unify public political judgment'.[18] He then reminds us that Rawls and his followers

[12] Raz, 'Postema on Law's Autonomy', above n 8, at 2.
[13] *Ibid.*
[14] *Ibid.*
[15] *Ibid* (footnote omitted).
[16] *Ibid*, 3.
[17] *Ibid.*
[18] *Ibid.*

defend the view that unified public political judgment is a necessary condition of political legitimacy.[19] Raz argues that this position is misplaced:

> In fact, a government can be legitimate even if many among the population do not accept the moral credentials of important aspects of the basic structure, as long as they accept it in the less demanding sense of being willing to live under it.[20]

Even if this criticism of Rawls is correct, Raz has not escaped Postema's main charge, he has only side-stepped it by recasting Postema's central criticism – Postema is not worried about the relationship between legitimacy and unity of judgment, but rather he is questioning the viability of the view that law offers us a set factually ascertainable reasons for action that unify judgment.[21]

While Raz had misinterpreted the argument from co-operation thus far, he hits the mark with his third and final attempt. It is this final possibility that echoes his own views in earlier works. Raz's writes:

> Possibly he means simply that it is one of the law's tasks, but unlike all the others which vary from country to country and from time to time, this task is universal. It is the only one of the law's tasks which is part of its nature to have, that by necessity all laws have.[22]

Raz adds that this 'is an intriguing thought, which I will not be able to pursue to its conclusion here, as it would take us far too long'.[23] Raz, does however, proceed to make several points. First, he notes that he does allocate a necessary 'task' to law: it is from the nature of law that it claims authority.[24] 'It follows that to be valid, and for its directives to have normative force, it must meet the conditions of legitimacy for authorities of its kind'.[25] Raz's second point is that providing a public framework of practical reasoning 'is not necessary for legitimacy, if it is a task that all law has by its nature, it is not the only one'.[26]

These two points are misleading. Raz is correct, of course; the conditions of the legitimacy he defends (namely, the normal justification thesis) are silent about law's order-engendering role. This does not mean, however, that Raz's theory of authority, as articulated in *The Morality of Freedom*, is not connected to an account of law's function. In order for law's claim to be realized, legal norms must be capable of serving as pre-emptory reasons for action. In chapters three through to five, I argue that the pre-emption thesis cannot be wholly

[19] *Ibid.*
[20] *Ibid.*
[21] I also question this view in ch 5.
[22] Raz, 'Postema on Law's Autonomy', above n 8, at 3.
[23] *Ibid.*
[24] *Ibid.*
[25] *Ibid.*
[26] *Ibid.*

disconnected from the account of law's function which Raz championed in both *Practical Reason and Norms* and *The Authority of Law*. The idea that law has a universal function is thus not simply an 'intriguing thought', it is a thought that is at the very centre of his conception of law in these early works.

Raz's adds that 'even if we assume that it is a good thing for a society to enjoy unity in its political judgment, it is not obviously the law's task to secure it, or even to contribute to that goal'.[27] He argues that the 'unity of judgment is a by-product of true judgment':

> If we all have (all the) true beliefs on certain matters then we are all united in judgment on these matters. It does not follow that unity of judgment is good in itself. To be that, it would have to be a good for the sake of which it is sometimes better to have false beliefs, or at any rate dubious ones. That is far from clear.[28]

This argument is little more than a distraction in the context in which it is offered. The account of law as a set of public practical reasons which Postema attributes to Raz assumes that law is the unifying force, irrespective of the moral standing of the beliefs of the lawmakers or law's subjects.

C. The Autonomy Thesis

Raz does not deny that he is committed to a certain version of the autonomy thesis (the sources thesis dictates as much). He does, however, deny that he is committed to the version of the autonomy thesis that Postema claims he is committed to. Raz argues that a distinction needs to be made between '(at least) two autonomy theses: the autonomy of law and of legal reasoning'.[29] Raz argues that he is committed to the autonomy of law, but not the autonomy of legal reasoning.[30] The thesis that the law is autonomous is little more than a restatement of the sources thesis: 'it is possible to identify the content of the law without recourse to moral reasoning'.[31] Conversely, 'legal reasoning' is

> normally used to include any reasoning to conclusions which entail that, according to law, if a matter were before a court the court should decide thus and so (or that since it is before the court this is how it should be decided).[32]

While law is autonomous, according to Raz, 'Legal reasoning is not autonomous'.[33] He explains that 'much of legal reasoning is interpretive reasoning,

[27] *Ibid.*
[28] *Ibid*, 3–4.
[29] *Ibid*, 4.
[30] *Ibid.*
[31] *Ibid.*
[32] *Ibid* (footnote omitted).
[33] *Ibid.*

and interpretive reasoning is not, in general, autonomous'.[34] Raz's response to Postema is to point out that he champions a theory of law that adheres to the sources thesis and a theory of adjudication that does not.[35] In other words, Raz supports the weak version of the autonomy thesis and rejects the strong version.

Raz expands on his understanding of the autonomy of law, which is limited to the act of law identification:

> Reasoning to establish the content of the law as it is at any given moment can proceed without resort to evaluative considerations – i.e., it is, in Postema's terms, autonomous. Such reasoning relies on the fact that certain actions took place, that they were undertaken with certain intentions, that the rest of the law is thus and so, etc. It includes assumptions regarding the moral or other evaluative views of lawmakers, courts, or others.[36]

While one might refer to moral arguments made by others, one is not thereby engaging in moral argumentation. This kind of detached reporting is not the same as engaging in moral argumentation. While one might agree with Raz on this point, whether this particular argument shores up Raz's sources thesis remains doubtful. I share Postema's take on the matter: the sources thesis is a valuable thesis insofar as it is a part of a particular account of the practical role such norms play in our daily lives. Of course, the importance of this account rests on its tenability. I have argued that the account, as Raz originally offered it, is not plausible and hence new ideas (or a return to older ones) is required.

Raz then argues that the 'rest of legal reasoning is (in shape and form) ordinary evaluative reasoning, which is undertaken according to law, for the law requires courts to reach decisions through such reasoning'.[37] He explains that in 'legal reasoning, legal rules and standards appear among the reasons inclining the argument toward one conclusion or another'.[38] Legal reasons are not decisive, however, as they must 'compete with other reasons'.[39] Raz is careful to stress the fact that reasoning about the content of law as it exists is not a 'separate species of reasoning' and although 'it can be undertaken in its own right, it is often but one aspect of legal reasoning'.[40] Raz proceeds to defend his distinction between 'reasoning about the law' and 'reasoning according to the law':

> I expect that it is now clear why we need to distinguish reasoning *to* the conclusions

[34] *Ibid.* For an alternate view, see T Endicott 'Legal Interpretation' in A Marmor (ed), *Routledge Companion to Philosophy of Law* (Oxford, Routledge, 2012)

[35] For a critical assessment of this distinction, see ch 3.

[36] Raz, 'Postema on Law's Autonomy', above n 8.

[37] *Ibid.*

[38] *Ibid*, 5–6 (footnote omitted).

[39] *Ibid*, 6. Compare with his comments on the matter in *Practical Reason and Norms*. See ch 1.

[40] *Ibid.*

> that the law as it exists at a certain time has a certain content, from reasoning *from* premises that the law, as it exists at a certain time, has a certain content. The first kind of reasoning, is – I suspect –autonomous, to use Postema's term. The second includes what is normally called legal reasoning, which is simply evaluative reasoning according to law. It is not autonomous in my view, nor do I know of any serious theorist who thinks that it is.[41]

Here Raz proclaims his agreement with the weaker version of the autonomy thesis by utilizing the same distinction he uses in his theory of adjudication – the distinction between 'reasoning according to the law' and 'reasoning about the law'. 'Reasoning according to the law' is judicial reasoning, which includes appeals to moral principles.[42] Conversely, 'reasoning about the law' is consistent with the sources thesis: the aim of this kind of reasoning is to identify the content of existing law, which, according to Raz, proceeds by ascertaining facts.

Postema acknowledges that most thinkers who endorse the autonomy thesis also share Raz's view that judges often appeal to moral considerations when making judicial decisions.[43] But recall it is this combination of a non-autonomous theory of adjudication with an autonomous theory of law which Postema is questioning:

> Of course, this raises the obvious question whether law's autonomy can be maintained, and whether the point of insisting upon this autonomy can be sustained in the face of extensive, non-autonomous judicial reasoning.[44]

In chapter three, I argue that Postema is correct to suspect that Raz's theory of adjudication sits in tension with his theory of law. I also demonstrate that when Raz introduces us to his morally robust theory of adjudication he aligns himself with the realists and not with the positivists. Moreover, when Raz states that he knows of no one who endorses the strong version of the autonomy thesis, he has clearly forgotten that he endorsed this position himself in *Practical Reason and Norms*.[45] Due to the interconnectedness of Raz's theory in *Practical Reason and Norms*, divorcing himself from the strong autonomy thesis is not a simple task. In chapters two through to five, I pinpoint the failure of Raz's attempts to maintain his key positivist theses without also committing to the strong autonomy thesis. But since the strong autonomy thesis is not a viable position (as a non-normative theory), Raz finds himself in a difficult situation from which there is no clear escape route.

[41] *Ibid.* See ch 5 for an additional discussion of this distinction.
[42] *Ibid.*
[43] Postema, 'Law's Autonomy', above n 1, at 87.
[44] *Ibid*, 88.
[45] See ch 1.

D. The Limited Domain Thesis

Raz's stance on the limited domain thesis is similar to his position on the autonomy thesis: he rejects the stronger version of the thesis (which states that the law is a limited domain both in identification and application) in favour of the weaker version (which states that law is a limited domain only in its identification). He maintains that the law is equivalent to a limited domain of pre-existing laws that serve (or can serve) as practical reasons for action: '*Limited domain thesis*: law defines a limited domain of practical reasons or norms'.[46] Raz proceeds to define the precise meaning of this thesis: 'As formulated, the limited domain thesis means that the law (e.g., the sum total of legal norms) is a limited domain'.[47] This thesis is easily established, argues Raz: all we have to do is establish the existence of non-legal reasons to prove that law's domain is not unlimited. For instance, if the payout of a lottery ticket is less than the price of the ticket, this is a good reason not to buy it but it is not a legal reason.[48] The limited domain thesis is 'trivially true'.[49] Theorists of all stripes can commit to this 'trivially true' characterization of the limited domain thesis. No one would argue against the existence of non-legal reasons.

This is a red herring. The limited domain thesis does not simply say that non-legal reasons exist. Raz eventually admits that its truth remains 'a necessary condition for the truth of the autonomy thesis'.[50] If law is to be autonomous (and the sources thesis is to hold true), then the law must be a limited domain in this weaker sense. As I have argued in this book, the problem with the sources thesis is that it is meaningful in the context in which it is originally introduced: that is as a part of the story of law as a set of public practical reasons. However, when Raz introduces his morally robust theory of adjudication, it is difficult to find a role for fact-based sources to play.[51] This leaves him a positivist in name only.

The strong version of the limited domain thesis states that the set of norms is a limited set *and* that judges (on the whole) must make decisions from this limited legal perspective and exclude non-legal (moral) considerations. Notice that the strong version of the limited domain thesis repeats the assertion of the strong autonomy thesis, which holds that judicial reasoning largely excludes extra-legal considerations such as moral considerations. Again, the problem is that Raz himself explicitly champions the strong version of the limited domain thesis in

[46] Raz, 'Postema on Law's Autonomy', above n 8, at 7.
[47] *Ibid.*
[48] *Ibid.*
[49] *Ibid.*
[50] *Ibid*, 8.
[51] See chs 3 and 5.

Practical Reason and Norms, even though he no longer supports this view.[52] It is not the mere fact that Raz has changed his mind that has occupied a central strand of argumentation in this book, but the impact these changes have had on the coherence of his theory has been ignored by Raz. Given the enourmous influence Raz has had on jurisprudential thinking, making sense of his position remains an important task. In addition to concerns about consistency and overall coherence, I have also worried about the apparent motivation for a number of the arguments forwarded in defense of Raz's account: namely, the desire to protect foundational commitments at any cost, often at the expense of an accurate characterization of legal practice. For instance, in chapter two I am critical of Raz's attempt to offer a theory of common law adjudication which accommodates his own definitions, whilst obscuring the nature of the practice. I also question the move to sever questions about law's function (or functions) from the domain of legal philosophy – this move, I have argued in chapter five, is motivated out of a desire to preserve methodological neutrality. The very fact that such foundational questions (questions that were at the very foundation of Raz's early accounts!) must be abandoned as they violate the methodological constraints speaks to the remarkable limits of this popular method.

E. The Argument from Co-operation

Raz proceeds to reject Postema's claim that he is committed to the argument from co-operation, which states that it is law's central function to provide a public framework for practical reason that will facilitate co-operation. Raz's rejection of this thesis is not surprising given that he has already rejected the possibility that law has one overarching function. Raz articulates an abbreviated version of Postema's argument before challenging it:

> The function of law is to facilitate social cooperation. The law fulfills its function through its conformity to the autonomy thesis. There are two obstacles on the road to cooperation. The problem of identification of what one should do as one's share in cooperation. And the problem of motivating people to do their share.[53]

Raz sums up Postema's position: the 'sources thesis enables people to establish how to cooperate; the pre-emption thesis solves the problem of motivation'.[54] Postema does not think that Raz will support this particular argument, and Raz makes it clear that Postema is correct on this point.[55] Raz admits that it is

[52] See ch 1.
[53] Raz, 'Postema on Law's Autonomy', above n 8, at 9. In his footnote to this passage Raz makes it clear that he will be using the terms 'co-operation' and 'co-ordination' interchangeably.
[54] *Ibid.*
[55] *Ibid*, 10.

'fairly obvious that the law plays an important role in securing some forms of social cooperation in well-ordered societies'.[56] The problem (from Raz's perspective) is that Postema is grounding the autonomy thesis in the argument from co-operation, whereas Raz thinks that if there is a connection to be made with the autonomy thesis then the argument from co-operation works in the other direction: we establish that the autonomy thesis is correct and then we can begin to see whether the existence of factually ascertainable legal norms helps to facilitate co-operation. Raz explains:

> If the autonomy thesis is correct then it is possible that it brings benefits in helping secure cooperation. But how could the fact that if it is correct it would solve the problem of social cooperation be a reason for its correctness?'[57]

The difficulty with this statement is that it contradicts one of Raz's arguments in *The Authority of Law,* where Raz grounds his sources thesis in an argument from co-operation similar, if not identical, to the one Postema attributes to Raz.[58] In *The Authority of Law* Raz argues that we should adopt the sources thesis precisely because it captures something important about the manner in which law works: legal norms are factually ascertainable reasons for action that unify judgment thereby facilitate co-ordination and co-operation. Recall that it is through the practical role that Raz allocated to fact-based legal norms that allowed us to see, at once, both what law does and why it is important to see law though the lens of the sources thesis. Once this argument is abandoned, and we see the myriad ways in which legal norms can and do impact on our practical reasoning process,[59] the value of the sources thesis ceases to be transparent.

Raz then goes on to consider the possibility that co-ordination is a necessary moral task that law performs. The problem with this suggestion, Raz contends, is that the correct argument proceeds in the reverse order from the argument Postema champions:

> But we learn of the moral and other tasks of the law in part from its nature. If we can show (1) that securing coordination is good, and (2) that the law is better at securing coordination than alternative methods, and (3) that its doing so has no adverse effects (or none serious enough to outweigh the advantage of its doing so) then we can conclude that it has the task of securing coordination.[60]

Raz argues that in order to prove the validity of the argument, we must 'establish the second premise'.[61] Postema assumes that the second premise is

[56] *Ibid.*
[57] *Ibid.*
[58] See ch 2.
[59] See ch 6.
[60] Raz, 'Postema on Law's Autonomy', above n 8, at 10.
[61] *Ibid.*

established once the sources thesis and the pre-emption thesis are established, but Raz claims he is incorrect to make this assumption.

The difficulty with this argument is the same as the one with the last argument: in *The Authority of Law* (and implicitly in *Practical Reason and Norms*) Raz grounds his sources thesis in just such a view of law's function.[62] He makes the same assumptions that he challenges Postema for making: in these early works his theory of what law is *is* grounded in an account of what law does. Furthermore, it is curious that Raz now thinks that championing the view that law's necessary function is to secure co-operation requires a *moral* argument. In *The Authority of Law*, Raz grounds his theory of law in a view of its function but the argument is not moral (at least not self-consciously so).[63] Insofar as Raz cannot excise the function-based aspect of his account (in chapter five I argue that he cannot) then the implications are clear: his positivist theses (the sources thesis and the pre-emption thesis) are part of a moral account of law's role in our lives. I reach a similar conclusion in chapter five.

Raz does, however, concede that 'It is true, of course, that *if* the law's essential function is to solve the problem of social cooperation then that would be an important aspect of the law and worth pointing out'.[64] Indeed, that 'would be a justification for including the autonomy thesis, or rather the sources thesis, in an account of the nature of the law' in that it would show that the sources thesis 'singles out important aspects of the law'.[65] However, Raz cautions, 'before we get there we have to have some reason to believe that the thesis (or the theses) is (are) correct'.[66] Once again, Raz has reversed the order of his claims: in *The Authority of Law*, he argues that the sources thesis is true *because* it captures an important social function that law performs; now he is arguing that we must have reason to believe that the sources thesis (or the autonomy thesis) is correct before we can tell if law plays a key role in co-ordinating society. Again, I am doubtful that such a clean separation of issues is possible.

F. Methodology and Law's Importance

While Raz agrees with Postema that 'one important way in which a theory is to be assessed is by its ability to deepen our understanding of the law', he disagrees with Postema about the precise method used to achieve this end.[67]

[62] J Raz, *The Authority of Law: Essays on Law and Morality* (New York, Oxford University Press, 1979) 51.

[63] Traditionally, it has been the positivists who point to the fact that co-operation is not necessarily a morally good thing in order to secure their morally neutral stance on law's function. See J Waldron, 'All We Like Sheep' (1999) 12 *Canadian Journal of Law and Jurisprudence* 169.

[64] Raz, 'Postema on Law's Autonomy', above n 8, at 10.

[65] *Ibid.*

[66] *Ibid.*

[67] *Ibid.*

Postema proposes that a theory of law 'should not only describe *how law works*, but also, and more importantly, explain *why it is important* to have it' (author's emphasis).[68] Raz disagrees with this approach: 'But while no one would doubt the importance of knowing why we should have law, if indeed we should have law, this cannot be an argument for the thesis that the law is one way or another'.[69] Raz adds that his stance is not connected to the view (often associated with legal positivism) that law cannot be a matter of morality.[70] He concedes that it 'is possible that the essential properties of the law are moral'.[71] Even if law has essential moral properties, this does not definitively answer the question of law's importance (and whether it is good to have law). The possibility still exists that law's 'disadvantages may outweigh its advantages'.[72]

There are two problems with Raz's dismissal of Postema's methodological approach. First, Raz fails to offer an alternative method: if a view of law's importance does not help to identify the key features of law, then how, precisely is Raz identifying the features of law that figure into his theory? This question becomes particularly pressing in light of methodological claims Raz makes elsewhere: as mentioned, in *The Authority of Law* Raz explicitly defends the sources thesis on the grounds that it captures the important function law plays in society.[73] Furthermore, a close examination of *Practical Reason and Norms* reveals that Raz adheres to the methodology that he explicitly rejects above: he bases his theory on a view of *why* law is important (see chapter one). Again, instead of suppressing essential questions to preserve the positivist methodology, the methodology must be rethought.[74] While there are a number of ways to proceed, one way, I have suggested, is to reflect on the similarities and differences between at least two types of legal orders. What emerges is an ideal of legality. This shift in approach does not amount to a rejection of the 'universal' in favour of the 'contingent' – but a wholesale rejection of the way in which these terms are currently used.

G. The Relationship between the Pre-emption Thesis and the Sources Thesis

When outlining the argument for co-operation, Postema identifies two problems: the problem of *identification* and the problem of *motivation*. In order for law to unify judgment through the provision of a public framework of practical

68 Postema, 'Law's Autonomy', above n 1, at 88.
69 Raz, 'Postema on Law's Autonomy', above n 8, at 11.
70 *Ibid.*
71 *Ibid.*
72 *Ibid.*
73 Raz, *The Authority of Law*, above n 62, at 52.
74 See ch 5.

reason, citizens must be able to identify the law and then they must be motivated to act in accordance with its demands. If either of these two elements is lacking, the danger of lapsing into a chaos of subjectivity and uncertainty will remain (as implied by the creation myth). Postema argues that the sources thesis solves the problem of identification while the pre-emption thesis solves the problem of motivation, and then he defines the relationship between the two: 'The Sources Thesis without the Pre-emption Thesis is inert; the Pre-emption Thesis without the Sources Thesis is blind'.[75] The sources thesis might identify pre-existing legal norms, but unless we are motivated to follow these norms (ie by the pre-emption thesis), then the sources thesis captures something of little relevance. Likewise, without the sources thesis the pre-emption thesis is useless: our judgment cannot be pre-empted by legal norms, unless these norms can be identified (ie by the sources thesis).

Raz rejects this view of the relationship between the pre-emption thesis and the sources thesis. To begin with, he denies that the pre-emption thesis is able to solve the problem of motivation:

> First notice that the pre-emption thesis as I understand it does not say that there are pre-emptive reasons for complying with the law. It merely says that if the law is morally binding then its subjects have pre-emptive reasons to comply with it.[76]

Raz wonders how the pre-emption thesis can solve the problem of motivation.[77] He notes that people are motivated to act in various ways for various reasons and, in addition, people 'can have reason to do what they are not motivated to do and they may be motivated to do what they have no reason to do'.[78] Raz concludes, 'even if the law's subjects have a pre-emptive reason to comply with the law, it is not clear how that can contribute to the solution of the problem of motivation'.[79] It is either the case that people are motivated to obey the law (and to treat legal norms as pre-emptive reasons for action), or people are not so motivated (even though the law gives them pre-emptive reasons): the pre-emption thesis does not solve the problem of motivation, as that is a separate issue.[80] It is not clear that it is, however. Unless Raz can explain why people may be moved to accord legal norms pre-eptive status, the pre-emption thesis is arid. Raz ends his discussion of the pre-emption thesis with the following words: 'I conclude that the pre-emption thesis is as irrelevant to the solution of the problem of social coordination as it is to the autonomy thesis'.[81] But again, this statement is far more difficult to substanti-

[75] Postema, 'Law's Autonomy', above n 1, at 92.
[76] Raz, 'Postema on Law's Autonomy' above n 8, at 11–12.
[77] *Ibid*, 12.
[78] *Ibid.*
[79] *Ibid.*
[80] *Ibid.*
[81] *Ibid.*

ate than it may appear. In chapter five, I have identified the way in which the question of motivation has figured into Raz's theories.

Raz proceeds to reject Postema's argument that the sources thesis solves the problem of identification. Raz begins by articulating the question at hand: 'What of the sources thesis? Does it not solve the problem of identification which is half the problem of social cooperation?'[82] Raz's answer to this question is implied when he reverses the order of the claims:

> I think that the sources thesis is true of the law, and that the law can contribute to achieving cooperation. Nor would I deny that the sources thesis is relevant to the way the law helps with cooperation. But all this is a long way from even claiming that there is a problem of social cooperation and that the law's function is to solve it.[83]

To prove his point, Raz identifies other mechanisms that help to achieve social co-operation: 'speaking the same language, and following rules of polite conduct are but two examples of complex social cooperation without which there can be no social life – indeed, no law – and to which the law usually contributes not at all'.[84] Surely these social forces are part of the story, but it does not negate a) the role law actually plays in engendering social cooperation or; b) the fact that Raz did indeed argue that 'there is a problem of social cooperation and that the law's function is to solve it'. Again, I address this issue in chapters one, three and five.

Raz admits 'there are circumstances and forms of cooperation where the law offers the most efficient (sometimes the only) way of securing cooperation', however, this 'does not show that there is a problem of social cooperation as such'.[85] Raz moves on to point out that not all co-operation is good, for example, co-operation with the aim of producing a nuclear arsenal in certain countries.[86] While it may be good for the law to secure some forms of co-operation, Raz argues, it is the specific form of co-operation that may be deemed to be good, not co-operation in general. And in order to, once again, deflect the idea that law's central and defining function is to secure co-operation, Raz draws our attention to the fact that 'there are various other goods it is right or even required that the law secure'.[87] Raz arrives at the following conclusion:

> The right conclusion is that if the sources thesis is true, then the law is morally binding if, and by and large only if, it secures valuable cooperation as well as other goods, better than they can be secured without it.[88]

82 *Ibid.*
83 *Ibid*, 12–13.
84 *Ibid*, 13.
85 *Ibid.*
86 *Ibid.*
87 *Ibid.*
88 *Ibid.*

Raz argues that Postema fails to see this point (and his previous related points) because he is 'mesmerized' by the argument from co-operation.[89]

Contrary to Raz's understanding of his own position, Postema is correct to see the co-ordination argument as essential to Raz's theory. As mentioned earlier, I agree with Postema that Raz's argument is grounded in a specific co-ordination engendering function. Only if Raz's theses are defended in isolation from each other does his series of deflections make sense. Once they are combined into a single theoretical account, Postema's charges find their target. Chapters three and four demonstrate how this ground is very difficult (indeed impossible) to replace with a different foundation once removed: serious tension exists between Raz's theory of law and his theory of adjudication. I have also argued that Postema is correct in thinking that Raz must account for the motivation of citizens with regards to the pre-emption thesis.[90] Furthermore, while the sources thesis does not solve the problem of identification, it does capture a key feature of Raz's exclusive positivist position: the content of legal norms must be easy to ascertain for judges and citizens alike. This point was touched upon throughout the book, but especially in chapter five.

H. The Certainty Thesis

The certainty thesis is the view that legal norms must have content that is easily ascertained – content that is *certain*, or at least relatively so. Raz also denies that his theory of law is committed to the certainty thesis: 'Has the sources thesis much to do with certainty? I do not think so'.[91] Given that the sources thesis claims that law is a product of facts, and not moral argument, Raz contests the suggestion that fact-based issues are less controversial than moral issues: 'I do not think e.g., that there are fewer, or less serious controversies among economists about the likely course of the economy under various circumstances than controversies among people regarding moral issues'.[92] Raz puts the point more generally: 'In other words, I know of no general reason to think that so-called factual issues are easier to resolve than moral ones, or that there are fewer controversies regarding them'.[93] Raz proceeds to clarify the nature of this central thesis stating, 'the sources thesis distinguishes not between ways of establishing the law with certainty and those open to doubt, but between non-evaluative and evaluative criteria'.[94]

[89] *Ibid*, 16.
[90] See ch 3.
[91] Raz, 'Postema on Law's Autonomy' above n 8, at 13.
[92] *Ibid.*
[93] *Ibid.*
[94] *Ibid.*

Raz notes that uncertainty is sometimes desirable, but admits that a large degree of certainty is often welcome.[95] He nonetheless maintains his stance that 'it is wrong to elevate it to a matter of unique and central importance for the law'.[96] An argument that elevates certainty in this manner will be unable to account for the existence of customary law or the common law.[97] Raz insists that 'both customary law and common law are sources of law, recognized by the sources thesis'.[98] According to Raz, the sources thesis is concerned with *finality* not certainty.[99] Raz returns to his argument that law claims authority to solidify this point:

> It is in the nature of the law that it claims authority, i.e. that it claims to be authoritative, and that means that it claims to have settled moral and other social issues (and not necessarily because they were controversial; sometimes there is simply a need for someone to decide, even when the matter is not controversial).[100]

In chapter five, I argued that Raz underestimates the extent to which his theory of law is committed to the certainty thesis. Postema stresses a similar point. He argues that Raz's emphasis on *finality* over *certainty,* in reference to the role of legal sources, 'somewhat understates the importance of certainty'.[101] I also argue throughout that Raz's theory of law, contrary to his own beliefs on the matter, does not account for the existence of common law systems. Notice that Raz's two arguments are interconnected: he wants to distance himself from the certainty thesis, but only in order to ensure that he can account for the existence of common law systems. In chapter six I offer a more accurate account of the sources of certainty and uncertainty. These modest observations I offer lead quickly to the articulation of a legal ideal rather than a non-normative account of law.

I. The Sources Thesis

The sources thesis states that the content of law is factually ascertainable: we do not have to use moral arguments in order to establish what the content of law is. Postema wonders whether the distinction between morally evaluative and non-evaluative arguments can be maintained.[102] He argues that, even if a

95 *Ibid.*
96 *Ibid.*
97 *Ibid.*
98 *Ibid.*
99 *Ibid.*
100 *Ibid,* 14.
101 Postema, 'Law's Autonomy', above n 1, at 92.
102 Note that when the distinction is made between evaluative and non-evaluative arguments, the former refers to morally evaluative arguments. A number of positivists, including Raz, champion the position that theory construction is necessarily evaluative, but evaluative does not mean

judge is reasoning in a detached manner, it does not mean that the reasoning is non-evaluative in the sense that the sources thesis demands. Postema provides an example: 'consider the rabbi who advises a Catholic about her moral duties as a Catholic regarding abortion – but this does not make the practical reasoning involved non-evaluative'.[103]

Raz admits that 'Postema is right that the same difficulties which engaged moral reasoning leads to, are equally encountered in the parallel detached reasoning' but insists that 'reconstructive reasoning is not detached reasoning'.[104] Detached reasoning, Raz argues, 'is like saying "I do not accept any of what follows but let us suppose it for the sake of the argument" and then proceeding to make statements and draw conclusions'.[105] Reconstructive reasoning, by contrast, seeks to understand the reasoning of a judge in order to determine what the law is in accordance with the sources thesis. Raz makes it clear that reconstructive reasoning does not involve the initial supposition that is made when one reasons in a detached way. Instead, it is a fact-finding mission of discovering what a judge says and what it means. Raz gives an example of how reconstructive reasoning proceeds:

> Judge A is known to believe in (let us say) tough punitive policy, and he wrote in his judgment that. . . . Those who have his views on penal policy often use the same words to express the view that. . . . We can therefore assume that in writing what he wrote, Judge A made the statement that . . .[106]

Reconstructive reasoning deals with the views of a few people '*insofar as they were expressed* in a particular document, *or are relevant to establishing what was expressed in it*'.[107] Conversely, detached reasoning (as described by Postema) 'deals with the implications of a moral or religious system of belief'.[108]

The next response to Postema indicates how difficult it is to maintain this line. Sometimes value judgments enter into one's interpretation implicitly through the reconstructive process. Postema argues that when reconstructing the reasoning of another, we inevitably rely on our own ideas of how to construct a good argument.[109] Raz concurs, but trivializes this point:

'morally evaluative' (J Raz, *Ethics in the Public Domain: Essays in the Morality of Law and Politics* (Oxford, Clarendon Press, 1994) 237). Julie Dickson argues that the terms 'descriptive' and 'evaluative' should be replaced by 'directly evaluative' and 'indirectly evaluative' in order to capture Raz's idea that one can make evaluative judgments that are not moral (J Dickson, *Evaluation and Legal Theory* (Oxford, Hart Publishing, 2001) 51). Given that I am sceptical about the prevalence of evaluative arguments that are not moral, I will continue to use the terms 'descriptive' and 'evaluative' in the manner just discussed.

[103] Postema, 'Law's Autonomy', above n 1, at 97.

[104] Raz, 'Postema on Law's Autonomy', above n 8, at 14.

[105] *Ibid*, 14–15.

[106] *Ibid*, 15.

[107] *Ibid.*

[108] *Ibid.*

[109] Postema, 'Law's Autonomy', above n 1, at 96–97.

> Such very general capacities, capacities which are among those that define personhood, are not to be confused with the deployment of evaluative premises of the kind relevant to the justification of legal standards, which are excluded by the sources thesis.[110]

Raz does, however, concede a less trivial point. Postema argues that, when reconstructing another's reasoning, one imports one's own standard of what is reasonable. Given that reasonableness is an evaluative concept, evaluations do play a role in reconstruction.[111]

Raz's response is to concede that this can, and does, happen: he agrees with Postema that 'we often rely on our ideas of what is reasonable in reconstructing other people's thought'.[112] He adds, 'But if we are any good at the task, we do so only when we have reason to think those others share our view of what is a reasonable opinion, or a plausible argument'.[113] Thus when 'assessing Postema's objection, the crucial test is not how we reason, but how we should reason, what we do when we reason correctly'.[114] Raz elaborates on this point using an analogy with morality:

> When we engage in moral reasoning we succeed when our conclusions are morally justified. But in establishing the ruling set in a previous case we succeed when our reasoning leads to the rule the court in that case really expressed in its judgment.[115]

The standard of evaluation is different in each case: for one, we ask whether it is a good moral argument and, for the other, we ask whether it is a good reconstructive argument.[116] This point is meant to prove that the sources thesis excludes evaluative considerations by operating with a different standard than the one that moral arguments rely on. If the standard is not different, then legal positivism collapses: the natural lawyers would therefore be correct to claim that legal judgment is an instance of moral judgment. Thus, Raz has a vested interest in maintaining a separate standard for legal evaluation.

While we can concede that a good moral argument requires a different standard of judgment, it does not mean that a good legal argument is measured by fact-based standards alone. (See chapters two, five and six for an exploration of this point.) Once Raz admits that non-evaluative reasoning is the legal *ideal,* rather than simply what happens when we ascertain the content of existing law, then the sources thesis is trivialized. Moreover, it is a significant concession to say that this is not what judges necessarily do, but what they should do. Such a concession directs our attention to an ideal of legal

[110] Raz, 'Postema on Law's Autonomy', above n 8, at 15 (footnote omitted).
[111] Postema, 'Law's Autonomy', above n 1, at 96–97.
[112] Raz, 'Postema on Law's Autonomy', above n 8, at 15.
[113] *Ibid.*
[114] *Ibid*, 16.
[115] *Ibid.*
[116] *Ibid*, 15.

reasoning that is incompatible with Raz's morally robust theory of adjudication, signalling once again that the sources thesis is at home in a theory of law that is captured by the strong autonomy thesis – Postema is correct about this point. I defend this position at length in chapters three and five.

Taking aim once again at the argument from co-operation, Raz thinks that Postema's line of argument is off the mark given that Postema is still connecting Raz's sources thesis with the argument from co-operation. Postema argues that, because the sources thesis is concerned with the '*uncertainty* of mutual identification of the practical rules that are supposed to govern our social interaction', the issue of whether or not moral evaluation is involved is peripheral.[117] Raz responds by re-articulating his rejection of the argument from co-operation and suggests that the truth of the sources thesis is not based on law's function but on law's objective characteristics or its nature. The sources thesis, Raz argues, is not addressed to the problem of co-operation 'nor to any other problem'.[118] He insists that 'It is true – if at all – because it captures an essential property of the law, not because it is a property which it would be useful for the law to possess'.[119] We can certainly doubt whether grounding one's theory in the statement 'this is how law is' is a sufficiently sound defence of one's position. Indeed when Raz introduces his theses to his readers in his major works he always offers reasons why we should share his view of law. As mentioned, Raz did not always adopt this strategy in reference to his sources thesis: in *The Authority of Law* he grounds the sources thesis in the argument from co-operation – the same argument he rejects above.

J. The Pre-emption Thesis

Postema's next target is Raz's pre-emption thesis. He challenges Raz's ability to account for the nature of adjudication whilst still maintaining the pre-emption thesis. Postema begins by outlining what commonly happens in courts:

> [I]t is not uncommon for courts to appeal to non-source-based principles to justify interpretations which set aside the settled or plain meaning of statutes, and to justify distinguishing (modifying by narrowing) or even overruling established precedent.[120]

Postema rightly points out that the pre-emption thesis can only be made consistent with the nature of adjudication if it is meant to apply only to citizens and not to the courts.[121] If one's theory holds that the pre-emption applies to

[117] Postema, 'Law's Autonomy', above n 1, at 97.
[118] Raz, 'Postema on Law's Autonomy', above n 8, at 16.
[119] *Ibid.*
[120] Postema, 'Law's Autonomy', above n 1, at 99.
[121] *Ibid.*

the courts as well, then the common practice of the courts referred to above would remain unaccounted for. Postema next identifies two problems with restricting the pre-emption thesis to apply only to citizens. The first problem is that such a restriction seems to be *ad hoc*: it is not grounded in an account of how law functions in society. The second problem is that once judges are outside the range of the pre-emption thesis, citizens will be less motivated to allocate legal norms pre-emptive power. Raz inadvertently concedes this second point (as I demonstrate in chapter three), which then confirms Postema's first point. I will outline each objection before considering Raz's responses.

i. Postema's First Objection to the Pre-emption Thesis

Postema's first objection is cited by Raz:

> First, the restriction of the subject scope of the law's pre-emptive force appears entirely *ad hoc* motivated by the need to fit legal practice, but not rooted in any normative argument for the restriction.[122]

The idea is that Raz has arbitrarily restricted the pre-emptive force of law in order to enable it to fit legal practice: he does not ground this restriction in an understanding of how law functions in society and why law must function in this way. When we view Postema's complaint in the context of the argument from co-operation, we are able to see Postema's point more clearly.

Postema has already argued that Raz's theory is grounded in a specific view of law's function: the law's function is to provide a public framework of practical reasons that facilitates co-operation.[123] (I argue for this point in chapters two, three and five). In this regard, there is yet another way to understand the creation myth that focuses on the co-operation-engendering function of law: law facilitates co-operation by providing a set of stable norms that citizens can turn to for guidance. In a society wracked by disagreement, these stable norms can serve to unify judgment insofar as the citizens assign them pre-emptive force. If judges apply these norms in administering the law whenever possible, then they preserve the stability of these pre-existing norms, which, in turn, gives citizens reason to allocate legal norms pre-emptive force. Why, after all, should citizens treat legal norms as pre-emptive reasons for action if they cannot count on judges to reinforce the authority of these norms? In sum, Postema's point is that if one's theory is grounded in the argument from co-operation (as articulated in the creation myth), then it only makes sense if the pre-emptive force of legal norms applies to citizens and judges alike. Raz (at least in his more recent writings) resists this extension of the pre-emption thesis to judges given that it does not cohere with the phenomenology of judicial

[122] Raz, 'Postema on Law's Autonomy', above n 8, at 17.
[123] Postema, 'Law's Autonomy', above n 1, at 80.

decision-making. The restriction of the pre-emption thesis is put in place to account for the nature of adjudication, but this restriction does not cohere well with the argument from co-operation. Postema wants a normative argument to justify the restriction, failing which his claim that Raz's argument is merely an *ad hoc* one stands.

Nevertheless, Raz thinks that Postema's charge misses the mark: he is adamant that he does not ground his theory in the argument from co-operation. Raz proceeds to deflect Postema's complaint in the same manner that he deals with the criticisms of the sources thesis just considered: 'Whether or not it is good for the law to have pre-emptive force is irrelevant to the question of whether it has such force'.[124] Raz is adamant that 'No desperate "rescue" of the original thesis about the pre-emptive force of law (at least as I advanced it) is necessary'.[125] Raz reminds readers precisely what his pre-emption thesis commits him to: the 'pre-emption thesis says, roughly, that if the law is valid and therefore binding then the fact that it requires a certain action is a reason performing that action, and a reason for not acting for certain conflicting reasons'.[126] The idea behind the pre-emption thesis, as Raz sees it here, is that valid law has pre-emptive force. Two difficulties come to light. First, Raz seems to be saying that the law has pre-emptive force, regardless of whether or not citizens believe it does or treat it as if it does: if it is valid, then it has this kind of force. The problem is that unless citizens treat law as having pre-emptive force, the pre-emption thesis becomes arid and does no useful work. Raz shows a keen awareness of this point in *Practical Reason and Norms* and *The Morality of Freedom*: in both works he argues that citizens do and/or should allocate law pre-emptive force. I explain and defend this point in chapters three and four.

The second problem arises when we isolate Raz's claim that *valid* law has pre-emptive force. Unlike many other legal positivists, for Raz 'valid' means 'morally valid'. The problem is that if we want to determine the (moral) validity of the legal norm in question, we must assess the reasons behind the rule; yet, if we do this we are not treating law as a pre-emptive reason. In *The Morality of Freedom*, Raz recognizes this problem and attempts to address it. In chapters four and five, I argue that Raz fails to offer an adequate response to this challenge.

Above, we looked at Raz's understanding of the pre-emption thesis in general; now let us see how he responds to Postema regarding whether or not the pre-emption thesis applies to the courts. Regarding the question of whether the pre-emptive force of the law applies to the courts, Raz replies: 'Of course it does'. He explains, 'just as I am only bound by the laws that apply to me, so

[124] Raz, 'Postema on Law's Autonomy', above n 8, at 17.
[125] *Ibid.*
[126] *Ibid.*

the courts are only bound by the laws that apply to them'.[127] Here Raz is likely referring to what he calls 'the ultimate laws of discretion'.[128] Postema, however, is not talking about rules that are directed at judges, he is talking about whether or not judges must treat the primary rules of the system as pre-emptive rules.

Raz acknowledges this point. He admits that Postema is not talking about rules that guide adjudication, but about the manner in which judges treat the primary rules that are supposed to guide the conduct of the citizens.[129] Thus, he is admitting that his initial response to the question – 'Of course it does' – is misleading. Once Raz admits his error, he proceeds to identify the key question: 'What does the law require the courts to do regarding laws which apply not to them but to the litigants in front of them?'.[130] Raz responds as follows:

> Roughly speaking, the answer is that courts must (and this is a requirement enjoying a pre-emptive force) apply the law to the litigants unless (a) they have power to change it, and (b) it would be right to do so. If they do not have the power to change the law they are subject to a duty (with pre-emptive force) to apply it.[131]

Raz adds that even if judges have the power to change the law, they may choose not to do so, recognizing that there are good reasons to enforce it as is.[132] He rightly notes that the 'reasons for not changing the law are not pre-emptive'.[133]

Raz then identifies the 'hard question', which I have explored in chapters one through three: 'When do the courts have power to change the law?'[134] In many common law jurisdictions, Raz argues, the courts have two kinds of powers: to distinguish and to overrule.[135] He directs us to *The Authority of Law,* where he attempts to give a detailed account of common law adjudication, but adds that the precise definition does not matter.[136] This account, as I have argued in chapter two, is untenable as not only does it mischaracterize the practice, it also collapses into a Dworkinian account. Moreover, as I argue in chapter three, the very fact that Raz directs readers to this theory is evidence that Postema is correct: he cannot use his very formalistic rule-plus-exception model of adjudication to shore up the issues that arise when he attempts to combine a morally robust account of adjudication with his positivist theses.

127 *Ibid.*
128 Raz, *The Authority of Law*, above n 62, at 96.
129 Raz, 'Postema on Law's Autonomy', above n 8, at 18.
130 *Ibid.*
131 *Ibid.*
132 *Ibid.*
133 *Ibid.*
134 *Ibid.*
135 *Ibid.*
136 *Ibid.*

'What does matter', Raz contends, 'is that Postema is clearly considering the very same power of the courts to change the laws'.[137] The significance is as follows: 'Consequently, he is right in thinking that those who believe in the pre-emptive force of the law do not believe it applies to courts when they have power to change the law'.[138] He adds that: 'To think otherwise makes as much sense as to believe the legislature cannot change the law, because once it made it it is binding and if it is binding it cannot be changed'.[139] The only puzzle remaining, as far as Raz can see, is why 'Postema should think this to be an "*ad hoc*" "rescue" attempt, rather than a statement of the core idea of the thesis of the pre-emptive force of law'.[140]

As mentioned above, in this book I argue that Raz is in need of a rescue strategy. In chapter one, I show that Raz is committed to the argument from co-operation and the strong autonomy thesis: it becomes clear that the removal of these elements poses a great problem for Raz. Indeed, in chapter three, I argue that Raz's theory of adjudication (which is committed to the weak autonomy thesis) sits in tension with his theory of law (as understood in *Practical Reason and Norms* and as formulated in his central claim that law necessarily claims authority). What is implied in this argument is that Raz's theory of law is fundamentally inconsistent with a theory of adjudication that adequately accounts for the nature of adjudication in common law systems. While he surely needs a rescue strategy, it is hard to conceive of one that will do the requisite work.

ii. Postema's Second Objection to the Pre-emption Thesis

Raz goes on to consider Postema's second objection to the pre-emption thesis. Postema writes:

> Legal norms have pre-emptive force only insofar as agents to whom they are addressed accord the norms pre-emptive force in their practical reasoning. However, I shall argue that agents will have reason to accord them that force only to the extent that they believe the *courts* reliably do so.[141]

Postema is making explicit the point that has motivated his discussion thus far: citizens have reason to treat legal norms pre-emptively only if judges do the same. This is simply another way to articulate Postema's overarching concern about 'whether the point of insisting upon this autonomy can be sustained in the face of extensive, non-autonomous judicial reasoning'.[142] Put generally,

[137] *Ibid.*
[138] *Ibid* (footnote omitted).
[139] *Ibid.*
[140] *Ibid.*
[141] Postema, 'Law's Autonomy', above n 1, at 100.
[142] *Ibid*, 88.

Postema's point is that the behaviour of judges impacts on the behaviour of citizens.

Raz identifies Postema's second objection as a 'serious question' and pinpoints the way it manifests itself in his account of law:

> 'My' problem arises out of the fact that the law is an institutionalized normative system. In particular, it is a system of norms coupled with a system of adjudication. The norms that belong to the system are those that the courts or other law-applying institutions have a special institutional duty to apply. So a legal standard does not bind its subjects unless the courts are bound to apply it. But if the courts can change the norm any time it comes up for adjudication, does it make sense to regard it as binding on its subjects?[143]

In answering this question, Raz concedes Postema's main point that judicial creativity saps incentive from citizens. Raz states, 'it is true that the easier it is for a person to get the law changed, the less motivated he is to comply with it'.[144] Raz, however, does not view this potential problem as pressing given that 'This is a reason, well appreciated by the courts, not to make it too easy for litigants to get the law changed'.[145] Raz attempts to shore up this point with an account of adjudication that suggests, in fact, that judicial creativity is a penumbral activity. According to Raz, the core cases (which are the majority of cases) do not afford judges this option:

> The limits on the intelligibility of the claim that a norm exists are transgressed when every occasion for its application is also an occasion for its modification or repeal. But when this is not so, when there are occasions of its application which are not occasions for its modification, there is no such problem. The case of being subject to revision by the courts is a long way from getting near the borderline of intelligibility. In the nature of things only an infinitesimally small proportion of the circumstances to which the law applies *can* ever be subject to litigation in the courts, the matter is decided after a significant time lag, and in deciding to take matters to court most people incur risks of considerable costs (not only financial).[146]

Raz adds that in 'such circumstances no problem regarding the binding force of the law arises out of the fact that it is revisable by the courts'.[147]

Although it might not be readily apparent, Raz is relying on two different argumentative strategies here. The first strategy says 'yes, judges have the power to change the law in any given case, but the system makes it difficult to achieve this end', while the second strategy argues that 'judges only have the

143 Raz, 'Postema on Law's Autonomy', above n 8, at 19.
144 *Ibid*, 20.
145 *Ibid.*
146 *Ibid*, 19–20.
147 *Ibid*, 20.

power to change the law in a small number of cases' so we need not worry about the impact that their discretionary activities might have on the citizenry. The existence of the first strategy signals that we do need to worry about discretionary activity after all. Raz's second strategy also encounters problems. He has retreated back to his positivist theory of adjudication – indeed he even points readers to the rule-plus-exception model in order to shore up this point.[148] In chapter two, I demonstrate how this model collapses from within (into a version of Dworkian interpretation). Raz cannot rely on this model to deflect Postema's criticisms. Furthermore, Raz cannot simultaneously maintain that judges rarely exercise discretion and that they often do. In other words, his comments here are at odds with his morally robust theory of adjudication – a point made in chapter three.

Only pages earlier, Raz agrees with Postema that 'it is not uncommon for courts to appeal to non-source-based principles to justify interpretations which set aside the settled or plain meaning of statutes, and to justify distinguishing (modifying by narrowing) or even overruling established precedent'.[149] The inconsistency found in this text is typical of Raz's entire canon of works explored in this book: he continually vacillates between a view of adjudication that limits the possibility of change (and which is thus consistent with his legal positivist stance) and a view that acknowledges that such change is likely to occur. Again, I explore these precise points in chapter three.

Raz finishes with a discussion of one final point made by Postema. He wants to distance himself from any understanding of the pre-emptive thesis that makes its validity hinge on the beliefs of participants. Raz begins his argument by identifying the issue: 'Postema's related problem arises out of the statement that "legal norms have pre-emptive force only insofar as agents to whom they are addressed accord the norms pre-emptive force in their practical reasoning"'.[150] Raz argues that he tends 'to think that something like this thesis is plausible [though] I am not sure that my reasons are the same as [Postema's]'.[151] Raz's reason for accepting a version of Postema's claim is that he endorses Hart's assertion that 'The legitimacy of many aspects of the law depend on its acceptance by the population which it purports to govern'.[152] Yet, Raz rejects Postema's version of the claim given that, on this view, 'whether or not norms have pre-emptive force does not depend on people's beliefs or attitudes'.[153] Instead, Raz proposes the following as an acceptable

[148] *Ibid*, 18.
[149] *Ibid*, 17.
[150] *Ibid*, 19.
[151] *Ibid.*
[152] *Ibid.*
[153] *Ibid.*

replacement: 'The legitimacy of norms as binding legal norms depends on their acceptance by the population to whom the legal system as a whole is addressed'.[154] Raz returns to Postema's original query:

> Assuming that the legitimacy of much of the law depends on its general acceptance by the population, the question arises whether anyone can accept the law as binding knowing that whenever a question relating to it arises before the courts, the courts may change it.[155]

I will refer to this as the 'acceptance-based argument'. This argument is inadequate for several interrelated reasons. First, if Raz wishes to maintain his thesis that legal norms are pre-emptive reasons for action, legal norms *must* be treated as such. Raz directly acknowledges as much in *Practical Reason and Norms* but he also does so implicitly in *The Morality of Freedom*. (Chapters one, three and four illustrate this point through a close reading of Raz's works). Raz wants to distance himself from the claim that the pre-emptive thesis hinges on whether or not people treat law pre-emptively, because he is wary about putting too much weight on the beliefs of participants.

The most significant problem with the acceptance-based argument, however, is that it loses sight of the pre-emption thesis. Law's legitimacy is dependent, so the argument goes, on the acceptance of the law by the general population. However, the population can accept the law for *any reason*: they need not allocate it pre-emptive force. But, as I argue throughout this book, if people do not allocate legal reasons pre-emptive force, then Raz's pre-emptive thesis is arid. Raz would not have to introduce the prohibition against 'double counting' unless he was concerned with how people reason with rules.[156] Unless legal norms are frequently treated as pre-emptive reasons, we will have good reason to think of legal norms as weighty first-order reasons rather than second-order exclusionary reasons. In *Practical Reason and Norms,* Raz argues against the acceptance-based argument (championed by Hart) for a similar reason: he argues that Hart's practice theory of norms is unable to 'distinguish between practiced rules and accepted reasons'.[157] Unfortunately for Raz, he must pay attention to the beliefs of participants if his pre-emptive thesis is to be viable. But, as chapter six illustrates, a more complex account of the role of legal norms in our daily lives must be told; and the pre-emption thesis does not belong at the centre.

It should now be clear that Raz cannot simply deflect criticisms. He must show how the pieces of his conceptual puzzle fit together. In my view this is a

[154] *Ibid.*

[155] *Ibid* (footnote omitted).

[156] In ch 6 I argue that 'double counting' is a good thing insofar as the system is itself good.

[157] J Raz, *Practical Reason and Norms* (Oxford, Oxford University Press, 1999) 55.

futile undertaking. I would, instead, urge those with the appetite for jurisprudential reflection to blaze new trails through this much travelled terrain.

> *We shall not cease from exploration, and the end of all our exploring will be to arrive where we started and know the place for the first time.*
>
> *TS Eliot*

Index

www.ingramcontent.com/pod-product-compliance
Ingram Content Group UK Ltd.
Pitfield, Milton Keynes, MK11 3LW, UK
UKHW020816290926
15470UKWH00003B/1199

9 781849 460996